Stories from Indian Wigwams and Northern Campfires

How I missed my first bear

Stories from Indian Wigwams and Northern Campfires

By EGERTON RYERSON YOUNG

The flowers will spring up in the hunter's trail,
and the birds will sing in the branches.

Lighthouse Trails Publishing
Eureka, Montana

Stories from Indian Wigwams and Northern Campfires
by Egerton Ryerson Young
©*2011 Special Lighthouse Trails Edition*

The text and photos of *Stories from Indian Wigwams and Northern Campfires* are in the public domain. Originally published
in 1892.

This special edition published by
Lighthouse Trails Publishing, LLC
P.O. Box 908
Eureka, MT 59917
(see back of book for publisher and author contact information)

Scripture quotations are taken from the *King James Version*.
Cover design by Lighthouse Trails Publishing.

Lighthouse Trails Publishing books are available at special
quantity discounts. Contact information for publisher in
back of book.

Printed in the United States of America

The Tearm
Great Spirit excet bothers me —

CONTENTS

CHAPTER I

CONTRADICTORY NOTIONS FORMED OF THEM—PHYSICAL AP-
PEARANCE—POWER TO ENDURE—HIGH IDEAS OF HONOR—SO-
CIAL LIFE—SELF CONTROL UNDER ALL CIRCUMSTANCES—ATA-
HULPA—MAXIMS—DECORUM IN THEIR COUNCILS—METHODS
OF WAR—ONLY VOLUNTEERS—HOW A CAPTAIN ENLISTED
FOLLOWERS FOR A BATTLE—NO PUBLIC COMMISSARIAT—EV-
ERY MAN FOR HIMSELF—OPEN WARFARE AND PITCHED BATTLES
ALMOST UNKNOWN—THE SECRET ATTACK AND AMBUSH PRE-
FERRED—EAGLE FEATHERS THE BADGE OF SUCCESS—SCALPING
CONFINED TO INDIANS—ROMANTIC STORY OF ITS ORIGIN

CHAPTER II

FORT GARRY—LAKE WINNIPEG—PRIMITIVE COOKING—PEM-
MICAN—THE TUMBLE IN THE LAKE—CORDIAL WELCOME—NO
LOCKS OR KEYS—VISITORS AT ALL HOURS—THE STARTLED BED-
ROOM CALLER—TEACHING BY EXAMPLE AS WELL AS PRECEPT—
LOVE OF THE INDIANS FOR OUR CHILDREN—BEAUTIFUL INDIAN
NAMES GIVEN THEM

CHAPTER III

SURRENDER OF THE HUDSON BAY COMPANY'S CHARTER—AN
INCREASE OF OUR RESPONSIBILITIES—REVERENCE FOR THE SAB-
BATH AND LOVE FOR AND GOOD ATTENDANCE IN THE HOUSE
OF GOD—PAPOOSES HUNG ON THE WALLS—STORY OF THE MIS-
SIONARY'S SERMON—THE SHATTERED HAND—THE WOUNDED
MAN'S TESTIMONY—HIS CONVERSION AND DEATH—THE BRAVE
SABBATH-KEEPING GUIDE—THE SINKING OF THE SHIP—INDIANS
DEEPLY IMPRESSED—ANOTHER ARGUMENT FOR THE SANCTITY
OF THE SABBATH—THE BRIGADE OF BOATS —THE INLAND FUR-

TRADE—PORTAGING—MARVELOUS STRENGTH AND ENDUR-
ANCE OF THE TRIP-MEN—DR. TAYLOR'S TESTIMONY—THE PRACTI-
CAL TESTING OF THE QUESTION BETWEEN THE SABBATH-KEEPING
AND NON-SABBATH-KEEPING BRIGADES—THE CAMP-FIRE STORY

CHAPTER IV

CHAPTER V

CHAPTER VI

OLD CAESAR—MY OWN TRAIN—VOYAGEUR, THE MATCHLESS
LEADER—HOW I UNFORTUNATELY BROKE HIS HEART—JACK
THE NOBLEST OF THEM ALL

CHAPTER XI

CHAPTER XII

CHAPTER XIII

CHAPTER XIV

UNDER PECULIAR CIRCUMSTANCES—ATTENTIVE HEARERS OF
THE WORD—ICE-RAFTS—THE SUCCESSFUL WILD-CAT HUNTER—
PREACHING THE WORD AS WE JOURNEY ON—SLEEPING TWENTY-
THREE STRONG IN A SMALL WIGWAM—A TROUBLESOME DOG—
HITTING OOJIBETOOS BY MISTAKE—AN ALMOST TRAGEDY
TURNED INTO A COMEDY—"ALL'S WELL THAT ENDS WELL."

CHAPTER XV

CHAPTER XVI

CHAPTER XVII

CHAPTER XVIII

CHAPTER XIX

CHAPTER XX

CHAPTER XXI

CHAPTER XXII

CHAPTER XXIII

Note from the Publisher

The stories you are about to read took place a long time ago, and we have attempted to preserve the writing style and language of the author. However, some of the terms used in this book would be considered out-dated and incorrect usage in today's society. We chose to keep Young's terminology for we knew of his great love and respect for the Native people he so diligently worked and lived with.

A note from Nanci Des Gerlaise (who wrote the foreword to this book): Many people today prefer to be called "First Nations" or "First Nations people" instead of "Indians." In Canada, generally, "First Nations people" is used to describe both Status (registered with the government) and Non-Status (not registered) Indian people. Indian and Northern Affairs Canada rarely uses a synonym for "Aboriginal peoples" because it usually doesn't include Inuit or Métis people.

There are three groups of aboriginal people in Canada who are recognized in the Constitution Act, 1982; they consist of Indian, Inuit, and Métis peoples.

Those described as "Indian" describe indigenous people in Canada which include: Status Indians, Non-Status Indians, and Treaty Indians.

Inuit are aboriginal people who live mainly in the most Northern arctic parts of Canada. Inuit means "the people" in the Inuktitut language. The singular of Inuit is Inuk.

Métis is the term for the people of mixed First Nations and European Ancestry.

About the Author

EGERTON RYERSON YOUNG
1840-1909

Egerton Ryerson Young, a biography written while he was still alive. [The following must have been written about 1905, because Mr. Young is no longer with us. He died 5th May 1909. Ed.] Canadian Methodist Episcopalian; born at Smith's Falls, Ontario, April 7, 1840. He was educated at the Normal School of the Province of Ontario, after having taught for several years, and in 1863 entered the ministry. Four years later he was ordained, and, after being stationed at the First Methodist Episcopal Church, Hamilton, Ontario, in 1867-68, was sent as a missionary to Norway House, Northwest Territory. There he worked among the Indians for five years, and in 1873 went in a similar capacity to Beren's River, Northwest Territory, where he remained three years (1873-76). In 1876 he returned to Ontario and was stationed successively at Port Perry (1876-79), Colborne (1879-82), Bowmanville (1882-85), Medford (1885-87), and St.

Paul's, Brampton (1887-88). Since 1888 he has been prominent as a lecturer on work among the American Indians, and in this cause has made repeated tours of the world. He wrote:

1. *By Canoe and Dog Train among the Cree and Saulteaux Indians* (New York, 1890);
2. *Stories from Indian Wigwams and Northern Camp-Fires* (1893);
3. *Oowikapun: or, How the Gospel reached Nelson River Indians* (1894);
4. *Three Boys in the Wild North Land* (1896);
5. *On the Indian Trail: Stories of Missionary Work among the Cree and Saulteaux Indians* (1897);
6. *Winter Adventures of Three Boys in the Great Lone Land* (1899);
7. *The Apostle of the North, James Evans* (1899);
8. *My Dogs in the Northland* (1902);
9. *Algonquin Indian Tales* (1903);
10. *Children of the Forest* (1904);
11. *Hector my Dog* (Boston, 1905);
12. *Battle of the Bears* (1907)

Illustrations

Foreword

IT is more than a small coincidence how it came to be that I was asked to write the foreword to *Stories from Indian Wigwams and Northern Campfires* by Canadian missionary Egerton Ryerson Young. I had recently signed a contract with Lighthouse Trails Publishing for my own book, *Muddy Waters: An Insider's View of North American Native Spirituality*. Because my book shows how Native spirituality is becoming increasingly popular, weaving its way into many facets of mainstream society particularly through the *emerging church*, Lighthouse Trails was interested in my book. What I did not know at the time was that Lighthouse Trails was about to publish this book by Young who ministered primarily to the Cree Indians in Northeastern Canada in the mid to late eighteen hundreds. What Lighthouse Trails did not know when they signed a contract with me was that I am a Cree Indian whose ancestors are from the very region Young was ministering at. Thus, the "coincidence" that led to writing the foreword to the *Wigwam* book.

Growing up, I lived a life full of darkness, steeped in Native spirituality. My grandfather was a medicine man, and later after I was grown, my father became a medicine man also. Later in my life, I began a search for answers because of a missing void I felt in my heart. In my search, I become involved in substance abuse and idolatry, among other things, believing that I would find this missing piece through these avenues. God's truth would later set me free from these chains. I became a born-again Christian after being convicted by the Holy Spirit when someone shared with me that Jesus Christ died on the Cross for my sins, so that I would have eternal life.

My childhood, living in a North American native community, certainly had its difficult challenges, humor, close familial bonds, and a culture intertwined with spiritual mysticism as spoken of in *Stories from Indian Wigwams and Northern Campfires*.

Reading this book has brought back a flood of memories of life at home and community.

Part of what is amiss from the culture today is the language, which is attributable to the Residential Schools forbidding the children to speak their native tongue. As well, the Cree language has changed somewhat from the old Cree. Much of the loving, sharing, and caring aspects of the culture are awash with substance abuse to numb the pain of atrocities suffered at the Residential Schools or the rejection suffered from parents when these young people no longer fit into the family mold following their return home from these institutions. These children, in turn, pass on to their children learned behaviors such as neglect and substance abuse.

This is perhaps why I was so thrilled to read Egerton Ryerson Young's book. It is very encouraging for me to learn that the Gospel was shared with Natives, including medicine men, which so often resulted in decisions being made for Jesus Christ. Psalm 16:28 states: "There is a way that seems right to man, but in the end it leads to death." This verse paints a very powerful warning to non-Christian cultures.

Mr. Young shares thrilling and entertaining stories regarding his experiences with native people both in Canada and the United States, and shares very extraordinary events as he journeys to the remotest parts of Canada sharing the Gospel to the lost. He describes witnessing boldly to medicine men regarding their pagan beliefs with very encouraging and positive results achieved by no other than the Holy Spirit.

As I read the *Wigwam* book recently, for the first time, I was very surprised to read about one lost Indian named Mask-e-pe-toon (Crooked Arm). Why surprised? Because I knew the name Mask-e-pe-toon. From research I had done years ago, I collected documentation and learned that my great, great grandfather Chief Kehiwin was Mask-e-pe-toon's best friend. This, of course, has made Young's book all the more meaningful to me.

Mask-e-pe-toon was the most powerful chief among the

Cree tribes and also a medicine man. His son was killed by an Indian of another tribe. When Mask-e-pe-toon was on his way to seek revenge, at the last moment he had an incredible change of heart electing to forgive his enemy instead, after hearing the missionary speak about forgiveness the previous night. When Mask-e-pe-toon came face to face with the one who had killed his son, he forgave him and did not seek revenge. As you will read about it in the coming pages, Mask-e-pe-toon went on to serve the Lord, until his life ended in a most dramatic heart-rending manner.

Young tells another story of an old Chief who was taught the truth by a missionary regarding his belief in paganism. The missionary urged him to renounce this pagan, mystical spirituality and become a Christian. The old Chief was aware that he was a great sinner and needed a Savior. What an illustration this story is to show that God has placed in each of our hearts a conscience to know right from wrong.

Stories from Indian Wigwams and Northern Campfires answers a myriad of questions, especially one that I would frequently ask myself, "If the Lord wants everyone to hear the Gospel, how could a loving God allow our people to pass on prior to learning that the Lord Jesus Christ died on the cross for their sins?"

This book is testimony that the Gospel is indeed for everyone, and a loving God desires that none should perish without hearing about the Gospel (2 Peter 3:9). God does not accept the diverse spirituality of all cultures as being locked into truth. For Him to accept false and contradictory spirituality, while the Gospel calls all to repentance and belief in the Savior, would make God a liar—because there can only be one truth. And God cannot tell a lie because He is just and holy.

I have noticed that many of the Cree believers today are returning to Native spirituality while others are syncretizing Christianity with Native spirituality and/or Roman Catholicism with a smaller population remaining in true Christianity. If you have ever wondered about Native spirituality, you will learn the truth about it in *Stories from Indian Wigwams and Northern Campfires* through the thrilling accounts of error corrected by God's Holy Word, the Bible.

Prior to my receiving the Lord Jesus Christ as my Savior and Lord, I tried to fight it but realized that Roman Catholicism and Native Spirituality could never assure me of entering the Kingdom of God. These paths do not lead to salvation. Today, I have inner peace, joy, and love that could come only through Jesus Christ.

This book is for all audiences and age groups. It will educate the reader in the ways of the early North American Indian, ways that included astounding and highly intelligent practices for survival in conditions, such as sub-zero temperatures and little to eat. It will also show the faithfulness of God, that He is looking throughout the earth to find those who are seeking truth, sending missionaries with the Gospel message for those who have ears to hear. And finally, because Native spirituality is becoming more and more popular in our society and in the church today, this book will unveil a Native spirituality that is not at all as is described in much of Hollywood and now the emerging church; rather you will see the Indians are in as much need of a Savior as anyone else. And a spirituality without Jesus Christ at the foundation is a false and futile belief system. This book is a must-read.

Nanci Des Gerlaise
Author of *Muddy Waters: An Insider's View of North American Native Spirituality*

For God will save Zion, and will build the cities of Judah: that they may dwell there, and have it in possession. The seed also of his servants shall inherit it: and they that love his name shall dwell therein. (Psalm 69: 33-36)

Introduction

NIGHT VISIONS AND HEART MUSINGS IN THE WILD NORTH LAND

So short are the wintry days in those "high latitudes" where for years we toiled that on our long trips with our dogs and Indians we were obliged to rouse ourselves up from our snowy beds in the cold and dreary forests, hours before day. Aided by the light of our camp-fire, we cooked our morning meal, packed up our robes and blankets, and tied them, with our provisions and kettles, on our dog-sleds. Before starting we sang, in the Cree Indian language, one of the sweet songs of Zion, and then, bowing at the mercy seat, with grateful hearts we offered up our prayers to the loving Protector who had watched over and shielded us from all harm, although our lodging-place was in the "forest primeval" and our bed was in the snow, with the temperature from forty to sixty degrees below zero. Our last camp duty was the capturing and harnessing of our dogs, which was an easy or difficult task according to their nature and training.

As much snow had recently fallen, we all tied on our snow-shoes; then, starting our dogs, we wended our way out from the light of the camp-fire and through the weird shadows of the fir and birch and juniper trees to the vast expanse of Lake Winnipeg, across which our journey lay. The stars shone down upon us with a clearness and brilliancy unknown in lands of mists and fogs. At times, meteors blazed along the star-decked vault of heaven, leaving behind them for a few seconds lines of silvery light that soon faded away. The Northern Lights flashed, danced, and scintillated with a glory and magnificence that paled into insignificance man's most wonderful pyrotechnic displays. Frequently a clear and distinct corona would be formed at the zenith, from which would shoot out long columns of various-colored lights, which seemed to rest down upon the snowy waste around us or on the far-off distant shores. Often have I seen a cloud of light flit swiftly across these ever-changing bars with a resemblance so natural to that of a hand across the strings of a harp that I have suddenly stopped and listened for that rustling sound which some arctic travelers have affirmed they have heard from these auroral displays; but although I have often watched and listened amid the death-like stillness of this dreary land, no sound have I ever heard. Amid all their flashing, changing glories they seemed as voiceless as the stars above them.

The morning crescent-shaped moon, the silvery queen of night, helped to light up our way as through the long, dreary hours we journeyed on. If the cold had been less terrible, nothing could have been more delightful than contemplating these glorious sights in the heavens. As it was, the words of the psalmist, "The heavens declare the glory of God, and the firmament showeth his handiwork," and Job's magnificent description of that God "who is wise in heart and mighty in strength, which alone spreadeth out the heavens, which maketh Arcturus, Orion, and Pleiades, and the chambers of the south," rang in our ears, and we were thankful that the Creator of all these things was mindful of us. Still, after all, on account of the bitterness of the morning, it being, as we afterward found, in the neighborhood of fifty degrees below zero, there was a disposition to lose our love of the sentimental, and in almost bitter anguish to cry out to these lights in the heavens, "Miserable comforters are ye all! Can none of you give us any warmth?"

But while we journey on, a dim, faint line of light is seen in the eastern horizon. At first it is scarcely visible. The brilliant meteors seem to say, "How much more exalted and beautiful are we than that dim, faint line down there so low!" The Northern Lights appear to cry out in derision, "Who for a moment would compare us in all our ever-changing, flashing splendor with that insignificant and modest beam?" The silvery moon, the queen of night, seems to consider that eastern light as an intruder as she gazes upon it with saucy stare. But that eastern light heeds them not. As we watch we see that it is rapidly increasing. The white line, extending round to the north and south, has risen, and underneath is one of crimson and purple. A flashing ray shoots up, and then the glorious sun bounds up from his snowy bed, "rejoicing as a strong man to run a race." Felix, my Indian guide, who ran ahead, shouted out, "Sagastao! Sagastao!" ("The sun rises! The sun rises!").

The poor shivering missionary coming next, toiling along on snow-shoes behind his dog-train, takes up the joyful sound, which is caught up and loudly shouted by William, my other Indian attendant, who at this glad sight casts off his usual stoicism and is as noisy in his words of welcome to the sovereign king of day as the rest of us. We turn our ice-covered, frost-bitten faces to the sun, and as its bright beams fall upon us like loving kisses, we rejoice that the light and brightness of another day has come, for "truly the light is sweet; and a pleasant thing it is for the eyes to behold the sun." But look around the heavens and behold the marvelous change his coming has effected. Every lesser light has gone, every competitor has left the field. The race is all his own. At first his bright rays gild the distant hill-tops, then they light up the fir-clad rocky isles, which, when burnished by his golden beams, bear some fanciful resemblance to old ruined temples or vast cathedrals. And while we gaze upon them, wondering, if God's footstool can be made to look so glorious what will the throne be? The sun has risen higher, every shadow of night has disappeared, and we are deluged in his glory.

I would have been a poor lover of the world's evangelization, and emphatically a poor missionary, if I could have gazed upon these marvelous transformations in the heavens and thought on the lessons they taught me unmoved. My heart grew hot within me, and while I mused the fire burned; then spake I with my tongue.

Meet emblem of a world shrouded in the chill and gloom of paganism seems Lake Winnipeg on this cold wintry morning. No sign of life is here. The ice and snow, like a great mantle, seem to have wrapped themselves round every thing that once had life.

The flashing meteors reminded me of the efforts of the old philosophers to reform and illuminate the world. There was a transient beauty in some of their theories, but the darkness to be dispelled was too dense, and so their lights, meteor-like, went out almost as soon as kindled. The fickle, ever-changing Northern Lights made me think of some of the various systems of false religions, or perversions of the true, which man has invented to dazzle the unwary or to lead the fickle astray. Whether it be Mormonism, or Spiritualism, or a mere sensuous Ritualism, changeable and inconstant are they as the auroras. Their revelations, their spiritual communications, rapped or written, their gorgeous vestments and illuminated altars are no more able to dispel the darkness and irradiate the world lost in sin and error's night than the auroras are to warm and comfort the poor shivering missionary and his Indian attendants, toiling through the wintry cold and longing for the morning.

The crescent-shaped moon reminded me of that vast system of error which for twelve centuries has waved its crescent flag over some of the fairest portions of God's heritages. Humiliating is the thought that even in the land once pressed by the dear Redeemer's feet the baneful cry is still heard that, although "God is great, Mohammed is his prophet." But the crescent must go down before the Sun of righteousness. As the moon is the last of the lights of night to fade before the sun, so Mohammedanism, although such a stubborn foe, must eventually succumb. Once her crescent-bannered armies made all Christendom tremble; now the mutual forbearance, or rather mutual jealousies, of Christian nations keep the only great Mohammedan nation from falling to pieces.

Soon, very soon, perhaps before we expect and before we are ready to enter in, the crescent will go down before the cross, and then many more of the dark places full of the habitations of cruelty shall open for the blessed light of the sun. Haste, happy day, day so much desired and so often prayed for, and for which we toil, when the Sun of righteousness shall shine upon every portion of the world polluted and darkened by sin, but bought with the Redeemer's blood!

> And shall not I, at God and duty's call,
> Fly to the utmost limits of the ball,
> Cross the wide sea, along the desert toil,
> Or circumnavigate each Indian isle?
> To torrid regions run to save the lost,
> Or brave the rigors of eternal frost?
> I may like Brainard perish in my bloom,
> A group of Indians weeping round my tomb ;
> I may like Martyn lay my burning head
> In some lone Persian hut or Turkish shed ;
> I may like Coke be buried in the wave:
> I may like Howard find a Tartar grave ;
> Or like a Xavier perish on the beach,
> In some lone cottage out of friendship's reach ;
> Or like McDougall in a snow-drift die,
> With angels only near to hear the dying sigh.

> I may but never let my soul repine:

> Lo, I'm with you alway! Heaven's in that line.
> Tropic or pole, or mild or burning zone,
> Is but a step from my eternal throne.

And it shall come to pass, that whosoever shall call on the name of the LORD shall be delivered: for in mount Zion and in Jerusalem shall be deliverance, as the LORD hath said, and in the remnant whom the LORD shall call. (Joel 2:32)

CHAPTER I

THE INDIANS

CONTRADICTORY NOTIONS FORMED OF THEM—PHYSICAL
APPEARANCE—POWER TO ENDURE—HIGH IDEAS OF
HONOR—SOCIAL LIFE—SELF CONTROL UNDER ALL
CIRCUMSTANCES—ATAHULPA—MAXIMS—DECORUM
IN THEIR COUNCILS—METHODS OF WAR—ONLY
VOLUNTEERS—HOW A CAPTAIN ENLISTED FOLLOWERS
FOR A BATTLE—NO PUBLIC COMMISSARIAT—EVERY MAN
FOR HIMSELF—OPEN WARFARE AND PITCHED BATTLES
ALMOST UNKNOWN—THE SECRET ATTACK AND AMBUSH
PREFERRED—EAGLE FEATHERS THE BADGE OF SUCCESS—
SCALPING CONFINED TO INDIANS—ROMANTIC STORY
OF ITS ORIGIN.

AROUND none of the subdivisions of the great human family does there cluster more of the romantic and picturesque than that which is associated with the North American Indian. Startling indeed to the Old World's inhabitants must have been the news brought back by the adventurous voyagers, toward the end of the fifteenth century, that across the great and wide sea there were found new continents inhabited by strange people with many striking characteristics and with customs altogether different from those possessed by any other of earth's heterogeneous races.

Amidst the thirst for gold and greed for land there were those who endeavored to study as well as benefit this newly discovered branch of the great Adamic family which had so long been lost to view. The research, which is not yet ended, has resulted in much that has not only interested the curious and added greatly to the knowledge of the ethnological and antiquarian student, but has also opened up a wide field for the philanthropist and Christian worker.

And yet of no race or people have impressions and views more different been formed than about these American aborigines. By some they have been painted in the darkest colors, as possessing every characteristic of fiends without a redeeming feature; and if these chroniclers could have their own way the stronger nations would long ago have civilized them off the face of the earth. Others have written in strains exactly the reverse of these. To judge from their descriptions of the Indians one would imagine that at length the land of Arcadian simplicity and innocence had been found, where the inhabitants without a vice or defect, and in possession of all those excellencies which make up the perfect ideal character, had been discovered. The result from the reading of these two descriptions so diametrically opposite, is that some people have become very much mixed and unsettled as what really to believe about the true Indian.

As with some other subjects about which much has been written, so it is here, the truth is generally to be found somewhere between the two extremes. Many years experience with and intimate study of the red man in his own haunts and surrounded by his natural environments have only deepened the conviction formed long ago that he is one of the sinning race of Adam suffering from the fall, not much better or worse than others, and needing as well as others the benefits of the great scheme of redeeming love to genuinely lift him up and so save him that there comes real and lasting peace in his own heart and fitness is given him to take his place among the other subdivisions of the great human family.

Physically the Indians are a fine-looking race. The men stand erect, and have, as a general thing, strong, stalwart frames, without any tendency to corpulency. In height they will average up with any known race. In ability to endure hardness the American Indian is perhaps without a peer. He has a stoicism that enables him to control his feelings under the most fiery ordeal, and a haughty pride and power of self-control that so sustains him that he can even taunt and exult over his enemies who are subjecting him to the fiercest torture. At times he seems fearless of all danger and capable of any heroic deed, and yet he so conducts his methods of warfare and attack that he appears to be the most cowardly of enemies. Yet, on the other hand, when the tomahawk is buried and peace declared he possesses high notions of honor and a sacred respect for treaties that nations and peoples professing to be vastly above him in the scale of civilization might with great advantage copy. In his social and domestic life he possesses a gravity and self-control which at first would give the impression that there was but little of love and affection for even his own family in his heart. The loving words of affection and the endearing caresses so prized and so abounding in the happy homes of other lands are very little known in the wigwam of the pagan Indian. Occasionally a bright little son may soften the stolid heart of the warrior-father and win from him some smiles and caresses, but this is the exception and not the general rule. To perfectly control himself, under all circumstances, is one of his most prominent characteristics. Priding himself on this trait, he steels his muscles to resist all expressions of emotion. To be apparently perfectly indifferent to whatever occurs is the goal he seeks. Hence he allows neither fear nor joy, loss nor gain, success nor disappointment, to have any effect upon him. With the most stoical indifference apparently, he looks upon the most marvelous inventions and the most ingenious contrivances without the least expression of surprise. To permit his face to indicate the slightest expression of astonishment would be considered a mark of childishness or cowardice. To this stern discipline of the mind and nerves the whole Indian race were accustomed to discipline themselves. In the cold North there abounded these characteristics, and in the sunny South the heat relaxed not what they ever considered the manly requirements.

When Pizarro invaded Peru the native ruler, Atahulpa, ordered the immediate execution of some of his soldiers because they exhibited signs of surprise or emotion at the sight of the Spaniard's cavalry, which had dashed and curveted before them for the first time, although the horse, then but recently brought into America, was known to be an object of special fear and dread to the Indian.

This perfect mastery over their emotions influences them in various ways. They are cautious and deliberate in the use of words. One maxim among the Indians is that the man of the fewest words in a dispute is the innocent one. Another one is that he who is sparing of his words in a quarrel is discreet. They draw a very great distinction between public speaking and ordinary talking. The orator, who on great public occasions may extend his address for hours, ordinarily only speaks in aphorism or in sententious utterances. This was especially seen in their councils even when there were great divergencies of opinion and perhaps revengeful feelings in the hearts of many. So, while there was noticed the lack of those demonstrations of affection so prized and prominent in other lands, there was also observed the absence of all wrangling and strife. Noisy quarrelings and wordy contentions were unknown among the chiefs and leaders of the Indians. While at times in their councils there were in the hearts of some of the members deadly animosities and hates which might eventually end in bloodshed and murder, yet such was the self-control of all that no loud, bitter, contentious words were heard, such as would characterize a similar gathering of some of the more hot-blooded races of the world.

Their methods of war differed from that of all other nations. All their warriors were volunteers for that one special campaign. The leader or captain who would raise a war-party must first of all have some reputation as a successful warrior to start on. He musters the warriors to the war-dance and there he appeals to the assembled ones to join him for the contemplated attack he has planned on some tribe with whom they are at war.

Deeply superstitious these would-be warriors are, and he knows that he must be thought under the immediate guidance of the Great Spirit, whose aid he informs them he has secured by some mysterious rites, and who in dreams has assured him of his protection. Various are his schemes to fire their enthusiasm and inflame their hearts. Springing into the midst of the circle, he seizes the vermilion-painted war-club and sings his exciting war-song. In it he repeats over and over again the story of his heroic deeds accomplished and those yet to be performed. His actions are now of the most frantic character. The staid decorum of ordinary days is laid aside. He stamps upon the ground as though then and there he could make the earth so tremble as to fill his enemies with terror. His language is of the most extravagant and symbolical character. He sings of his having the good-will of the spirits and of the favorable omens that he has seen. He says his voice fills the forests and reaches up to the clouds and his strong arms reach to the horizon on every side.

Frequently does he stop in his song and in the most exciting manner sound the piercing war-whoop. We know of nothing more calculated to fire an Indian's soul than one of these exciting war-dances. The strange contortions, the intense muscular energy, and the weird rhythmic movements are in perfect unison with the wild music of the drum and rattle.

Thus in poetic language and in startling pantomime this would-be commander of these red warriors pictures to their excited imagination the enemy, the march, the ambush, the attack, and the victory. In unison with the rude music he stamps his victim under his feet and tears off the bleeding scalp. All his physical as well as mental energies are brought into play. This is no time for stately oratory, and so, under intense excitement, he utters in short sentences his prowess, his anger, his defiance, and what he is to accomplish. His spirit generally becomes contagious, and warrior after warrior rises from his place and joins the war dance. This act constitutes him a volunteer for the contemplated attack, and no warrior who thus joins the circle can honorably withdraw. No other enlistment is known among them. Each volunteer arms and equips himself and provides his own subsistence. There are no paid warriors among them. All are but as volunteers. Even the most warlike tribes had no compulsory military service. No man was compelled to serve, and even if a warrior became discouraged and faint-hearted after starting on the warpath and returned home he suffered no punishment for his desertion except being held for a long time after as an object of ridicule. Each warrior must look out for himself. Hence they have no public debts, and to these facts must be attributed the unique character of Indian warfare. Having no arrangements for supplies, they cannot keep a large force at one point for any length of time. So that even if a goodly force under some great excitement or provocation may assemble together and start off on the war-path, it is not many days ere the limited supply of food carried by each one becomes exhausted, and they are obliged, even, it may be, in the enemy's country, to begin hunting for game.

Open warfare in the field as generally understood among the civilized nations was hardly known among the Indians. They ever preferred the secret attack, generally just before sunrise. No particular order was observed. When the war whoop was sounded and the rush upon the unsuspecting enemy took place each man was expected to do the best he could. They generally divested themselves of the greater part of their clothing as they rushed into the fray. In some of the tribes the warriors painted themselves with vermilion and other striking colors in the most hideous manner, the object being to strike terror into the hearts of their foes. They advance generally in Indian file and use the greatest precaution on the march. Several of the most skillful scouts are sent on ahead to watch for and report on every suspicious sign. When the battle begins all order or system ceases. It is every man for himself. If successful they return home in company. If obliged to retreat each survivor makes his way home as best he can.

The badge of an eagle's feather is the sign of being a successful warrior, and the number he wears is indicative of the scalps he has taken from his enemies. The custom of scalping their enemies is peculiar to the Indians. We know of no other people who ever were guilty of this horrid practice unless it was our remote German ancestors and the Vandals and Huns. They have a strange romantic legend accounting for its origin. They say that hundreds of years ago, perhaps thousands, when the Indians were all one tribe and under one great chief, a dispute arose in the tribe as to who should become chief, the old chief having died without leaving a son to succeed him. There were two principal aspirants for the chieftaincy, and each of them had a strong following. The dispute ended in dividing the tribe and in war. Previous to this time scalping was unknown, as there were no enemies to scalp, the land being occupied by only one people. Peace was never made between the two factions.

The chief on one side had a beautiful daughter, and one of the leading warriors was a suitor for her hand. The chief, as a condition to consenting to give his daughter to her warrior-lover, required him to kill the chief of the opposing tribe (his old-time rival for the chieftaincy), and to bring him proof of the act. The warrior accepted the condition. It was many long miles to the camp of the enemy and the snow was deep, but he immediately set out upon his mission. After lying in wait near the enemy's camp for days and undergoing great suffering from the extreme cold without having an opportunity of carrying out his plan, he finally one night boldly entered the camp, walked into the great chief's lodge, slew him, and, cutting off his head, to take back with him as proof, started to return to his own people.

The next morning the murder was discovered, also the murderer's tracks in the snow, and drops of blood which had fallen from the dead chieftain's captured head. Two hundred warriors started in pursuit of the murderer. They almost overtook him, and he could hear them on his track. He was almost tired out, and the dead chief's head was growing heavy, yet he struggled on with it through the snow and cold, determined not to relinquish the proof which would win for him his bride. The pursuers pressed him so at length that he threw away every weight but his trophy. They finally gained on the weary brave so fast that it seemed that he must either relinquish his prize or be captured, which, of course, would be death. Whipping out his rude stone knife (it was before the time of steel knives among the Indians), he hurriedly stripped off the scalp from the dead man's head and sped on. Thus lightened of his load, he made his own camp in safety, the scalp was accepted as sufficient proof that he had fulfilled his mission, the old chief no longer withheld his consent, and the bright-eyed daughter of the forest became his own. Thus originated the custom of scalping among the American Indians, according to the tradition of some of the tribes.

CHAPTER II

ON THE WAY TO OUR MISSION FIELD

FORT GARRY—LAKE WINNIPEG—PRIMITIVE COOKING—
PEMMICAN—THE TUMBLE IN THE LAKE—CORDIAL
WELCOME—NO LOCKS OR KEYS—VISITORS AT ALL
HOURS—THE STARTLED BEDROOM CALLER—TEACHING BY
EXAMPLE AS WELL AS PRECEPT—LOVE OF THE INDIANS FOR
OUR CHILDREN—BEAUTIFUL INDIAN NAMES GIVEN THEM

In the year 1868 a party of about fifteen, comprising several missionaries, teachers, and adventurers, started out from the city of Hamilton, Canada. Of this company some were going to seek their fortunes in the then almost unknown Northwest. Others, at the call of their Church, were going out as missionaries and teachers among the Indian tribes of the wild north land. The destination of the writer and his young wife was to be among Cree Indians at Rossville Mission, near Norway House, far up in the yet unexplored regions north of Manitoba.

With the primitive means of transportation of those days two months were consumed in the journey to the city of Winnipeg, then known only as Fort Garry. The days spent on the great lakes, rivers, and prairies were full of adventures and strange experiences. At Fort Garry the party that had so long traveled in company broke up, some to push on twelve or fifteen hundred miles westward, some to remain in the Red River Settlement, which has since developed into the Province of Manitoba. The writer and his wife were under the necessity of waiting for a few days for some mode of conveyance by which they could get northward. The longest delays end sometime, and the summons to get ready and start came abrupt and sudden. We hastily packed up our camp-bed and traveling outfit and hurried down to the bank of Red River, where we found waiting for us the boat in which our long, perilous journey was to be made. It was nothing more nor less than a large skiff, sharp at both ends, and known as a Hudson Bay Company's inland boat. It had neither deck, awning, nor cabin.

Its crew consisted of eight Indians, one of whom was called the guide, and whose duty it was to act as steersman. His place was in the stern of the boat, and he used as his steering apparatus a long, heavy oar. Into this little boat our traveling outfit was quickly thrown and a snug little place was assigned to us in the stern near the guide. The Indian boatmen, with their oars, soon pushed out the boat from the shore, and, rowing with a precision and dash that won our admiration, we started down the Red River of the North under happy auspices and with exhilarated spirits.

At Lower Fort Garry, which is a massive stone structure, we stopped to get the mails for the Northern Hudson Bay Company's ports and also to receive Indian supplies. Then off again we started, leaving behind us the Selkirk Settlement, with its romantic history and its baptism of blood. The flourishing Indian Mission, with its comfortable homes and cozy church and well-clad, fine-looking natives, flitted by as a moving panorama. Observing Tom, the guide, heading for the shore, I asked what was the matter, and got in response the answer, "We are going to take on board another passenger." Fancy our amazement and disgust at finding that this additional *compagnon de voyage* was a large ox. Aided by some stalwart Indians who had brought him down to the shore, our crew soon had him in the boat, and to him was assigned a position directly in front of us with his head over one side of the boat, and his tail over the other. Putting it mildly, we would have preferred his room to his company.

We camped for the night at the border of the great marsh, or lagoon, through which the Red River by many channels finds its way into Lake Winnipeg. This vast morass of reeds and rushes

TAKING ON BOARD ANOTHER PASSENGER

is the home of innumerable flocks of ducks and other aquatic birds. It is a paradise for sportsmen and mosquitoes.

The primitive picturesque camping of our Indians and the utter absence of conventional ideas in the preparation of their meals very much interested and amused us. They were furnished by the company with an abundance of pemmican, flour, and tea. The far-famed pemmican was for many years the staple food of the hardy Indian voyager and the trip-men of the great Northwest. But with the buffalo, of whose meat it was made, it has disappeared. Perhaps it may not be out of place to give it a description here, as it is worthy of remembrance for the prominence it once held. The writer and his wife used it, off and on, for years, and they hereby testify that in it there is more nourishment, pound for pound, than in any other kind of food they ever used. The method of its preparation was something like this: When the Indian hunters succeeded in killing a large number of buffaloes, after being skinned the meat was skillfully cut off in large thin flakes and strips. These were placed on a frame staging. Utilizing the heat and warmth of the sun above, and a small, steady fire made of buffalo chips below, these thin sheets of meat were soon as dry as they could be. The next step in the process was to pound this dry meat as fine and small as possible. Large bags, capable of holding from one to three bushels, were made by the Skwews* out of the fresh buffalo hides, with the fur side out. Into these green hide-bags this pounded dry meat was packed. To aid in the packing down an Indian, in his dirty moccasined feet, would frequently jump into the bag and stamp and dance around in it as it was held up by two other strong, sturdy fellows, while a fourth kept shoveling in additional meat until no more could be packed in. Then the melted buffalo tallow was poured in until it permeated the whole mass. The top of the bag was then skillfully sewed together with sinew, and it was ready for use. If well prepared it would keep for years. This pemmican was the most nourishing food I ever ate,

---

* The name for Indian women—pronounced: skwoh (long o)

but a little would go a long way, for it often smelled like rotten soap-grease. Still there were many times in our after-life when we were glad to get it.

But let us return to our camp. We were joined at Lower Fort Garry by several other boats, each with a crew of eight Indians, and so our camp-fires were numerous. While every phase of this new life was interesting, we were specially amused with the operations of one of the Indian cooks who had been detailed to cook the "cakes" for his party. He had neither bake-board, pan, dish, nor oven. Our curiosity was excited to observe his methods, and so, without seeming to attract his attention, with great interest we followed his various movements and expedients and admired his inventive skill. Truly, "necessity is the mother of invention." Having no baking-pan in which to pour out his flour, he proceeded to clear away the dust and leaves from a granite rock that cropped up to the surface near by. His moc-casined foot performed this operation sufficiently to suit his simple taste. Then from the bag he poured out fifteen or twenty pounds of flour on this spot. Having no dish in which to bring water from the river to mix with his flour, he found a capital substitute in his dirty old greasy felt hat. Several trips down to the river gave him sufficient, and soon he had the whole deftly mixed into dough. His next move was to build up a capital fire, and then, from the willows near the shore, to supply himself with quite a number of sticks about the size and length of ordinary walking-canes. Then spitting on his hands he attacked that pile of dough. He tore off a piece weighing about a pound, and after kneading it and rolling it between his hands he stuck the lump on the end of one of those cane-like sticks ; then skillfully working the dough down a little way he flattened it out into the shape of, and what is really called, a "beaver's tail." Carefully pushing the other end of the stick down into the soft ground near the fire, the trowel-like cake was slanted to the right distance near the fire to be cooked. When one side was done brown it was turned over, and soon the "beavers' tails" were ready for the hungry men. Pemmican cakes and tea were considered by these hardy men as the best of living. The evening pipe was smoked, pleasant chat and bright repartee went around, and then these Christian Indians sang their evening hymn and reverently bowed in prayer. Some wrapped themselves up in their blankets and curled down under the stars, on the rocks, to rest. Others of us, more fortunate, retired to our little tent to try and sleep, but we found it hard work after the excitement of this adventurous day.

Between three and four o'clock the next morning, the musical cry of the guide, "Koos-koos-kwah!" ("Wake up!") was heard. Every body sprang up, and all was hurry and excitement. Although so very early in the morning, it was broad daylight, for we were getting up in the high latitudes. "Sou-wa-nas!" ("South wind!") shouted the glad Indians, for that meant that instead of laboring all day at the oars the favoring gale would waft us on northward toward our destination. A fire was hastily prepared. Our kettles of tea were made, and then all bowed down at morning prayers. Tents were quickly taken down, and, with the bedding, were soon stowed away in the boats. Then all embarked, and we pushed out into the river. Each boat was furnished with a mast, which, when not in use, was kept tied alongside under the rowlocks. These were quickly stepped and securely fastened. The single big square sail was hoisted, and as it caught the southern breeze, we were soon out of the river and gayly dancing over the waves of the great Lake Winnipeg. While two or three of the crew "trimmed the sail" the rest of us attacked our provision-bags, and with the kettles of hot tea we made out a capital breakfast, as we were being so rapidly, yet so pleasantly, wafted along.

"Winnipeg" is an Indian word, and literally means "the sea." It is well named, as it is one of the largest and stormiest lakes on the continent, being about as long as Lakes Erie and Ontario combined. It is indented with many large bays and has in it many rocky islands and sandy bars. As our boat was such a frail one we went ashore every evening to camp and cook our meals. Generally the water was deep, and our little boat could come in close to the shore and we could easily step out on to the dry land. But there were places where the water was so shallow that our boat grounded in the sand a hundred feet or more from the shore. When this happened a broad-shouldered man named So-qua-a-tum would jump into the water and, coming around to the stern of the boat, would take Mrs. Young on his back or shoulders safely to the shore. I would undress my feet and wade ashore. One day the big guide, as he saw me about to take off my shoes, said: "Missionary, let me carry you ashore like So-qua-a-tum carried your wife."

"All right, Tom," I replied.

He jumped into the water and, coming around to the side of the boat, placed himself in position for me to get on his back. Just as I let myself go to catch hold of him, he suddenly ducked down, and I went over his head into the lake, amid roars of laughter from the men. He said he slipped, and urged me to try again, but I preferred ever after to wade ashore.

After fourteen days of varied experiences on the lake, we reached our northern home. We were cordially welcomed at the

**HE SUDDENLY DUCKED DOWN,
AND I WENT OVER HIS HEAD INTO THE LAKE**

Norway House, Hudson Bay Fort, and after tea we were taken over by the chief factor of the fort to the Indian village two and a half miles away, which was for years to be our home, and our real missionary life had begun. For the first five years of our missionary life we lived among the Cree Indians. Noble men had done good service for the Master here, and we were permitted to see at once some of the blessed results of their labors. While there were still many pagan Indians around, there were also many genuine followers of the Lord Jesus. Very cordial was the welcome given us by them, and we very quickly began to feel at home among them, although we were four hundred miles from the nearest post-office or other signs of civilization.

We let it be known immediately after our arrival among them that we did not intend to lock a door or fasten a window, that nothing was under lock and key, that to do them good we had come from a far-away happy home to live among them ; and we told them that in return we expected them to be honest and true to us. This confidence in them was never abused; we never had any thing stolen from us. And yet, Indian-like, they loved to come to our house and visit every room and examine every thing strange to them.

As they all wear moccasins on their feet, and so move around like cats, it did at first seem strange to have them, sometimes in large numbers, flitting around through the different rooms in their quiet way. As our acquaintanceship became more intimate through the increasing knowledge of their language, our opportunities for aiding them were enlarged. Ultimately we were considered not only their missionary but their doctor, dentist, lawyer, and many other things besides. Often with heavy satchel, carrying food and medicine, did I go from wigwam to wigwam ministering, as well as I could, to the sick of all ages, from the old, decrepit ones to the little children, the mortality among whom, owing to their wretched abodes, was very great. As a natural consequence the mission-house was the general resort of any or all who had business with us which called for the exercise of our abilities, imaginary or real, along any of these lines. And so they came with their troubles and sorrows and perplexities by day or by night. The door was never closed against them, and as Indians have a natural aversion to knocking they would quietly come in and if they could not find us in one room, they would search through the whole house, or until successful. We have been aroused at midnight or during the small hours of the morning by the noise of a chair being violently thrown down or the slamming of a table-leaf. Springing up from my bed, I would go out into the kitchen or dining-room and would there often find four or five big Indians.

Perhaps my nervous friends would be startled at the thought of this unceremonious midnight visit. But we got to consider it as an almost every-day, or rather every-night, occurrence. Inquiring the cause of their coming, we heard the following from among the almost endless variety of reasons:

"Missionary, you know George went out shooting deer?"

"Yes," I replied, "I heard him say that he knew where a herd of reindeer had passed along and he thought he would go and have a shot at them."

"Well, he did go," they said, "and when he came up to them and fired, his gun exploded and blew off part of his hand. Will you please come quick over to the wigwam where we have brought him? Bring your instruments and bandages, please, and fix him up."

Of course, I would dress and hurry away with them to do the best I could for the badly wounded man. Occasionally I have been aroused by the loud, forced cough of some one in the room. I hurry out to this night visitor, and, inquiring the reasons of his coming, my sympathies are at once aroused by his words and his emotions.

"Missionary," he says, "my wife he very sick." (They never use "she" when speaking of their wives.) "He going to die. He say to me, 'William, you go to our missionary, and you ask him to come and bring with him the great book, to read to me, and to pray with me before I go out into the great beyond; for I will not see another sun rise.'"

Quickly do I respond to this appeal, and soon we are hurrying through the gloom to the little home, where he of whom

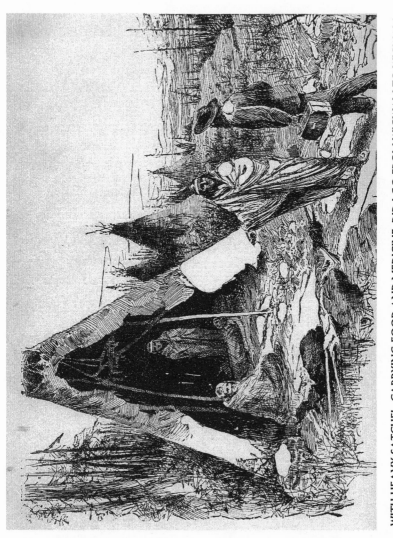

WITH HEAVY SATCHEL, CARRYING FOOD AND MEDICINE, DID I GO FROM WIGWAM TO WIGWAM

Horace sings when he says, "He comes alike, with equal fate, To palace door or cabin gate," is feeling for the heart-strings of the dying woman. We stay in the little home until the quiet, trustful spirit flits away into the presence of Him in whom, in her child-like faith, she so calmly trusted. Thus they came, and they ever found an open door, even if at times their reasons for coming seemed trivial or unnecessary.

Once, through a great storm, and at an unseemly hour, came an old Indian.

"Well, Oo-see-me-mou, what is it?" I asked.

"Missionary," he replied, "you know my cow was very sick?"

"Certainly," I said, "did I not give you a condition powder for her?"

"Well, missionary," he answered, with all the glee of a young-ster with his first pair of trousers, "my cow she all well again, and I thought I must come over and tell you." I congratulated him and sent him off happy to his home miles away.

They were grateful for our open door and for our interest in them, and they never betrayed our confidence in them by pilfering or by any dishonorable action. But we really would have been glad if we could have got them into the habit of knocking at the door when they came. This seemed, however, to be an impossibility; so, as a natural result, the situation was sometimes a little awkward, as the following will show.

One morning I arose very early and went off to help a couple of Indians about their line fences. Soon after one of the big Indians, wishing to see me, came to the mission house. He quietly opened the front door and went in. Not finding me in the first room, he noiselessly opened the next door and inspected that room. Failing there to find me, he pushed on to the next door, which happened to be that of our bedroom. Mrs. Young had just risen, and, throwing a shawl over her shoulders and night-dress, was combing her hair at the mirror, which was op-posite to the door. Fancy her amazement at seeing reflected in the glass before her the head and shoulders of the Indian, who had quietly opened the door and was looking round the room. She turned on him indignantly and shouted, "A-wus-ta kena!" ("Get out, you!"). He quickly got out.

I met him an hour or two after, and not having yet been home I had to hear the story from him. He seemed very much crestfallen in his manner, and told me that Ookemasquao (Mrs. Young's Indian name) was very cross to him, and said "A-wus-ta kena!" so very cross to him that it made him jump. I laughed at him in his troubles and humiliation at having been spoken to so sternly by the dear woman they had all learned to love so well, and told him that perhaps in the future, when he wanted to find me, he had better knock at each door before he entered.

The Indians are quick and observant, and so there was ever a disposition to see if in the home of the missionary there were practiced the teachings which were enunciated from the pulpit or which entered so largely into the advice and counsel which we gave them as we made our pastoral rounds at their little houses or wigwams.

Frequently there were scores of them in the mission-house, each one with some request or reason for coming, and all alert and watchful to see how this or that was done. Of course, it required time and patience for many of them to be skillful in the performance of some new domestic duties. Very easily were some of them discouraged and downhearted at their lack of ability to do as well as the missionary's wife, which was ever their ideal of perfection. All Mrs. Young had to do to cause their faces to brighten was to say, "Persevere, and try again. I wish I could scale and cook the fish as skillfully as you can, and who knows but you will soon be able to beat me at this new work also." Thus encouraged they would try and try again, until in their simple household duties and with their needle and thread, many of them were not inferior to some of their more highly favored sisters in other lands.

Great indeed was the love which they had for our dear children born while we lived among them. The watchful solicitude of the Indian women over the precious mother, both before and after the darling ones were born, was beyond all praise. Their loving care and skill in that isolated land, where no physician was within four hundred miles of us, could not have been surpassed.

Great indeed were the rejoicings among the Indians when it was announced that a child was born at the mission-house, and many were the callers with congratulations, from the dignified chief and principal men to the dear old grandmas of the people.

Our children were considered as of the tribe and treated as to the manner born. It was often quite amusing to see how great an interest some claimed in them. It was no uncommon thing to have a couple of great stalwart Indians come into the house in their noise-less way, and without even saying, "By your leave," or even giving us the morning salutation, to pick up our little ones, from two years old and upward, and, quickly seating them on their shoulders, to quietly flit away with them to their wigwams in the forest.

Never did our children seem happier than when thus riding on the shoulders of these big Indians and holding on to the tresses of their coal-black hair, and never did the black eyes of these red men seem to beam with a softer or happier radiance than when they saw the confidence and trust which these darling children of the pale-faces reposed in them as they prattled out their childish joy in both Cree and English.

We were fortunate in having children who were not nervous or timid, and who seemed just about as fond of the swarthy Indians as of their pale-faced parents. Of course, they were all given Indian names. Egerton, our first-born and only son, they called Sagastaooke-mou, which means "the sunrise gentleman." Lilian, ever full of mirth and brightness, they called Minnehaha, or "Laughing-water." To precious Nellie, who was born when the leaves were falling, and who tarried with us hardly a year, they gave a beautiful name that seemed to be but a sad prophecy of her short life. They called her a beautiful Indian word, which literally meant "the rustling of the falling leaf." Florence, born in the pleasant spring-time, when the birds were returning after the long, cold, quiet winter, and filling the air with their melodies, they called Souwanahquanapeke, which means "the voice of the southwind birds."

We give the pictures of our two eldest children as they appeared when at the call of the missionary authorities we first came out to civilization for a round of missionary anniversary services from Sarnia to Quebec. The Indian women, who loved to dress them up in the beautiful bead and silk worked leather costume of their country, would hardly recognise them as they here appear in their first suits of civilized apparel.

MINNEHAHA AND SAGASTAOOKEMOU

CHAPTER III

HAPPY ROUTINE DUTIES

SURRENDER OF THE HUDSON BAY COMPANY'S CHARTER—
AN INCREASE OF OUR RESPONSIBILITIES—REVERENCE FOR
THE SABBATH AND LOVE FOR AND GOOD ATTENDANCE
IN THE HOUSE OF GOD—PAPOOSES HUNG ON THE
WALLS—STORY OF THE MISSIONARY'S SERMON—THE
SHATTERED HAND—THE WOUNDED MAN'S TESTIMONY—
HIS CONVERSION AND DEATH—THE BRAVE SABBATH-
KEEPING GUIDE—THE SINKING OF THE SHIP—INDIANS
DEEPLY IMPRESSED—ANOTHER ARGUMENT FOR THE
SANCTITY OF THE SABBATH—THE BRIGADE OF BOATS
—THE INLAND FUR-TRADE—PORTAGING—MARVELOUS
STRENGTH AND ENDURANCE OF THE TRIP-MEN—DR.
TAYLOR'S TESTIMONY—THE PRACTICAL TESTING OF THE
QUESTION BETWEEN THE SABBATH-KEEPING AND NON-
SABBATH-KEEPING BRIGADES—THE CAMP-FIRE STORY

SOON after our arrival we were on friendly terms with all, and the blessing of Heaven rested upon our efforts. The good work begun by noble men and women who years before had penetrated into these remote regions and amid many privations had commenced the seed-sowing was now yielding the welcome harvest. May the sowers and the reapers by and by rejoice together!

With my faithful interpreter, Timothy Bear, I visited from house to house and wigwam to wigwam. An almost universal desire to accept the white man's way had taken possession of these Indians, and so there was but little opposition. Even old Tapastanum, the conjurer, became friendly and frequently called to have a talk over a cup of tea.

Thus the blessed work extended and increased until the

Sabbath congregation amounted to several hundreds and the Sabbath and day schools were in a prosperous condition. As the Indians have so little literature in their own language we had both Indian and English taught in the day-schools, the latter, however, with but indifferent success.

A few years after our arrival the charter of the Hudson Bay Company was bought up by the government of the Dominion of Canada. This charter had given them the right to the exclusive trade in furs with the Indians in all this great Northwest country. The loss of their charter was the signal for an influx of traders and adventurers to the country to barter with the Indians for their valuable furs. The coming in of these persons, many of whom, we are sorry to say, were without much principle or character, gave us a good deal of anxiety and very much added to our duties. To keep our people pure and sober we were resolved, if possible. A system of native police was organized, and every effort was put forth with a good degree of success to keep all intoxicating liquors out of the land. Soon after the government took up the matter, and we ever after, up in that land, at least, could rejoice that there were prohibitory laws that really did prohibit.

Another thing that very much pleased us was that the Indians so easily and almost universally accepted the teachings of the good book in reference to reverencing and keeping holy the Sabbath day. Very confidently can I say that I never in any land saw the sacred day better observed. Such a thing as hunting or fishing on the Sabbath was unknown. The day was one of rest and religious worship; every body able to attend the house of God was at all the services; all the family attended. I always encouraged the Indian mothers to bring along their babies. They brought them well wrapped up in moss-bags strapped on a board. This primitive contrivance is called a cradle. The outer cloth covering of this cradle is often decorated with the most beautiful bead-work. With the babies lovingly stowed away in them, the mothers carry them on their backs supported by a strap from their foreheads. When they bring them to church they frequently stand them in the windows or hang them on the walls. It seemed at first a little novel to me to preach in a church where not only were there scores of Indians seated on the floor in preference to using the benches, but where in addition there were a goodly number of fat-faced, black-eyed papooses hanging up on the walls around me. Usually they were very good babies and seldom cried. When one did begin, the watchful mother generally succeeded in quickly quieting it again. I have no sympathy with the nervous preacher who cannot stand the music of a baby's voice, whether the child is red, black, or white.

What sight is there more delightful than to see the parents and all the children together in the house of the Lord? And especially cheering was the sight to us in that land where the people had but lately emerged from a degrading paganism which taught very different things.

This love for the services of the sanctuary was not only a blessing to the people themselves, but it produced a deep impression on many of the unconverted natives around, who were still refusing to accept of Christianity. Several things also occurred which tended to impress upon the minds of the people the beneficial results which follow from keeping the day sacred.

The following story was told me as we rested one quiet Sabbath day on one of my long canoe trips at a camp-fire on the bank of a river very near to the place where the event occurred. The narrator was present when the incident took place. He said:

"A zealous missionary who was passing through this part of the country, finding these Indians were without a missionary, stayed here for several days and conversed with them about the Christian religion. Many became quite interested in his message and gathered a number of the people to hear him. He spent a Sunday with them, and in his sermons he urged them to listen to what he had to tell them out of the great book. Among other things, he told them that the Great Spirit had appointed one day in seven for quiet rest and worship. He did not wish them to hunt or fish on that day, and if they desired his favor they must keep holy the Sabbath day. He also said the Great Spirit was angry with those who disobeyed him, and that he would punish those who did not listen to his words. While the missionary was thus talking an old chief sprang up and said: 'I don't believe it. I am not afraid to hunt or fish on this day. I will do as I like on every day.' And to show how little he cared for the missionary's words he rushed off and, seizing his gun and ammunition, sprang into his canoe, which was only a few yards away from where the people were gathered together on the bank of the river. He quickly paddled away, and as he rounded the point and disappeared he shouted back his defiant words.

"The missionary had not heeded the interruption, and went on with the service. Soon after a shot was heard. Then after a while the Indian was seen coming back in his canoe. It was observed that he returned very slowly and was only paddling with one hand. As he came to the place of landing some of his friends went to him and found that he was in trouble. However, he said but little until he had landed from his canoe and had come up among the little company of people to whom the missionary was still talking. Then lifting up one of his arms, from which it was seen the hand was nearly shot off, he said in a loud voice: 'It would have been a good thing for me if I had listened to the words of the missionary and stayed here instead of rushing away to hunt on this day. See here,' he said, as he shook the shattered arm, around which he had tightly twisted his sash-belt to stop the bleeding, 'see how I am punished for my sin! Now I believe there is a God who is angry with and can punish those who do not keep his day.'"

The incident produced a very great impression upon the people at the time. However, as the missionary's stay among them was but a short one, and they were not visited again for years, no apparent results for good were then seen. Years after, when I took up this place as one of my outstations from Norway House, no Indian more cordially welcomed me than the old man with only one hand. Earnestly did he listen to the truth and strive to obtain all the information possible for his soul's comfort.

I could only visit his land twice a year, once in summer in a birch canoe, and then again in winter with my dogs. He drank in the truth and tried to live as a Christian should. On one of my visits I missed him from among the company that had gathered to welcome me on my arrival. In answer to my inquiries as to his absence they told me that he was dead, but that about the only wish he had had during his sickness was that he might live until the missionary arrived to talk with him about Jesus and pray with him. When the end drew near his mind at times seemed to be wandering, and he talked about various things, but most of the time he seemed to be in prayer. At the close he raised himself up and said to his son Jacob, "O, I wish the missionary were here!" Then he laid back and died.

The missionary was a hundred and fifty miles away, but he firmly believes the omnipresent Saviour was there and poor old Cha-koos found as he left his old maimed body behind that he had exchanged his old wigwam for a mansion in the celestial city.

Another event that produced a profound impression upon the Indians as regards Sabbath observance was the smashup on the Lord's day of the first steam-boat ever built on the great Saskatchewan River. This boat was built at the foot of the Grand Rapids, which are near the mouth of this great river, which, rising in the far West near the Rocky Mountains, pours its vast flood of waters into Lake Winnipeg.

When the steam-boat was being built a number of our skillful Christian Indians, who were clever with tools, were employed by the white builders to aid in the work. As some difficulty was expected in getting the boat up the rapids the most skillful guide on the river was sent for to act as pilot. He had for many years been employed as guide by the Hudson Bay Company to take charge of their brigades of boats which annually carried up the cargoes of goods for traffic and returned laden with the rich furs from the interior trading-posts. As the result of his long years of duty on the river he knew more about its treacherous shoals and dangerous rapids than any other man. When the boat was finished it was loaded with its valuable cargo, being the outfits for all the trading-places in that great Northwest. Steam was got up and word was sent for the guide to come on board and take his place as pilot and direct their course up the dangerous rapids. The answer of the man was characteristic and worthy of remembrance: "I am a Christian. My missionary has taught me to remember the Sabbath day, to keep it holy. Never since I have become a Christian have I traveled on the Sabbath day on this river, and I do not intend to begin now."

Of course, there was annoyance and indignation in the hearts of the officials of the great company that had built the boat. The bold, fearless words of the brave Christian Indian surprised and startled them somewhat, but, standing on their dignity, they thought it would never do to yield to this fool and fanatic, as they called him. However, knowing something of the firmness of the man, they did not by bribes or cajolery try to induce him to yield, but immediately began to try and secure a man to take his place. As the reward promised was considerable, they succeeded in finding in the crowd of Indians on the shore a man who professed to have sufficient knowledge of the rapids to steer the boat safely up to the smooth waters beyond.

With a few sarcastic flings at the brave Christian man who had thus lost his pay for the sake of his conscience, the men embarked and the boat moved out from the shore and began to stem the current of the great river. The new guide, so hastily secured, turned out to be the possessor of more presumption than knowledge of the river. Soon he had the boat in a wrong channel, and in spite of all that could be done, even by the aid of strong hawsers on the shore, the vessel swung round broadside in the stream, and such was the force of the current that the ropes snapped and the steamer was carried back down the rapids, and, collapsing like an egg-shell, went to the bottom with its valuable cargo. Fortunately, many Indians with their canoes were close at hand when the accident occurred, and, paddling to the rescue, they succeeded in saving the lives of all. As some of the poor, dripping white men landed near the Christian guide who had refused to break the Sabbath, he quietly said to them, "If you will make another boat next year and will send for me I will safely take it up for you any day but the Sabbath." Then turning away he left them, now mortified and annoyed that they had not respected his feelings and waited until the Sabbath was ended and thus have had the benefit of his knowledge of the river. They would have been a good many thousand dollars better off, much less ruffled in spirit, and decidedly drier in their persons.

While studying the question of Sabbath observance and doing what we could to retain it in its sanctity among our people we were more and more impressed with the fact of its value to man, not only spiritually, but also physically. The following fact will bear us out in this assertion. For nine years we saw men who rested on the Sabbath day do better work in less time, with better health, than those who kept no day of rest but toiled on continuously without cessation.

The following is the detailed account of the contest between the rival Sabbath-keeping and non-Sabbath-keeping brigades which has enabled me to make the above strong assertion.

Years ago all the Hudson Bay Company's supplies for the Northwest territories were shipped in London in their own vessels to York Factory, on the west coast of Hudson Bay. From this port they were taken by Indians up the great rivers into the interior of the country in heavy boats made for the purpose. These boats, which will carry on an average of about four tons of cargo, are strongly made, that they may not only stand the strain in the frequent rapids of the rivers and outride the storms on the great lakes, but also endure the rough usage of being dragged overland through the rough portages which have to be made around the falls and other obstructions in the rivers. So wild and rough are some parts of the country that as many as seventy portages have to be made in a trip of four or five hundred miles. The packages of goods and bales of furs are done up in

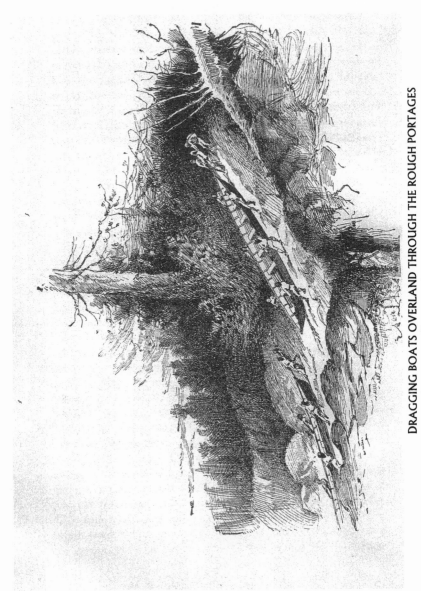

DRAGGING BOATS OVERLAND THROUGH THE ROUGH PORTAGES

bundles weighing from sixty to a hundred pounds each. When a portage has to be made the whole cargo of the boats is carried on the backs of the Indian boatmen, supported by straps from their foreheads. From one to three packages constitute a load. When carrying a load an Indian seldom or never walks, but swings along on a kind of a jog-trot.

So vast is this country that some of the interior posts were two thousand miles away from where the goods were landed on the coast. The result was that on account of the difficulties in the way of getting in supplies for trade, and then in taking out the furs to the home market, often seven years elapsed from the time the goods left London ere the furs obtained for them reached that market. Hundreds of Indians were employed every summer in this work of freighting in goods and bringing out the furs.

The Hudson Bay Company's fort at Norway House was a great depot and distributing center for many years. During a few weeks in our short and brilliant summers it was a place of excitement and activity owing to the arrival and departure of the different brigades, as the collection of boats from each post is called.

One of the great events of the summer was the departure of the different brigades of boats loaded with supplies for the posts in the Athabasca and Mackenzie River districts. These brigades were obtained in different parts of the country, and each boat was manned by the picked men of the tribes, as this trip is not only the longest but the hardest in the country. Many a stalwart man broke down from the hardships of that slavish work, and many a noble life was there lost.

I have seen coal-heavers in Lancashire and in other parts of the world; I have gone down in some of the deepest mines of earth, and have there watched the toilers at their task; I have stood on the massive docks at London and Liverpool, amid the vessels from almost every land, and have there watched how the poor fellows wrought at their tasks; I have looked at the "navvies" at work in the construction of new railroads in our western country; I have been out with the brave fishermen who have toiled all night at their nets amid treacherous breakers and dangerous waves; I have seen the colored sons of Africa as to the rhythm of some weird melody they toiled at the unloading of steam-boats on great western rivers; I have been in the backwoods of Canada where the lumbermen were felling great trees in her magnificent forests and cutting them up for the lumber markets of the world, but I know of no work more trying or severe than that of portaging cargoes in the wild Northwest country, and I know of no laborers who could surpass or even equal the Indians at this exhausting work. Especially was it exciting to spectators when two rival brigades reached a portage at the same time, and the strife was to see which could get their cargoes and boats across in the shorter time.

Once when taking the eloquent missionary secretary, the late Rev. Lachlan Taylor, down to Oxford Mission, we witnessed at Robinson Portage one of these contests between a Norway House and Red River brigade. Although the portage is several miles long, yet some of the men, carrying three pieces, would run from end to end without once stopping. The doctor became intensely excited, and among other things said: "I have traveled all over the world, and have seen men at work every-where, but these men could beat any I ever saw, not even excepting the famous porters at Constantinople."

The brigades selected for this long trip were from both pagan and Christian sections of the country. From our mission a strong brigade went up every year. It was ever to me an interesting sight to watch these scores of active men as they made their final preparations and then started off on their long, adventurous journey. As boat after boat was rapidly loaded and these magnificent specimens of physical manhood took their places, and at the word of command their long, heavy oars rose and fell with clock-like precision, propelling their crafts along with a speed that was surprising, I could not help but think of the times of long ago when propelled by no other power the ships of the

Phenicians, Carthaginians, and even of the Greeks and Romans had met in battle array and fought for the mastery of the seas.

Although the brigades with their valuable cargoes of supplies started together from Norway House for the Mackenzie River and Athabasca districts, I noticed each year that our own Indians of the mission were the first to return with their loads of furs. On talking with them about it they at once and unanimously declared that it was because they *remembered the Sabbath day and kept it holy* that they were able to make the trip in a shorter time than the other brigades that had no Sabbath.

With great pleasure I recall the following account of one of their trips as told me one fall as a camp-fire story by some of the stalwart fellows who had been on the trip themselves. Their simple story is another argument for the day of rest.

"You remember, missionary," said the narrator, "as you were there at the fort to see us off, how all the brigades left together. That was on Wednesday. We went down Sea River to Lake Winnipeg and then turned to the west and crossed over to the mouth of the Saskatchewan River. Up that great river we went until we turned up north toward the height of land. We kept well together for the first few days, and camped not far from each other the first Saturday night. As we from the Christian mission did not intend to travel the next day we selected as safe and pleasant a spot as we could find and made our boat's cargo secure from rain or storm. We gathered sufficient wood for our Sabbath fires, and after supper and prayers lay down to sleep. The next morning the other brigades went on and left us. We put on our Sunday clothes, which we always carried with us, and spent the day as nearly as possible as we would have spent it if we had been at home at our Christian village. We held two services during the day, for you know there are now many of our people who can lead us in these meetings. We had our Bibles and hymn-books with us. We sang and had prayers, and read from the good book and talked of its truths. We had a good rest between the services. Then after supper and prayers we were soon asleep again. Monday morning we were up very early, for you know that daylight comes soon in summer in this land. Soon were our kettles boiled and prayers over, and we were off. Refreshed by our Sabbath's rest, we bent to our oars and made our boats spin along at a great rate. In the portages we could work the harder and get over them the more quickly because of the rest. On we pushed day after day. We passed the different camping-places of the brigades ahead of us, for there is only the one route. When we reached those where the ashes were still warm, or there was a log still burning, we knew that they were now not very far ahead of us. We caught up to them this year Thursday afternoon, and then there was great excitement, as we tried to get ahead of them. They kept us back in the portage into which they had first entered, but when afterward we got out into the river again, where it was a trial at the oars, we managed to get in the lead, and camped that night as the head brigade. Very early were we up and off the next morning, and thus we did not let them pass us before the next Sabbath came. On that day we rested as usual. The other brigades passed us on Sabbath afternoon and pushed on a few miles further, and there camped.

"We were up very early on Monday morning, and came up to the others while they were at breakfast. With a cheer we rowed by, and they did not catch up to us again. We pushed on week after week until we reached the post where we found the brigades that had come down from the Mackenzie River district waiting for us with a cargo of furs. We quickly exchanged loads with them and commenced our return journey. We were three days down on our way home when we met the other brigades going up. We rested every Sabbath day during the whole trip of about two months, and yet were home about a week before the Indians returned who kept no Sabbath but pushed on every day."

As I looked upon the bronzed yet healthy faces, and contrasted them in their manly vigor with some worn-out, spiritless men in the other boats, as their missionary I rejoiced at their story. Deeply interested in the question, I watched, and as well as

I could I studied it for a number of years on these severe testing grounds. Physically our Indians were no larger and apparently no stronger than were those of other places, and yet here is the fact, witnessed and commented upon by others as well as myself, that the men who kept the Sabbath did their work in less time and returned in much better health than those who knew no day of rest.

Gladly then have I recorded this so fully, as another of the unanswerable arguments of facts, that the Sabbath is not only a blessing to man spiritually, but that in its observance he is so aided physically, that he can do more work and keep in better health than those who know not of it.

Return unto thy rest, O my soul; for the LORD hath dealt bountifully with thee. (Psalm 116:7)

A ROCKY MOUNTAIN GLACIER

CHAPTER IV

THE HALF-BREEDS OF MANITOBA*

SCOTCH HALF-BREEDS—LORD SELKIRK—REV. MR. BLACK—DONALD BANNERMAN—"ONLY PEMMICAN"—EARLY STORMY TIMES—THE INDIAN RAID—SINGULAR STRATAGEM—CAUGHT IN THE LOG—RAPID PROGRESS OF THIS THRIFTY PEOPLE—FRENCH HALF-BREEDS—RIEL REBELLION—ANCESTRY—CHARACTERISTICS—POOR FARMERS—SPLENDID HUNTERS—LONG DISCONTENTED—RED RIVER CARTS—THE GREAT BUFFALO HUNT—ANNIHILATION OF THE BUFFALO—WONDROUS CHANGES WROUGHT BY CIVILIZATION—DR. SUTHERLAND'S ELOQUENT WORDS—CANADA'S GREAT FUTURE

THE first indications we had that we were again reaching the abodes of civilized beings, after we had left the frontier settlements of Dakota and Minnesota, in 1868, were the humble log-cabins of the Red River French half-breeds. Their settlements extended along on both banks of the Red River, from Pembina up to the old massive Fort Garry of the Hudson Bay Company. Their number was variously estimated at from six to eleven thousand.

The rise of this semi-civilized half-breed colony in the heart of the American continent is one of the many interesting phenomena similar to other strange ethnological experiments which have been in progress in this New World since its discovery.

In addition to this colony of French half-breeds, we also passed through a large and flourishing settlement of Scotch half-breeds. Their location was farther north on the Red River, and

---

*Today, the term half-breed is not used. Métis people is the correct modern-day term, which stands for those of mixed First Nations and European Ancestry. (see note from publisher).

was known as the Selkirk Settlement. This colony was begun by Lord Selkirk, a Scottish nobleman, early in this century. From the Orkney Islands and the Highlands of Scotland the principal number of his colonists came. They were an industrious, hardy lot of people, and, as has generally been the case at each stage of colonization or of pioneering on this continent, but few of them took with them wives or daughters, and so, like others, when they had settled on a home amid the prairie wilds of that northern river, they took to themselves wives from the native tribes with whom they formed treaties of friendship. Those living there today are the third or fourth generation from these marriages, and they are among the best people in that interesting and rapidly increasing country.

Although during the three quarters of a century, there was a large infusion of Indian blood among these Scotch halfbreeds, yet they were ever a thoroughly civilized people, retaining all the best characteristics of old Scotia. They are very industrious and thrifty, and are the contented owners of large farms and comfortable homes. It was, indeed, a very great surprise to us when, years ago, we penetrated into that then almost unknown land, after passing for many days through the lands of roving wild Indians, and imagining ourselves hundreds of miles from civilization, to enter into this Selkirk Settlement and find here, in the wilderness, a counterpart of a Highland Scottish parish, with a church which was well attended by a devout people. The illusion seemed the more perfect by our frequently hearing the droning of the bag-pipes and several of the half-breeds fluently talking Gaelic. Scottish thrift, rather than Indian shiftlessness, had been paramount among them, and as the result many of them are the possessors of considerable wealth.

We were very much pleased to meet with their worthy minister, Rev. Mr. Black. He was greatly beloved and respected by his people. He was a thorough Scotchman still in all his sturdy independent ways, yet withal was full of quaint humor and loved a pleasant joke and a happy repartee. The Indian blood in the veins of his excellent wife did not make her the less a lady of kindly heart and noble life. Here in this isolated parish they had devoted their lives to the spiritual upbuilding of this interesting people, whose origin and history have in them so much that is romantic and unique.

Human nature is very much alike the wide world over. This good Mr. Black had found out as regards his own isolated flock. While happily exempt from some of the peculiar evils incident to more populous regions, yet there were others which required constant watchfulness on his part to keep in check. Hence he had his clouds as well as sunshine, his anxieties as well as rejoicings.

"Why, what do you think?" said he, one day to some of us when we had been conversing on the subject of the trials and discouragements of ministerial and missionary life. "Now there are my people down in the settlement. Gude people they are in many respects, yet last Sunday morning, while I was preaching to them the sober truths of the Gospel, they dinna seem to try to keep awake, but went to sleep all around me, in spite of my most earnest efforts. The only encouraging thing about it was that some of them *nodded assent* to my remarks. So I had to stop in my discourse to admonish them. I told them that if they did not arouse themselves and hear me out to the end I would keep them in until four o'clock in the afternoon. That aroused them," said the good old man, with a merry twinkle in his kindly eye, "and so I was enabled to finish my sermon to a wide-awake congregation."

From one of these wealthy Scottish half-breeds, a Mr. Donald Bannerman, we purchased a keg of excellent butter. About this Mr. Bannerman, his pastor, Mr. Black, told us a story that had much amused him, and for a time upset the gravity and marred the solemnity of one of his week-evening prayer-meetings.

It seems this Mr. Bannerman was in the habit of taking contracts from the Hudson Bay Company for freighting large quantities of their valuable furs from Fort Garry down to York Factory, on Hudson Bay, for shipment thence to England. Then he would bring up return cargoes of goods or supplies for the next year's trading operations of the company with the Indians and half-breeds. To carry out his contract he used to hire hundreds of Indians and half-breeds as boatmen, or "trippers," as they are generally called. As York Factory is at least eight hundred miles from Fort Garry, and the river route part is full of "portages," the greater part of the summer would be required for a single trip.

The building of the Canadian Pacific Railway, which now stretches its long lines of glittering steel rails through those wild, romantic mountainous regions of the country, as well as across the almost boundless prairies of that goodly land, has about done away with the old primitive methods of tripping except in the remote northern regions, where the solitudes are as yet untouched by civilization. The buffalo from the prairies having disappeared, the far-famed pemmican described elsewhere has also become a thing of the past. But in the time when Mr. Bannerman commanded his brigades it was the principal, and, at times, the only, article of food. On it, with plenty of good black tea, I have lived well for weeks.

One summer, when Mr. Bannerman was going down to York Factory, he very largely strengthened his brigade at Norway House by hiring a number of the Christian Indians from the Methodist mission there. These stalwart men were every-day Christians, and began and closed every day with prayers.

Mr. Bannerman, himself a worthy communicant in Mr. Black's church, was very much pleased with the consistent piety of these converted Indians, as well as very thoroughly satisfied with the thorough way in which they did the work for which he had engaged them. So he and some of his good people gladly joined in with the Indians at morning and evening prayers. Although he was naturally a timid man and always refused to take any active part in religious services, such as praying in public in his own church in the Red River Settlement, yet here, as they journeyed along down the wild river and across the picturesque lakes, he several times, at the request of the Indians, conducted the services and led in prayer.

When he returned home with his brigade his minister, Mr. Black, was delighted to hear that this worthy member of his church had been so "exercising his gifts," and was anxious to have him continue in this good way, and so at the next prayer-meeting at which Mr. Bannerman was present, when a suitable time came, Mr. Black said, "Will Brother Bannerman please lead us in prayer?"

To this request there came the quick response, "I canna do it."

"Why, Brother Bannerman, you prayed with the Christian Indians, and we were delighted to hear of it. Now we want you to pray with us in our own church."

Still he would not comply with his pastor's request, but said decidedly, "I canna do it; I canna pray in English."

Mr. Black, with true Presbyterian perseverance, was loath to give him up, and so he said, "Well, brother, pray in Gaelic or Indian if you cannot in English."

"I canna do it," was the answer still.

A little annoyed at the man's timidity or stubbornness, and wishing to find out in what language he had prayed when among his boatmen, Mr. Black said, "Well, what did you use when among the Indians?"

Quick as a flash came the answer, "*Only pemmican!*"

Of course the minister and people were convulsed with laughter, and the service soon closed.

These Scotch half-breeds, now so comfortably settled, and, as a general thing, in good circumstances, have had their times that tried men's souls and showed the stuff of which they were made. Extermination, at one period of their history, seemed to be their doom, and during the hostilities between the great rival fur companies they had to put up with much persecution.

During those exciting times when the tribes were up, war parties of hostile Indians hovered in their vicinity, ready to swoop down upon them if they thought they could be caught off their guard. The warlike Sioux, hunting for scalps, sometimes came up from his Dakota prairies filled with his horrid designs. But it more frequently happened that his body, pierced by bullets, became the prey of wolves than that he succeeded in his purposes. In spite of the greatest vigilance and care occasionally lives would be sacrificed in those stormy times. Sometimes one of the adventurous hunters, in his excitement, would follow too far on the track of a wounded deer, and perhaps when, as he fondly hoped, he was near success, as he entered the dense forests which then fringed these western rivers, he would be struck down by the gleaming tomahawk of the blood-thirsty villain who had secreted himself in ambush until he could in so cowardly a way deal the treacherous blow.

Still, on the whole, considering their position, so early in the century, in the very heart of the northern Indian country, they had but little to complain of as regards the general conduct of the Indians. The occasional lives lost were mostly in retaliation for some wrongs or cruelties inflicted upon the Indians by whites somewhere. The Indian law of revenge taught the survivors of those shot down by whites that if they could not kill those from whom they had suffered directly they were expected to kill wherever they had a chance. Thus it sometimes happened there, as it has in other lands and other ages, the innocent have suffered for the guilty.

Peace and goodwill generally abounded. The Indians were early taught some lessons they never forgot of the courage and bravery of these white people from over the sea who had come to live among them. Then they had nothing to complain of in reference to broken treaties. Every treaty these white men had made they had honorably kept; and now, having ample farms in that beautiful Settlement, they did not covet the broad prairies or forest regions of the Indian and try to legislate him out of existence. However, they had their baptism of blood as a community, and many of them personally could tell strange tales of marvelous escapes.

An old half-breed told me the following story as really having happened to his father. I had seen the story in print years before, and, as I had associated it with another place, I was at first inclined to question his veracity. However, he stoutly contended that he could not be mistaken, and others afterward stated to me that, although the incident had occurred many years ago, all the old men affirmed that my narrator's father was really the hero of the tale.

It seems that during the stormy times in the early formation of the Settlement some of the Indian tribes became uneasy and excited about the coming into the country of these hundreds of white settlers. Not knowing their motives in coming, and being instigated and poisoned in their minds by some miserable fur-traders and others who were jealous of the formation of the Settlement, the Indians allowed war parties to go out and harass the settlers. Among them was a party of half a dozen who skulked along among the timbers of Red River, waiting in their cowardly way for an opportunity to make an attack.

The father of my informant, being anxious to secure rails with which to fence in a little field of grain which he had sowed, took his ax, maul, and iron wedge, and went down to the woods to try his hand as a rail-splitter. He had already, before this day, felled a large elm-tree and cut up its trunk into logs twelve feet long. He was getting on well with his work, for he was a strong, vigorous man. Several of the smaller logs had been split up, and he was now vigorously driving the iron wedge into the largest one, when he was startled by the war-whoop of the Indians as they sprang at him from their ambush. Holding on to his heavy maul, he only had time to spring upon the prostrate log ere he was surrounded by them. Anxious to capture him alive that he might be reserved for ransom or the torture, rather than kill him at once, they hesitated to shoot their arrows or close upon him with their tomahawks or knives. So, pretending to be friends, and saying, "How! How!" they wanted to shake hands; but the threatening way in which that heavy maul was lifted warned them

to keep their distance. Among them was one villain who understood a little English, and so, after the white man found out that
they wanted him to go with them, although well knowing their
horrid designs, he, seeing nothing else but death if he refused,
at length very cheerfully consented on condition that they would
help him finish splitting that log, that his family might have the
rails for the fence. Strange to say, to this they consented. So, still
retaining his position of advantage upon the log, he showed them
where the large crack was which he had already made by driving
in the iron wedge before they came. He directed them to go three
on each side of the log, and, putting their long thin hands into the
great crack, to pull as hard as they could, while he with the maul
would drive in the wedge and the work would soon be done. No
sooner said than done. Sure of their victim, they were ready for
a little sport, and so they took the assigned positions and pulled
most vigorously. To throw them off their guard the white man
struck the wedge a vigorous blow or two, and thus perceptibly
widened the crack. Then, as his quick eye saw that every hand was
well in the crack, he gave his wedge a side blow so vigorous that it
instantly flew out of its position, and six simultaneous yells, from
so many imprisoned and most thoroughly captured Indians, told
of the success of his little scheme. Those Indian warriors did not
again return to disturb that colony.

After sharing in the stirring events and vicissitudes inevitably
incident to "Western border life, these regions are now largely
partaking of the advantages of the older settled communities.
Years ago many of their promising young men, after exhausting
the educational advantages of their home schools, went out to
other lands and in first-class colleges or universities have credit-
ably held their own against all competitors. They are now to be
found in many places of honor and responsibility in the growing
provinces of the West, and also in the Dominion government
employ. To the casual observer there is no peculiar trait or look
to distinguish them from other people. Intellectually and physically they are the peers of the noblest of the land.

SIX SIMULTANEOUS YELLS . . . . TOLD OF THE SUCCESS OF HIS LITTLE SCHEME

"Westward the course of empire takes its way."

And so, as the waves of our Anglo-Saxon civilization roll on and on farther west, Time works his marvelous changes for weal or woe. With the evils of this busy age come the blessings. Very evidently has it been so here. The long, straggling settlement of cabins and log-houses, surrounded by partially cultivated fields, has been transformed into a land of beautiful rural homes and magnificent farms. At one end of this little colony not more than a generation ago there stood, almost solitary and alone, the trading-post of Fort Garry. To it, at certain seasons of the year, there came to trade the wild Indians, in single file, along the narrow trail. The half-breed settlers, often with their families crowded into their rude, primitive carts, combining business with pleasure, appeared at its counter to exchange some of the produce of their fields for different things essential to supply their simple wants. Flowers bloomed everywhere in wondrous beauty, and the luxuriant prairie grasses, several feet high, as the gentle breezes swept over them, rose and fell like mimic waves far as the eye could reach.

Now, more than the touch of the enchanter has been here. The trail along the bank of Red River has become the main street of a flourishing city, the capital of a great province, the home of many thousands of people, who are enthused with the possibilities of the future of their country. To pick out of that energetic mass of humanity those with Indian blood in their veins is an utter impossibility. The intermixture of the races, however, is there, and doubtless in sufficient amount to aid in the development of characteristics which, it is to be hoped, will not be defects, but blessings, in the coming generations.

The news of the Riel Rebellion, a few years ago, suddenly brought into prominence the fact that there existed in the heart of this American continent a proud, high-spirited people of mixed French and Indian origin. Of that war and its causes I am not now going to write. However, it was very evident that "some one had blundered." Happily those days are over. Treaty rights have been respected, and wisdom is being learned by experience, although the Métis was at first treated with scant courtesy by the never over polite incrowding English-speaking immigrant, who looked upon his poor attempts at farming with disgust, and listened to his *patois* with contempt. Then his moc-casined feet and brilliant-colored scarf -belt, beaded cap, firebag and leggins, and distinct Indian face seemed to so ally him to the native tribes that too many never for a moment thought he could have any grievances to be redressed. They little dreamed of the blood that flowed in his veins. The two "uprisings" and the difficulty experienced in quieting these fiery spirits will not soon be forgotten.

Whatever may be the cause, the French half-breeds have retained in their looks and also in their habits much more of the peculiar characteristics of their Indian ancestry than the Scotch half-breeds. Many of these French half-breeds are descendants of the early employees of the Hudson Bay and Northwest fur companies. These hardy voyagers and trappers were obtained at the French settlements in Lower Canada. Many of them have some of the most aristocratic names of France, and profess to have in their veins some of the best blood of some of the noblest families of that old historic country. As a natural result not a few of them inherited both the traditions and feelings of the past; for were they not the descendants of those adventurous warriors who, long years ago, had left their native land and, tinder the guidance of such men as La Salle, Champlain, De Tracey, and Frontenac, had come to carve out their fortunes here in the New World? They well knew that there was a time when their French ancestors were rulers from Quebec to the Mississippi. Some of their forefathers, humiliated by the English victory on the Plains of Abraham and the subsequent surrender of Que-bec and then of the whole of Canada, had hurried away into the vast wilderness, and there, amid the excitement of almost savage life, had kept alive in the hearts and memories of their

children and grandchildren, as the years rolled by, the story of
their humiliation and hatred of that race which had made the
fleur-de-lis of France go down before the red cross of England.
With such antecedents it is no wonder that these half-breeds
were ever vastly superior to the Indian tribes around them,
with whom they had become so allied by marriage. The word
"Métis" is the one used by themselves to designate the children
of these peculiar marriages. The word, which means "mixed," is
much more accurate than "half-breed," now that the European
and the Indian blood is mixed in every degree. These Métis are
physically superior to their Indian and French ancestors, and
from personal observation I can indorse what Mr. Dawson of the
Red River exploring expedition has said when he writes of them
as follows: "I know from my own observation that the French
half-breeds at Red River are a gigantic race as compared with
the French Canadians of Lower Canada." Although having in
their veins so much Indian blood, they can hardly be regarded as
approximating to the wild nomadic Indian tribes. Although not
at all equal to the Selkirk settlers as farmers, yet they have their
own large farms and work them very much as do the *habitants*
of the Province of Quebec. They adhere to the Roman Catholic
Church. They are well supplied with priests under the guidance
of the venerable Archbishop Tache, a gentleman who has played
a very prominent part in that young country's history.

For many years the half-breeds were at open war with the
Sioux and other Indian tribes, and frequently imitated their op-
ponents in the methods of carrying on the contest. But they ever
manifested their superiority, and displayed a discipline, courage,
and self-reliance that made them such victors in every conflict
that it has become a habit with them to look with contempt upon
their Indian foes. And yet, while from the beginning the Métis,
by their superior discipline and force of character, have ever been
able to dominate the red men, they have never had any ambitious
designs to conquer them. They always preferred to live in peace
and harmony with them; while at the same time they were prompt,

when necessary, on account of some murderous or thievish raids, to teach them wholesome lessons of their power to punish. To the credit of the Métis it can be said that they in all their century's existence were never known to indulge in unprovoked or aggressive war. Their Indian wars were only those of self-defense or for the protection of their rights of property, and they gave proofs of some infusion of civilization into their methods of war, in that they never scalped or mutilated the dead or tortured their prisoners. Victorious in every conflict, and then magnanimous to their foes, they extorted from them their respect as well as their fear.

Under the despotism of the Hudson Bay Company, which kept the whole country subservient to its interests as solely a fur-producing region, all extensive efforts to develop the agricultural resources of the land were discouraged. Only what could be absorbed in the country, in the prosecution of the fur trade, was raised, as there were no markets for any surplus. Under this system many chafed, and as a natural result there was an abolition of the monopoly of the company, and freedom of trade was accorded to all. Long trains of Red River carts, loaded with the produce of the country, wended their way to St. Paul's, although it was many days' journey. Very picturesque looked these long lines of adventurous traders as they entered into the then flourishing little city. Their carts were manufactured by themselves, and had not in their construction a single particle of iron. Then, in addition to their primitive appearance, as they were never oiled or greased, the discordant music made by them attracted a good deal of attention and caused no little amazement to the wide awake citizens. Each cart was drawn by one ox that was harnessed up like a horse and placed between the two shafts.

The almost gigantic half-breeds, dressed in picturesque tanned deerskin suits, and bronzed by the wind and sun of the long prairie trip of many hundreds of miles, were shrewd traders and quick to make as profitable bargains as possible. The result was that when, after a good deal of excitement, the Dominion government of Canada assumed authority of that

THE OLD RED RIVER CART

Northwest country in 1870, it found a people, although living so remote from civilization, in comfortable circumstances and in possession of every thing they needed for the requirements of their simple habits.

In years gone by, the great annual event in the life of the Métis was the grand buffalo hunt. It occurred toward the end of summer, after the crops had been harvested, and there was but little work to do on the farm. All is excitement among them, and nothing is heard but the din of preparation. Old men rehearse their past triumphs, and young men boast of what they intend to do. Women and children are huddled into the capacious carts, while the men mount on their well-trained horses, which are justly called "buffalo runners." In semi-military array, the long cavalcade, numbering hundreds of persons, sets out for those distant regions where the scouts report the buffaloes are feeding. Every year, since the waves of the Anglo-Saxon civilization crossed the Mississippi, these Métis hunters had to go farther west in order to find the game.

I have picked up the skulls and bones of the buffaloes on the banks of the Red and Assiniboine Rivers, but long years have now passed since they quenched their thirst in those streams. Hunted and slaughtered incessantly by Indian, Métis, and white man, they were driven backward and westward until in the shadows of the Rocky Mountains the last herds of these noble and valuable animals have been ruthlessly destroyed. It does seem a pity that the strong arms of the United States or Canadian governments were not stretched out for the protection from extermination of these really valuable animals. But in the days about which I am writing they still roamed in countless multitudes over those western prairies and furnished the Indian and Métis with the principal part of their food. When the great hunting party to which we have referred was fairly under way a great council was held at a camp-fire, and a leader or president was appointed. Then a number of the most trusted men were elected as captains, and these selected others, who were called constables, to aid them in carrying out the rigorous laws which governed the whole party. The hunt being thus organized every member of it was considered under military law. Implicit obedience was demanded from all. No hunter was permitted to return home or go out shooting on his own account; and when the region of country was reached where the great herds of buffaloes were feeding no gun was allowed to be fired until the leader had given the word. The hunting was done on horseback, and the well-trained horses thoroughly entered into the excitement of the sport. It was, indeed, a wondrous spectacle to see those hundreds of stalwart men, as fine horsemen as the world ever produced, dressed in their picturesque garments and holding back, until the word to advance is given, their neighing, dancing, excited, fiery racers that, having by sight or scent detected the presence of the buffalo, are longing for the fray.

How admirably the men are dressed for such exciting work! Every thing about them, and also the accouterments of their horses, are exactly suited for the hour. Their little saddles are

DRESSED IN THEIR PICTURESQUE GARMENTS AND HOLDING BACK UNTIL THE WORD TO ADVANCE IS GIVEN

made of deerskin, strong and enduring, yet soft as flannel. Under it is the far-famed saddle-cloth, extending beyond the saddle on every side and beautifully ornamented with bead or silk-thread work by the fond wife or bright-eyed sweetheart. On they move, their highly ornamented whips swinging by a loop over their wrist. In one hand is held the trusty carbine, and with the other they restrain their fiery steeds until they get well in range of the buffaloes and hear the welcome signal for the charge from the captain. Then they dash forward with a deafening yell. The great herds of buffaloes, bewildered and excited, rapidly rush away, but are speedily overtaken by the swift runners. Pell-mell into the herd of wild animals dash the horsemen, and at once there is the greatest rivalry among these hunters as to who can, in the shortest time, kill the greatest number of these splendid beasts. All are firing and all trying to hit buffalo and not one another. It is intensely exciting sport. Both men and horses seem almost wild. How they escape as they do is simply marvelous. Bullets are flying everywhere; for some of the fiery horses have carried their riders so far into the herd that they turn in their saddles and shoot at the maddening, excited crowd of animals behind them. Then frequently some of the old bulls, maddened by wounds and excited by the smell of blood and the presence of the hunters, suddenly turn and, with lowered heads and fearful roars, charge the too adventurous hunters. Well is it for them that their well-trained chargers are quick of eye and nimble on their feet. If it were not so no unfortunate Spanish bull-fighter and his horse were ever more quickly or cruelly gored and tossed than would be this fiery Métis of the plains and his gallant steed. Often hundreds of buffaloes were slaughtered in one of these wildly exciting charges.

After the skins had been taken off the women skillfully sliced off the flesh in large, thin layers of meat, which they carefully dried by the heat of the sun or well-managed fires. In this way many bundles of dried meat were prepared, which was pleasant to the taste and would keep sweet and good for many months.

Thousands of pounds of pemmican would also be prepared, and great quantities of the buffalo tallow were melted down into large cakes and carefully preserved for future use. When sufficient supplies had been obtained the expedition returned home. The same watchful care had to be used to prevent surprise or sudden attack from their alert and cunning enemies. Every night the tents were pitched in a circle, while the carts and other things were so arranged that the whole encampment was made into a perfect network of defense. All these precautions were necessary, for the French half-breeds and many of the wild Indian tribes were not always on the best of terms, and if one caught the other napping—well, somebody suffered.

Great and marvelous are the changes which have in these later years come over these great plains and fertile prairies. The days of vast herds of buffaloes thundering along, with plumed and painted Indians or excited French half-breeds in full chase, have gone forever. Civilization, with its attendant blessings, and, alas! on account of its imperfection with some of its evils, has driven back the game and the picturesque hunters, and is dotting the land with dwellings of the industrious white man, who has evidently come to stay. Many are the transformations which he is making. His iron roads are already made across the matchless prairies, and up and on through mountain glens and glacier passes, by placid lakes of crystal beauty, set like gems of "purest rays serene," with their glorious background of mountains whose snowy tops lift themselves forever above the fleecy or tempestuous clouds. Already with an eye to the beautiful has man marked out parks and pleasure resorts of wondrous beauty and sublimity, where, amid scenery more entrancing, beautiful, and grand than any that Europe can offer, the weary over-worked ones in multitudes will yet come for health and renewed vigor into the glorious air and to the healthful springs which bubble up rivaling in reality the fabled nectar of ancient times.

But while those glorious Rockies, with their mountain lakes and wondrous glaciers and the emerald rivers of ice will attract

WITH THEIR GLORIOUS BACKGROUND OF MOUNTAINS

additional tourists by thousands, it will be on the boundless fertile prairies that the busy multitudes will find their happy homes and make their comfortable livelihood. Of the numbers who will yet come, and of the possibilities of the future of that land, no man can judge. The wildest dreamer may fall short of what may still be accomplished. The changes of a few short years have been simply wonderful. Greater things are yet in store. On a career of progress and prosperity that land has started. May nothing occur to mar its bright upward growth in every thing calculated to make it as its great Creator himself desires! I cannot better close this chapter than by here quoting from the fluent pen of the Rev. Alexander Sutherland, D.D., the honored senior secretary of one of the great missionary societies, words written by him on his return from, and published in his interesting book, *A Summer in Prairie Land*. He says:

"As I pen these lines I stand again in fancy where a few months ago I stood in fact, on the summit of a lofty foothill of the Rocky Mountains. Behind me rose the mountain range, beyond which the sun was sinking toward the western sea, and I thought of the vast treasures embedded in these rocky fastnesses which the hand of human enterprise would one day bring to light; of the towering forests on the Western slopes, vast enough to supply the markets of the world; of the teeming fisheries with food supply for a continent, and fertile valleys where millions would yet find a home. Before me stretched the rolling foot-hills, and beyond these the distant plain; but imagination passed swiftly onward to where the Atlantic surf breaks on our Eastern coast, and I thought of the splendid harbors and rich fisheries and mineral wealth of Nova Scotia, the fertile acres of Prince Edward, the pine forests of New Brunswick, the commerce of Quebec, the agricultural wealth and growing manufactures of Ontario; of our mighty lakes, those highways of commerce that link together the East and the West; and then again my eye rested upon the varied panorama of hill and vale and distant plain spread out at my feet. Far as the eye could reach there was no sign of human habitation, and no sound of human activities broke the stillness; but as thought took in the possibilities of the future I stood intently listening like one who:

Hears from far the muffled tread
Of millions yet to be—
The first low dash of waves where yet
Shall roll the human sea.

"In fancy's ear I heard the lowing of cattle from the hill-sides, the hum of industry from a hundred towns and villages, the merry shout of children returning from school, and in the distance the thundering tread of the iron horse as he sped swiftly across the plain. As I looked again the whole scene was transfig-ured. Everywhere quiet homesteads dotted the plains and nestled among the hills, the smoke of factories rose thickly on the air, a hundred village spires glittered in the rays of the setting sun, while golden fields of ripening grain filled up the interspaces and waved in the passing breeze; and I said in my heart: 'Lo, here is a dominion stretching from sea to sea, and from the river unto the ends of the earth, with the garnered experience of the centuries behind it, with no fetters of past abuses to cramp its energies or hinder its development, with no outside jealousies ready' to take advantage of its weakness, or avaricious neighbor covetous of its wealth. Starting thus in the career of empire, with unfettered limbs and a hearty 'Godspeed' from the great sisterhood of nations, surely nothing short of persistent folly or deliberate wickedness can mar the future of its hopes.'"

CHAPTER V

THE INDIANS' GREATEST CURSE— THE WHITE MAN'S FIRE-WATER

TERRIBLE RESULTS WHICH HAVE FOLLOWED FROM ITS INTRODUCTION AMONG THEM—PATHETIC PROTESTS OF THE INDIANS AGAINST IT—AN ELOQUENT BUT FRUITLESS ADDRESS—SAD SCENES WITNESSED—CUNNING TRICKS OF WHISKY-TRADERS TO BRING IN THE LIQUOR AMONG THE INDIANS—QUEER METHODS OF "TREATING"— DISAPPOINTING VISIT TO AN INDIAN TRADING-POST— INDIANS ALL DRUNK ON THE WHITE MAN'S RUM—OUR LIVES IN JEOPARDY—SIGENOOK'S WILL-POWER—PROHIBITION NOW THE LAW IN MANY PARTS OF THE COUNTRY

NOTHING has done more to impede the progress of Christianity and the blessings of a genuine civilization among the Indians than the introduction of spirituous liquors among them by the white people. In their original state, the red men of America had no intoxicating liquors. The wholesome water from the springs, streams, and great lakes furnished them all the beverage they required. And yet no people of whom we have any knowledge can be more infatuated by this terrible evil when it once gets the mastery over them than the red Indian. When once he gets a taste for the fire-water, his burning, craving appetite seems to have no bounds, and he will do any thing and part with every thing in order that he may obtain the accursed stuff. I have known them to part with their furs, guns, traps, blankets, yea, even sell wives and children, for the unprincipled white man's fire-water. A woman by the name of Norwich, when half intoxicated, in her mad frenzy for more liquor sold her only child, a bright-eyed little girl, for a quart of whisky.

When drunk the generally phlegmatic, stoical Indian often becomes a fiend incarnate. The quiet decorum of an Indian village is changed into a pandemonium when the white traders, with their poisonous compounds called fire-water, get possession and cunningly scatter it among the hunters ere they begin to trade with them for their valuable furs or skins. I have in my missionary wandering had to witness scenes that filled my heart with sorrow for the poor Indians who were so foolish as to have any thing to do with the wretched stuff. Toward the white men who brought in the liquor, no words of indignant protest were too severe; but little cared they for a missionary's pleadings. The demon of gain had so taken possession of them that Indians, morals, character, health, life, or family were nothing to them if only they could so excite the Indian's appetite for drink as to rob him of his natural shrewdness and carefulness in bargaining and thus get his rich furs for a trifle.

When infuriated with drink the men used to terribly beat their wives, and often drag them for many yards by the hair of their head. The helpless children came in for their full share of suffering from their enraged or maddened fathers or older brothers. Fortunate was it if, in the beginning of the drunken debauch, some of the women had been successful in gathering up the guns, tomahawks, axes, knives, and other deadly weapons, and carrying them away and concealing them in the woods for the time being as precautionary measures. And yet, notwithstanding this, murders frequently occurred during the carnival of sin. If one of the drunken bouts happened in winter, during the bitter cold, dreadful sufferings and often much fatality resulted. Twelve children have been known to have perished in one drunken frolic.

Here is an earnest and pathetic address which was made by a chief called Little Turtle to some noble members of the Society of Friends, who have always been the friends of the Indians. It was delivered as he was passing on his way to Washington to plead with the President of the United States to put a stop to the traffic in fire-water among his countrymen. Though uttered many years ago it is still applicable:

"BROTHERS AND FRIENDS: When our forefathers first met on this continent your red brethren were very numerous; but since the introduction of what you call spirituous liquors, but what we think we may justly call poison, our numbers have greatly diminished. It has destroyed a great number of your red brethren. It is not an evil of our own making. We had it not among ourselves, but it is an evil placed among us by the white people, and so we look to them to remove it out of our country. We tell the traders to fetch us useful things—bring us goods that will clothe us and our women and children, and not this liquor that destroys our health, our reason, that destroys our lives. But all I have said thus far has been of no service, and has given us no relief from this curse. My friends and brothers, I rejoice to find that you agree in opinions with us, and are anxious, if possible, to be of service to us in removing this great evil out of our country—an evil which has destroyed so many of our lives that it has caused our young men to say: 'We had better be at war with the white people. This liquor which they introduce into our country is more to be feared than the gun or the tomahawk. There are more of us dead by this fire-water since the treaty of peace than we lost by the six years of war before.'"

This is a terrible indictment against the abominable traffic, that more should have been killed by the white man's liquor than were cut off in those bloody wars. Continuing his address to these Baltimore Friends, Little Turtle described the execrable methods of the unprincipled white traders in their selfish dealings with the Indians:

"Brothers, when our young men have been out hunting and are returning home loaded with skins and furs on their way it often happens that they are met by the white traders with this whisky. The traders tell the young hunters to take a little drink. Some of them would say, 'No, I do not want it.' They go on till they come to another house where they find more of this same kind of drink. It is there offered again. They refuse, and again the third time; but finally the fourth or fifth time it is offered one accepts of it and takes a drink, and, getting one, he wants another, and then a third or fourth, till his senses have left him. After his reason comes back to him, when he gets up and finds where he is he asks for his furs and skins. The answer is:

'You have drunk them.'

'Where is my gun?'

'It is gone.'

'Where is my blanket?'

'It is gone.'

'Where is my shirt?'

'You have sold it for whisky.'

"Now, my white brothers, figure to yourselves what condition this man must be in. He has a family at home, a wife and children who stand in need of the profits of his hunting. Think of what must be the wants and sufferings when even he himself is without a shirt!"

While I was out in the Northwest laboring among the Indians, the following occurred: The Canadian government in its efforts to protect and save the red men, as well as to keep them in order, had established a large company of mounted police in the great region west of Manitoba. They tried faithfully to do their duty, and as a natural result peace and quietude abounded. Still, in spite of all their alertness and care, there were times when the whisky traders were too sharp for them, and trouble followed.

One day the guard of police near the boundary-line between the United States and Canada saw coming across the small river which there separated the two countries a number of traders. According to their instructions they visited their carts and carefully looked through the supplies to see if there were any intoxicating liquors, which, if they had found, they would have quickly spilled on the ground. Their diligent search, however, revealed nothing that was contraband. In these western prairies there are often long stretches between streams where no water is. The result is the carts are furnished with a five or ten gallon keg, according to the number of persons and horses traveling. This keg is filled at each stream for use till the next is reached. When these traders saw the police coming one of them leisurely picked up the keg and carried it down to the stream of clear, beautiful water which they had just crossed. While the police were looking through the cart he was apparently filling up his keg. When this was done he lifted it up with great effort, and, putting it on his shoulder, he brought it up and threw it among the goods which were being overhauled in the cart. As nothing objectionable was found they were allowed to proceed to the camp of the Blackfeet Indians, where they wished to trade.

Several days after word came to the police barracks that there had been a terrible time in the Blackfeet village, that some traders with liquor had got in among them, and, after setting them crazy and mad with the fire-water, had succeeded in getting eight or ten thousand dollars' worth of furs from them, and had escaped across the boundary-line into Montana. The police were of course indignant at having been so overreached. It seems that the keg which with so much ado one of the wretches was observed to apparently fill with water was already full of the horrid western whisky, and his ruse was only to throw the policemen off their guard, and unfortunately in this succeeded all too well. In the carnival of death that resulted among the Indians, four men were murdered, and others were so wounded that they died soon after, and some were maimed for life.

It is indeed a cause of thankfulness that the liquor traffic has been suppressed among the northern tribes of Canadian Indians most effectually. But it was not always so. While the great fur-trading company that long held absolute rule in that land boasted that they never sold a glass of rum to an Indian, it was notorious that many barrels every year were distributed among them in a way equally pernicious. Such sights as this I have seen at an interior trading-post: A number of Indians laden with valuable furs have come in from their distant hunting-grounds and are gathered around the little store of the great fur company. The heavy door is opened and six or eight only of the men are admitted at once. Then the door is closed and the rum is pro-duced. To each man is given a large tin cup full, which he drinks with great gusto. When all have been served and they are about to be let out, that another squad may come in, one says to the clerk in charge, "Please give us a little more." If he is an obliging fellow he will generally comply, as he well knows the purpose for which it is wanted. From this last supply each man fills his mouth as full as possible, and then with cheeks distended turns toward the door which is opened for his exit. As they come out their friends rush round them with open mouths and from each of these well-filled ones a little rum is squirted into this open mouth and that open mouth until all is thus fired out. And, as turn about is fair play, when these later ones are admitted in they come out with full mouths also and treat those who in this primitive way had treated them.

Not always did the distribution of rum end so well or have such a ludicrous aspect. I well remember one summer after traveling many days in a birch canoe with a couple of faithful Indians, when on the journey we had been drenched by the rains, tormented by the mosquitoes, and nearly wrecked in some of the great rapids, to find on our arrival at a pagan Indian village where we had long desired to preach the Gospel, that a so-called Christian white man with his wretched fire-water had got in before us. Most of the Indians were in a maudlin state of drunk-enness and were clamoring for more liquor. I was annoyed and indignant at what I saw, but was powerless to do any thing. The trader had around his trading-post, which consisted of several small log-houses, a stockade fence about twelve or fourteen feet high. This fence was made by digging a trench several feet deep and placing in it the stockades, which were the trunks of small trees about a foot thick. From these the bark was peeled off and the upper end sharpened to a point. These were placed side by side in the trench and securely fastened by transverse bars spiked on the inner side. When well made as this one was, such a wall affords a good deal of protection. Fortunately for this trader, he had treated the Indians to his rum on the outside of his wall, and seeing danger when they began to call for more, he handed them more liquor and then with his three or four men took refuge inside of his walls. In this inclosure with my canoe-men I had also gone, as I saw that trouble was brewing. The additional liquor given the Indians only seemed to make them clamor for more, and they were resolved to have it. The trader was now very much frightened, and at this I must admit I rejoiced. Fortunately for him, he and his men had succeeded in closing the gates before any of the mad, drunken, yelling fellows had got in. Night was now coming down upon us. Inside the stockade were we, a few white men and my Christian Indian boatmen. Outside was the crowd of drunken, yelling savages changed by this poisonous compound, the white man's rum, from being quiet, sedate, wood Indians, into furious demons. Wives and children were terribly beaten or chased away into the forest gloom. Some, fortunately for us, were so under the influence of the liquor that they fell off into a drunken slumber. A number of others, with appetites excited by what they had had, resolved to have more, and so they made a desperate effort, which was continued for hours, to get inside of the high stockaded wall. It was well for us that they were so drunk that they were incapable of combining for any organized effort. All they seemed capable of doing was to try and climb over the stockade, with dire threats of vengeance. The trader and his men armed themselves with long poles, and as fast as a head was seen emerging above the top they quickly caught the unfortunate transgressor under the chin with the end of these poles and hurled him to the ground below. The din and threats from outside at times were terrible, and the trader was quaking with fear, and I must candidly add that I rejoiced to see him frightened at his own wretched work, although I well knew if the angry Indians should use fire or other harsh means to conquer we would all be involved in the common disaster.

Toward sunrise they sobered off and the danger was over.

Of course, my visit was a complete failure, and with a heavy heart, with my faithful canoe-men, who were about as grieved and saddened as I was at what we witnessed, we turned our faces homeward and after several days of hard paddling reached our homes, having to admit that the wicked white man, with his rum and whisky, was the Indian's greatest curse, and that one such unprincipled man with his spirituous liquors could do much more injury than a dozen missionaries could do good.

It is pleasing to read such incidents as the following, and to find that there are even among the Indians some who have enough force of will and regard for their self-respect to break loose from the fetters that intemperance would bind around them.

Sigenook, of Manetouwaning, was a great warrior and orator, but unfortunately he became so fond of the white man's whisky that he became a terrible sot. He was a man of gigantic strength and had an ungovernable temper when drunk. So dangerous was he that when he began to drink the only way of safety was for his attendant to ply him with drink until he became insensible. Then only did his companions and attendant feel safe from his knife or tomahawk. One day, when he was in one of his drunken stupors, a Canadian Indian agent, knowing Sigenook's good qualities when sober, thought he would by a novel method try to reform him. The plan he adapted was this: Obtaining a quantity of rope, he very securely bound hand and foot the helpless, drunken, gigantic man, and then left a little miserable, feeble, decrepit boy to watch over him while he slept, with orders that just as soon as the Indian awoke he was to hasten to him with the news, but by no means was he to tell the chief who had bound him.

After some hours Sigenook awoke, and of course was furious at finding himself bound. He angrily demanded of the boy who had dared to bind such a mighty warrior as he was. The little lad gave him no answer, but at once hobbled away to the white man with the news that the chief was awake. The gentleman hurried over to the furious man, who was making the most desperate efforts to escape, but all in vain. The not overly conscientious white man told him that the helpless little boy had bound him and that he had lain for hours exposed to the derision and contempt of the whole village. Then he gave him a great lecture on the disgrace and degradation a great warrior like he professed to be had brought on himself by thus lowering himself below the brutes to gratify his vile appetite and thus making himself so helpless that he could not even protect himself from insult or annoyance. Sigenook's pride was humbled, and he was greatly mortified at his humiliation and disgrace in the eyes of his own people and before the whites, and he then and there resolved that he would never again be found in such a condition. When released he at once took the pledge of total abstinence, and he was ever after true to his resolution.

This was, however, not always the case with those who tried to reform. As with the whites so it is with the poor Indians. When once the appetite has been formed for strong drink it becomes a terrible tyrant, and is ever striving for the mastery. We had all the trouble, in one form or other, at our missions, in the days when liquors could be obtained, that afflict and harass missionaries in other lands, where the white man's intoxicants are ruining more immortal souls than the missionaries rescue.

So terrible is this evil among the Indians, and so liable are they to fall, if once they begin to tamper with intoxicating liquors, that I always made my mission churches total abstinence societies. I insisted on every man who wished to be called a member of the church that he should be a total abstainer. Some were at first a little inclined to think I was too strict, but afterward they rejoiced that this law was made and rigidly enforced. Many temptations were put in the way of the Indians by vicious and unprincipled rum-sellers, but as a general thing our converts were true and steadfast, and all rejoiced when the proclamation of the government of the Dominion of Canada arrived declaring that all traffic in intoxicating liquors should cease in those northern territories.

CHAPTER VI

THE RELIGION OF THE INDIANS

THEIR RELIGIOUS INSTINCTS STRONGLY DEVELOPED—
SIMILARITY OF BELIEFS AMONG ALL THE TRIBES—A
GOOD AND A BAD SPIRIT—MULTITUDES OF INFERIOR
GODS—MARVELOUS SIMILARITY BETWEEN MANY INDIAN
AND ANCIENT JEWISH CUSTOMS—BELIEF IN AND FEAR OF
WINDAGOOS, OR MAN-EATERS—STORY OF A MISSIONARY
SPEECH—REFERENCE TO CANNIBALS BRINGS UP THE DREAD
OF WINDAGOOS—PEOPLE ALL FLEE TO AN ISLAND—
BROUGHT BACK BY THE MISSIONARY

MAN has been defined by a certain philosopher to be "the religious animal." And very strange indeed is it that no tribe or nation of any size has been found on this broad earth of ours without the instincts of worship. To this universal belief the Indians are not exceptions, but on the contrary are endowed with what may be called the religious instincts in a remarkable manner. Pope correctly grasped the trend of the Indian's mind when he wrote:

> Lo, the poor Indian! whose untutored mind
> Sees God in clouds, or hears him in the wind;
> His soul, proud Science never taught to stray
> Far as the solar walk or milky way;
> Yet simpler Nature to his hope has given,
> Behind the cloud-topt hill, a humbler heaven;
> Some safer world in depths of woods embraced,
> Some happier island in the watery waste.

Their superstitious fears (called their religions) influence their impressible and fickle spirits in a manner that at times is almost incredible, and cause them to inflict sufferings upon themselves as severe as any inflicted by the devotees in the worst regions of India or Africa. The religion of the red Indians is mixed up with all they see or hear or do. It is associated with various confused beliefs and often accompanied by many complicated and magical rites. These religious beliefs of the different tribes of Indians bear a striking analogy one with the other, and in this we see a strong argument of the oneness of the race. Long years of separation as tribes and the lack of a written language in which to keep an accurate record of their belief must naturally tend to cause many divergences. The wonder is that with very few exceptions through these long centuries the whole of the tribes have with such very slight variations retained the same religious beliefs and the same forms or symbols of worship more or less elaborate. The Crees, Saulteaux, Ojibways, and some other of the northern tribes of Indians believe in the existence of a great Supreme Being, whom they call the *Keche-Maneto*, which means the Great Spirit. They believe that he is full of love and pity toward the human race, but that he is too exalted above them and has too many things occupying his attention to care more for them than merely to give them food.

The tribes in the West believe that the Good Spirit does more than this. They believe that he is the "good medicine" that aids them in their various schemes and plans; that he delivers them from the bullets of their enemies, and is anxious that they should have success in war and adventure and every thing that tends to their prosperity. As their ideas of right and wrong are very vague, and are prompted by their own selfishness, so their idea of the good God is that he is the one to aid them in stealing horses or successfully raiding the camps of their enemies. He directs their bullets and turns aside the whizzing arrows of their foes.

All the tribes believe in what they call the *Muche-Maneto*, or Bad Spirit. They affirm he is the enemy of every Indian and is ever trying to injure and to harm. He is to them the source of all the troubles and misfortunes and annoyances of life. He brings the summer drought that burns up all the grass, and then from him comes the terrible cold. He drives away the game, twists the bullets, and prematurely snaps the traps before the animals are in. He has power, they say, to injure or kill all who dare excite his ire, and he is very easily offended. Some tribes do not scruple to offer sacrifices to the Bad Spirit in order to retain his friendship and appease his anger. Many of the Indians also believe in the existence of innumerable inferior spirits or subordinate deities that have certain power or influence over the destinies of human beings. Then they have gods who control the game, others the fish, and others who bring up or hush the storms. Their vast forests, lakes, rivers, and prairies, in their excited imaginations, are inhabited by multitudes of these inferior spirits ready to do good or ill to the human race, as they feel disposed.

The early Virginian Indians believed in the existence of one God, but they also believed that the sun, moon, and stars were subordinate gods, and that offerings should be presented to them. They believed the Great Spirit rode on the clouds and his voice was heard in the storms.

The Sacs and some other tribes believed in a living God, active and interested in the affairs of men. They reverently worshiped him, regarding him as the giver of all their good things and the sure avenger of all their wrongs. Their religion, like that of many of the other tribes, partook largely of the Jewish character. Feasts were held and prayers were offered before the crops were planted, and then there was the offering of the first-fruits with invocations when the harvest was gathered. At the birth of a child there were prayers and thanksgiving. When the loved ones died, at the grave there were special invocations that the departed ones might be safely transmitted to the happy spirit-land.

A few years ago there were some prominent persons who, from observing many of the habits and especially the religious beliefs and customs of the Indians, firmly believed that they were descended from some of the lost tribes of Israel. While this belief does not now so prevail, still there were some arguments so striking that the subject was, and still is, one of interest and must ever come to the front when discussing the probable origin of these races. The parallel is remarkable and worthy of being preserved. The Indians lived in tribes as did the ancient Israelites. The personal resemblance in many instances is most striking. We have seen many Indian faces that were very Jewish indeed. They acknowledged one God, the Great Spirit, who created and upholds all things. They believe in a Bad Spirit, the source of all evil. By some of the tribes the Good Spirit is called *Ahe*, the old Hebrew name of God. He is also by some called *Yehowah*, sometimes *Yah*, and also *Abba*. They have a tradition that the time was when their fathers were in very close covenant relation with the Great Spirit, before the Bad Spirit obtained the power and influence he now has. They all acknowledge an overruling Providence, and believe that when we have done the best we can we must passively submit to what comes to pass. Many of their feasts bear a great similarity to those of the Mosaic ritual. The ceremony of the offering of the first kettle of green corn is exactly as the Jewish offering of first-fruits was. When successful in shooting a number of deer one was cut up and burnt as a thank-offering on an altar of rough stones, great care being taken that not a bone of the animal sacrificed should be broken.

Generations ago the Iroquois and some other tribes practiced the rite of circumcision, and although they have given up the custom, having lost the tradition why it was practiced, yet that it was customary among them is also attested by the fact that even to this day when the Munceys and Iroquois quarrel the former in derision reproach them with having practiced this rite in olden times.

That these remarkable analogies should exist is an interesting study, and also that these Indians should have in many of the tribes a most remarkable tradition of a great deluge, in which the world was overwhelmed, and the whole human race perished except one family who escaped either in a big canoe or on a great raft, is very suggestive and instructive.

Among the many errors and superstitions into which they have fallen is the belief in the existence of windagoos, or gigantic creatures half satan and half human, whom they represent as being of great size and dwelling in the dark, dreary forests. They describe them as being so powerful that when they march along they can brush aside the great pine-trees as an ordinary man does the grass of the prairies as he strides along through it. We found the Saulteaux Indians especially living in dread of these imaginary monsters. At many a camp-fire they used to tell us with bated breath that these windagoos were terrible cannibals, and that whenever they caught a lonely hunter far away from his home they soon devoured him. When I tried to disabuse their minds of these fears they proceeded to tell me of this one and that one who had been seized and devoured. The instances they brought before me were of hunters who had gone away on long journeys down dangerous rivers and treacherous rapids. On my expressing my opinion that the poor fellows had been drowned or had met with some other accident, the Indians refused to be convinced. They will never admit that an accident could happen to any of their great hunters, and so the one theory always before them is that those who mysteriously disappear have been caught and devoured by the windagoos.

Of the power and grip this superstition had on these Sault-eaux, I had a startling and somewhat amusing illustration shortly after I had gone as their first missionary to live among them. Very cordially were we received, and much encouraged were we by the attention given to our words and the really sincere desire manifested to improve their circumstances socially as well as religiously. As there were many of their countrymen still without missionaries, they used to frequently ask why it was that more missionaries with the great book were not sent among them. So one Sunday afternoon I held a kind of a missionary meeting with them. I took into the church my large maps of the world, with a number of pictures of heathens of many lands. I explained the map to them and showed them their own country, and told them that while we had a great land as regards size, yet there were many single cities with more people in them than all the Indians in our land put together. Then I showed them pictures of the cannibals of the isles of the Pacific, and described others of the wild, wicked nations of the earth, and told them that good white people were sending missionaries to a great many of these lands, and they must not expect to have them all come to them. "For," said I, "as bad as you and your forefathers were, some of these other people were much worse;" and then I particularized by describing some of the vilest and most degraded of the sinful races. I dwelt on cannibalism especially, and told of the man-eaters of the Pacific islands, who did not even object to a roasted missionary and some of his people cooked up with him. They were intensely interested, and also became very much excited before I finished, especially at what I had said about the cannibals.

The service closed and the people quickly returned to their little houses and wigwams at the Indian village, which was a little distance from the mission-house and church. The next morning, bright and early, I was up, and after breakfast and prayers started off to continue the work in which I had been engaged, namely, acting the part of a surveyor and helping the men run the dividing-lines between their little fields. To my great surprise, when I reached the first home I found that every body was away, and a stick tied across the door was the sign that they did not soon expect to return. On to the next and the next houses I went, and thus on through the whole village, and found, to my amazement, that I was literally a shepherd without a flock, a missionary without his people. Not a man, woman, child, dog, or canoe was to be found. After about an hour of aimless wandering around and wondering what had happened I returned to my home and told my good wife of the loss of our flock. Like myself she was perplexed, and neither of us could make out what it meant.

The Indians had often, in large numbers, gone away on their great hunting excursions, but they never all went at the same time, and never without telling us of their going. So we were indeed perplexed. Toward evening I saw a solitary Indian coming from a distant island in his canoe. I quickly hurried down to the shore, and as he stopped paddling a few hundred feet from the beach I shouted to him to come to land. He immediately came in, and when at the shore I said to him:

"Where are the Indians?"

"Out there far away on that island in Lake Winnipeg," he replied.

"Why are they there?" I asked.

"Very much afraid," he said.

"Very much afraid! Of what are they afraid?" I asked.

"Windagoos! Cannibals!" he answered.

"Did any of you see any windagoos?" I asked.

"No, I don't think we did, but what you said about them in your address in the church made our hearts melt like water, and then the winds began to blow, and there from the dark forests, with the sighing winds we seemed to hear strange sounds, and some said, "Windagoos! windagoos!" and that was enough, so we all got so alarmed that we launched our canoes, and, taking our families and dogs, away we paddled out to that distant island, and there the people all are now."

I confess I was amused as well as annoyed at the startling effect of my moving speech, and picking up a paddle I sprang into the canoe, and telling the Indian to show me what he could do as a canoe-man I struck in with him, and in less than an hour we had traversed the distance of several miles that lay between the main-land and that island. The Indians crowded down to the shore to meet us, and seemed delighted to see me. They wanted to shake hands and make a great fuss over me, but I repelled all their advances and would not shake hands with one of them. At this they were much crestfallen and surprised.

"Why did you leave us in this way?" I asked of the principal ones.

"Windagoos, windagoos!" they fairly shouted. "When you

told us about those windagoos who used to eat the missionaries and their people you made us very much afraid, and our hearts got like water, and the more we talked the worse we got, and so we all hurried over here."

Did I not tell you that those windagoos were more than a hundred days' journey away, even with your best canoes?" I asked.

"O, yes, you did, missionary," they said; "but we did not know but some of them might have started many days ago to come and catch us, and so we hurried out here."

"And you left your missionary and his wife and their little ones, whom you profess so to love, behind to be eaten by the windagoos, did you? And yet you say you so love us and are so thankful we have come to live among you and teach you the good way. Why, I am ashamed of you. Suppose the windagoos had come and no stalwart men had been there to help the missionary fight them off. What would he have thought of your love when he heard you had all, like a lot of old grandmothers, run away?"

Heartily ashamed of themselves, they speedily launched their canoes and returned with me to their village, and very little did we hear after that about the windagoos.

CHAPTER VII

THE SEARCH FOR THE BIBLE

TRUTH STRANGER THAN FICTION—THE VISIT OF THE
FLATHEAD INDIANS—THEIR REQUEST FOR THE BOOK
DENIED—POPERY STILL REFUSES THE BIBLE TO THE
PEOPLE—PATHETIC SPEECH OF AN INDIAN—THE TRIBE
DISHEARTENED AND SOURED—STORY OF MASK-E-PE-
TOON—THE WARRIOR CHIEF INTERESTED BY HEARING
THE STORY OF CHRIST'S FORGIVING LOVE—HIS ONLY SON
MURDERED—MURDERER FORGIVEN—MASK-E-PE-TOON
A CHRISTIAN—HIS USEFUL LIFE—HIS TRAGIC DEATH—
STORY OF THE OLD CONJURER—THE MISSIONARY'S
VISIT—STRANGE DINNER AND ITS RESULTS—POISONS
DESTROYED—THE CONJURER CONVERTED—HIS LOVE
FOR THE WORD

LONG years ago, in the depths of winter, there appeared in
the city of St. Louis four Flathead Indians. They carried in their
persons the evidences of many hardships and of the severest
privations. Bronzed and scarred were they by the summer's
heat and winter's pitiless blast, for many moons had waxed and
waned since they had commenced their long and dangerous
journey from their own land, which lay not far from the shores
of the Pacific Ocean. Their trail had led them through the domains of hostile Indian tribes. Thrilling indeed had been their
adventures, and many had been their risks of losing both their
scalps and lives. For weeks when crossing the broad ranges of
the Rocky Mountains, where gloomy defiles and dark recesses
abound for hundreds of miles, they had ever to be on the alert,
lest in an unguarded moment there should spring out upon
them the panther or mountain lion or rush upon them the
more dreaded grizzly bear.

THE BROAD RANGES OF THE ROCKY MOUNTAINS

But although their very appearance bore pathetic evidence of their privations and sufferings, yet very little had they to say about themselves or their personal sorrows. An all absorbing longing had got into their hearts to be the possessor of one thing, and this passion had dwarfed into insignificance every thing else to them. There had been implanted by some chance seed-sowing such a craving for something to satisfy their spiritual natures that in order to get this for which their souls now longed they had unflinchingly faced all the storms and dangers of that fearful journey. Yet to the thoughtless white men to whom they first addressed themselves, very strange and meaningless seemed the importunate request or petition of these gaunt, wearied red men. They came, they said, from the land of the setting sun; across the great snow-clad mountains and the wide prairies for many moons they had traveled; they had heard of the white man's God and of the white man's book of heaven; a stranger had visited them and had told them things that had excited the whole tribe. He had told them of the great God who had made all things, and that the white man had a book which told all about him and what they were to do to have his favor. So that they might obtain this book they had come from their home far away across the Rocky Mountains. Thus strangely they pleaded for a copy of the word of God.

Some persons, becoming interested in the appearance of these strange Indians and their remarkable request, took them to the commanding officer of the military post in that city, and to him they told their simple story and besought his aid. Unfortunately for them, although the general was a kind-hearted man, he was a Roman Catholic, and so when he took them to the bishop and priests of his Church, while they were received with the greatest hospitality and shown the pictures of the Virgin Mary and of the saints, they were steadily denied their oft-repeated request for the Bible. Caring for none of these things, importunately did they plead for the book, but all in vain. So exhausting had been the journey that two of the Indians died in St. Louis from their sufferings and hardships. The other two after a time became discouraged and homesick and prepared to return to their far-off home. Ere they left the city a feast was gotten up for them and speeches were made, and the general and others bade them "Godspeed" on their journey. During the addresses at the close of the feast one of the Indians was asked to respond. His address deserves not only to rank among the models of eloquence, but should be pondered over as an expression of the heart-cry of very many of the weary, longing souls who, dissatisfied with their false religions, are eagerly crying out for the true. *They want the book.* In this English version, like all of these highly figurative poetical Indian orations, it loses much in the translation. He said:

"I came to you over the trail of many moons from the land of the setting sun beyond the great mountains. You were the friends of my fathers, who have all gone the long way. I come with an eye partly opened for more light for my people who sit in darkness; I go back with both eyes closed. How can I go back blind to my people? I made my way to you with strong arms through many enemies and strange lands, that I might carry back much to them. I go back with both arms broken and empty. Two fathers came with us. They were the braves of many winters and wars. We leave them asleep here by your great water and wigwams. They were tired in many moons and their moccasins were worn out. My people sent me to get the white man's book of heaven. You took me where you allow your women to dance as we would not allow ours, and the book was not there. You took me where they worship the Great Spirit with candles, but the book was not there. You showed me images of the good spirits and pictures of the good land beyond, but the book was not among them to tell us the way. I am going back the long, sad trail to my people of the dark land. You make my feet heavy with gifts, and my moccasins will grow old and my arms tire in carrying them, yet the book is not among them. When I tell my poor blind people after one more snow in the big council that I did not bring the book no word will be spoken by our old men or by our young braves. One by one they will rise up and go out in silence. My people will die in darkness, and they will go on the long path to other hunting grounds. No good white man will go with them, and no white man's book to make the way plain. I have no more words."

How sad and pathetic are these words, and how unfortunate it was that these Indians should have fallen into the hands of the members of that Church which refuses to give the blessed book to the people! However, a young man who was present was so impressed with the address of this Indian that he wrote to friends in the Eastern States an account of this strange visit and the pathetic appeal of the Indians for a Bible. Some earnest Protestants became much interested in the matter, but it was two years before a missionary started with the Bible for that land which then lay many hundreds of miles beyond the most western shores of Anglo-Saxon civilization.

Meanwhile what had become of the two remaining Indians? After leaving St. Louis for their western home they fell in on the plains with George Catlin, the celebrated Indian artist. But although they traveled with him for many days, whether it was from Indian reserve and stoicism, or that they had become disheartened and discouraged, they did not mention the object of their visit to him. However, he painted their portraits, and in his famous collection they have become historic and are to be seen numbered 207 and 208. After leaving Catlin, one

George Catlin painting #207.
"Hee-Oh_'Ks-Te-Kin," (The Rabbit Skin Leggings)

Catlin painting # 208.
"H'co-A-H'co-a-H'cotes-min,"
(No Horns On His Head)

more of the Indians died, and so there was but one survivor of the four to return and announce to the Great Council the death of his companions and that the white man had refused them the book. The tribe was embittered, and gave up all hope of aid and comfort from the white man's God. From a condition of eager longing to hear and accept the teachings of the good book they swung over to the opposite extreme, and so when the missionaries at length found these Indians they received no welcome from them, and found it almost impossible to overcome the feelings of despair and bitterness which had sprung up in their hearts against the white man. However, other tribes in that same land were more docile, and a church and manual labor schools were established, and many of the Indians become Christianized and civilized. Rome refuses the Bible. Our glorious evangelical Protestant Churches love to give to all tribes and nationalities the blessed book. With the open volume in their hands our missionaries go forth, and at many a camp-fire and in many a wigwam they read and expound its blessed truths. Many are their trials and discouragements, but glorious are their triumphs and genuine are the trophies won. The following story is full of encouragement.

In missionary work among the Indians of North America it is a well-known fact that one of the most difficult things to banish out of the hearts of those who are influenced by the truth is the spirit of revenge which they harbor against all who have done them any real or imaginary injury. Very few, except those who have been for years in actual contact with the North American Indians, can have any conception of the extremes to which this feeling is carried and the expedients to which these red men will resort, so blood-thirsty and cruel are they to retaliate with accumulated interest. Some of these blood feuds are handed down from generation to generation, and the dying father, who in his life-time had not been able to wreak that vengeance upon his enemies which he desired, will transmit his quarrel to his son, with threats of direst maledictions if he fail to carry it out if the opportunity to do so ever presents itself.

The following incident occurred years ago on the great plains of the Canadian Northwest, long before the waves of Anglo-Saxon civilization began to surge over those glorious fertile prairies which for so many generations were hid from the gaze of the outside busy world. Among the Indian tribes that roamed over those vast regions the Crees in those days were perhaps the most numerous and powerful. The terrible small-pox and other epidemic diseases had not entered in among them, mowing them down by thousands, leaving them, as they are to-day, but a shadow or a wreck of their former glory. The most powerful chief among this tribe was called Mask-e-pe-toon, or "Crooked Arm," from the fact that one of his arms had been so hacked and wounded in his hand-to-hand conflicts with his neighbors, the Blackfeet Indians, that, in healing, the muscles had so contracted and stiffened that the arm remained crooked. He was a warlike chief, and his delight was in all the excitements of Indian conflicts, in cunning ambuscades, and, when successful, in the practice of unheard-of barbarities upon the captives of other tribes who fell into his hands. Very picturesque was the dress of many of these warriors of the plains. The quills of the eagle, which with them is considered the royal bird, formed the head-dress. Their shield was generally made of the tough leather of the neck of an old buffalo bull. The clothing, which was most elaborately ornamented and fringed, was made of the skins of the deer or moose, most beautifully tanned and prepared by the Indian women. Some of their horses were really magnificent animals, and marvelously trained for Indian warfare.

The Rev. Mr. Rundle, of the English Wesleyan Missionary Society, was the first missionary who at great personal risk visited the Cree tribes and faithfully declared the message of salvation to them. It was news indeed, and startled those wild prairie warriors; and the question went around among them, "Where did this little man come from with such strange tidings?" The conjurers were called upon to solve the question, and the answer was that he had come direct from heaven wrapped in a large piece of paper.

The Rev. James Evans, also, in some of his marvelous trips through that land of "magnificent distances" journeys that, as regards the miles traveled, very much exceeded any of the apostolic journeyings of Paul, the preaching tours of John Wesley, or the episcopal itinerating of Bishop Asbury, visited Mask-e-pe-toon and faithfully preached to him and his people. Some accepted the truth and became Christians, but Mask-e-pe-toon was too fond of war to quickly receive the message of peace.

A number of years later the Rev. George McDougall went out, in prosecution of his missionary work, to those mighty plains, on one of which in after years he so mysteriously died. That he might be more successful in his efforts to bring them to Christ, Mr. McDougall frequently left his own home, and for months together lived with these red men as they wandered over vast stretches of country, hunting the buffalo and other game. His custom was always to have religious service every evening where they camped for the night. These camp-fire services are quite an institution in connection with work among the Indians of the different tribes. Their habits are so migratory that it is necessary that the missionary should follow them up in their various haunts where they have gone hunting the various kinds of game, and gather them together in larger or smaller numbers as is possible and there preach to them. At these camp-fire services hymns were sung, prayers were offered, and God's word

MAGNIFICENT IS SOME OF THE ROCKY MOUNTAIN SCENERY

was read and expounded. One evening Mr. McDougall read as his lesson the story of the trial and death of the Lord Jesus. He dwelt particularly upon the prayer of the Saviour for his murderers, "Father, forgive them, for they know not what they do," and, well aware of the Indian spirit of revenge that was so prominent in the hearts of his hearers, he dwelt strongly upon it, and plainly told them that if they really expected forgiveness from the Great Spirit they must have the same mind that was in Christ, and forgive their enemies. Mask-e-pe-toon was observed to be deeply moved under the sermon, but nothing was said to him that evening. The next day, as the great company, consisting of many hundreds, was riding along over the beautiful prairies, an Indian chief rode quickly to the side of Mr. McDougall, and in quiet but excited tones asked him to fall back in the rear, as they did not wish him, the missionary, to witness the torture and killing of a man who was in that little band of Indians that was approaching them, although still so far away as to be almost indistinguishable to the eyes of a white man.

It seems that months before this Mask-e-pe-toon had sent his son across a mountain range or pass to bring from a sheltered valley a herd of horses which had there wintered. Very sublime and magnificent is some of the Rocky Mountain scenery. Travelers who have visited the Alps and other picturesque mountainous regions declare that some of the views in the Canadian "Rockies" are not excelled in any other part of the world. Tourists in ever-increasing numbers are availing themselves of the opportunities presented by the completion of the Canadian Pacific Railway through and across those sublime mountains to there see these magnificent fir-clad, snow-capped objects of the Creator's handiwork. Among the foot-hills of these mountains are many beautiful valleys, where the grass and herbage abound all the year, and it was in one of them that Mask-e-pe-toon had kept his reserved horses. He selected one of his warriors as his son's comrade to aid him in the work. From what afterward was found out it seems that the man, having a chance to sell the horses, his cupidity was excited, and so he murdered the chief's son, disposed of the horses, and hiding for the time his booty returned to the tribe with the plausible story that when they were coming across one of the dangerous passes in the mountains the young man lost his foothold and fell over one of the awful precipices, and was dashed to pieces, and that he alone was unable to manage the herd of horses, and so they had scattered on the plains.

Knowing nothing at the time to the contrary, Mask-e-pe-toon and his people were obliged to accept this story, improbable as it seemed. However, the truth came out after a while, for there had been, unknown to the murderer, witnesses of the tragedy. And now, for the first time since the truth had been revealed, the father was approaching the band in which was the murderer of his son. That the missionary might not see the dire vengeance that would be wreaked upon the culprit was the reason why this subordinate chief had requested Mr. McDougall to slacken his pace and fall into the rear of the crowd. Instead of doing so he quickened the speed of his horse and rode up to a position a little in the rear of the mighty chief, who, splendidly mounted, was leading the van of his warriors. On they galloped over the beautiful green sward, the missionary's heart uplifted in prayer that the wrath of man might be turned to the praise of God. When the two bands approached within a few hundred yards of each other the eagle eye of the old warrior chief detected the murderer, and, drawing his tomahawk from his belt, he rode up until he was face to face with the man who had done him the greatest injury that it was possible to inflict upon him. Mr. McDougall, who still kept near enough to hear and see all that transpired, says that Mask-e-pe-toon, with a voice tremulous with suppressed feeling, and yet with an admirable command over himself, looking the man in the face who had nearly broken his heart, thus sternly addressed him: "You have murdered my boy, and you deserve to die. I picked you out as his trusted companion and gave you the post of honor as his comrade, and you have betrayed my trust and cruelly killed my only son. You have done me and the tribe the greatest injury possible for a man to do, for you have broken my heart and you have destroyed him who was to have succeeded me when I am not among the living. You deserve to die, and but for what I heard from the missionary last night at the campfire before this I would have buried this toma-hawk in your brains. The missionary told us that if we expected the Great Spirit to forgive us we must forgive our enemies, even those who had done us the greatest wrong. You have been my worst enemy, and you deserve to die." Then, in a voice tremulous with deepest emotion, he added, "As I hope the Great Spirit will forgive me I forgive you." Then, speaking up sternly, he added, "But go immediately from among my people, and let me never see your face again." Then hastily pulling up his war-bonnet over his head his forced calmness gave way, and, quivering with the suppressed feelings that tore his heart, he bowed down over his horse's neck and gave way to an agony of tears.

> Talk not of grief till thou hast seen
> The tears of warlike men.

Mask-e-pe-toon lived for years afterward the life of a devoted, consistent Christian. All his old warlike habits were given up, and, mastering the syllabic characters in which the Cree Bible is printed, the word of God became his solace and his joy. He spent the remainder of his days in doing good. Very earnest and thrilling were the addresses which he gave to his own people as he urged them to give up all their old sinful ways and become followers of that Saviour who had so grandly saved him. Many listened to his words, and, like him, gave up their old warlike habits and settled down to quiet, peaceful lives. Anxious to ben-efit his old enemies, the Blackfeet, and to tell to them the story of the Saviour's love, he fearlessly and unarmed went among them with his Bible in his hand. A blood-thirsty chief of that tribe saw him coming, and, remembering some of their fierce conflicts of other days, and perhaps having lost by Mask-e-pe-toon's prowess some of his own relations in those conflicts, he seized his gun, and in defiance of all rules of humanity he coolly shot the converted Christian chieftain down.

Thus sadly fell Mask-e-pe-toon, a wondrous trophy of the cross, and one whose conversion did a vast amount of good, showing the power of the Gospel to change the hardest heart and to enable the warlike savage to conquer so thoroughly the besetting sin of the Indian character, even under the most extreme provocation, where very few indeed could have found fault if the price of blood had been exacted and the murderer summarily executed.

Far away in the forest wilds, several hundreds of miles northeast of the city of Winnipeg, there dwelt in an Indian village a notorious old conjurer. His reputation was very bad among the people. To the deadly effects of his poisons the sudden deaths of numbers of the Indians were ascribed, and many a maimed and disfigured Indian in secret muttered his denunciations against this wicked old man and blamed his "bad medicine" as the cause of all his troubles.

When reports reached him that the missionary with the great book was going around through the land among the Indians, traveling in summer in a birch canoe and in winter with his dog-trains, and that scores, and in some places hundreds, of the people were gladly listening to his words and giving up the old habits as well as the old religion of their fathers and accepting Christianity, the heart of this old conjurer was filled with wrath, and he declared that if ever that missionary came to their village neither he nor the Indians who brought him should leave the place alive.

So remote and apparently inaccessible was the Indian band that years passed away before it seemed possible for the missionary to make the long journey to that place. It so happened, however, that the same year the missionary heard of the old conjurer's threat, that summer the way opened by which two Christian canoe-men could be secured to go with him on the perilous journey—perilous in more ways than one. The dangers of the way and the old conjurer's threats were all talked over, and then with their eyes open as to the character of the undertaking, and earnestly seeking the divine blessing, they began the trip. They were twelve days on the way. Of course it was impossible to carry in a birch-bark canoe sufficient food to last for such an extended trip.

However, as they were armed with a good rifle and shotgun, and had plenty of ammunition, and much game abounded in that part of the country, they had abundance of food. So full of rapids and falls were the rivers that they had to make over fifty portages during the trip. At these obstructions one Indian would carry the canoe on his head around the rapids until he reached the smooth water beyond. The other Indian and the missionary would carry the blankets, kettles, guns, and other things which made up the load. Then all would be re-arranged and on they would go. It was not an unpleasant trip during the fine weather, although the mosquitoes and flies were very numerous. When it rained, however, it was somewhat trying. They had no tent, and there was not to be met with on the whole trip a single house. Several times were they drenched to the skin and had to remain so, which was on one occasion for several days, until the warm sun came out and dried them with its welcome rays. Their bed was made where night happened to overtake them. A smooth granite rock was preferred, although there were times when even this could not be found. At length, after a variety of adventures they drew near the end of the journey. When about six miles from the Indian village the hearts of the two Indian canoe-men seemed to fail them, and, to the missionary's surprise, they wanted to turn around and go back.

"What!" said the missionary, "come at least two hundred and ninety-four miles and not travel the other six! Never! Let us go on."

Vainly they pleaded their fears of the old medicine-man and his terrible deeds and threats. However, the missionary was firm, and so the men yielded, while he appealed to their manhood and promise to him ere they left home. He also cheered them with quoting some of the promises of God, whose servants they all were, and for whose glory and the good of these poor people this journey was undertaken. Encouraged by these things, the paddles were resumed until the wigwams of the Indians were visible in the distance. Then resting on their paddles the faithful Indians said:

"Missionary, there is one thing we want to ask of you. You know we, like you, have left our wives and children behind and came on this dangerous journey. How could we think of going back if any thing should happen to you? We think we can take care of ourselves, but our great fear is about you. This old conjurer with his 'bad medicine' is very wicked and cunning. What we want you to promise us is that you will not eat any food except as we prepare it for you."

While admiring their devotion, the missionary only laughed at their fears and said: "You make my heart very warm toward you for your love and anxiety about me, but I have another plan in my mind. I think I will eat with that wicked old conjurer before the sun goes down." They were amazed at this, and protested most earnestly. Very blood-curdling were some of the things they had heard about this bad man and his medicines, so powerful that a little dropped into the food would cause death in a few minutes. However, the missionary was firm, as he had decided on another method for dealing with this old Indian, whose reputation was so bad, than that very timid one suggested by his faithful canoe-men.

Another half-hour's paddling brought them into the Indian village. It was small and poor and looked like a place blighted and cursed. Quite a number of careworn and sad looking women and children were around; but very few men were visible. However, the majority of them seemed pleased to see the missionary, although some quickly began to speak out their fears that his life was in danger on account of the threats of the old medicine-man. "Where is the wigwam of this old medicine-man about whom I hear so much?" said the missionary. His tent was pointed out. It stood off by itself in a gloomy-looking place, and toward it the missionary, taking with him a few things, immediately started alone.

When he reached it he pulled aside the blanket which served as the door, and, stooping down to avoid striking his head against the poles, he entered. So gloomy and dark was the interior that it was a few seconds before the missionary, coming in out of the bright, dazzling sunlight, could clearly make out, or rather take in, the situation. However, he soon observed the object of his search sitting on the ground directly opposite. With some tea and tobacco the missionary went over in front of him, and, reaching out his right hand, he cheerily addressed him in the Indian way, saying, "What cheer, mismis?" which in English is, "How do you do, grandfather?" But the old man, who by some fleet runner had already been informed of the missionary's arrival, with a growl of disapprobation refused to shake hands with the white man who had thus dared to brave his wrath and crowd himself into his wigwam. But the missionary was not to be thus easily rebuffed, and so, stooping down quickly, he caught hold of the Indian's hand and shook it heartily in a pump-handle sort of a style. While vigorously doing so he began talking to the old man, saying, among other things, "What cheer, mismis, what cheer? I am not your enemy, but your friend. I have come all this long way to do you good. Our feet have been sore and our hands blistered. Our bones have ached with the hardships of the journey. We have been drenched by the rains and have tried to sleep in our wet clothes as we lay down on the rocks, while in the distance we have heard the howlings of the gray wolves. We came not to buy your furs or to trade with you, but to do you good. The Great Spirit has given us white people his book, and as its wonderful story is for his red children too we have come to tell it to you. You had better listen and let us be friends. It is true you will have to change your life, and you will have to stop your drumming and conjuring and burn your bad medicines and make your own living by hunting and fishing as do the other Indians." Still he refused, and so the missionary adopted another plan. He took a large plug of tobacco and placed it in his hands. Tobacco among Indians is like salt among the Arabs. If he accepted his tobacco he must be his friend, and would not dare to injure him while in his wigwam. For a time he refused to accept it, but the white man continued talking kindly to him, but all he could get in response were his growls of annoyance. "Take it, grandfather," he said; "I never use the stuff myself, but those who do say this is a very good kind."

Perhaps fortunately for the missionary the old man's supply had run out a few days before, and so his appetite was proportionally keen for the narcotic, and after a little more persuasion his hand closed upon it and the missionary knew he had him. Then taking up a pound package of tea the missionary said, looking up to some dirty dried meat that hung in shreds like straps across a pole, "You have meat and I have tea. You furnish the meat and I will the tea, and we will eat together."

A gleam of malignant triumph passed over his face as he seemed to say to himself, "Is this missionary such a fool as to thus put it into my power to so easily poison him?" The missionary had observed that look and had read its meaning, and so he said, "Never mind your poisons. I come as a stranger and challenge you to a dinner, if you furnish part. Never mind your fire-bag with its bad medicines about which you are thinking, and let us as friends eat and drink together."

The old fellow fairly quailed under those words, especially at the reference to his bad medicines, and began to think that the man who could thus read his innermost thoughts must be a bigger conjurer than he was himself. So turning quickly to his old wife, who was crouched down on the ground a little way from him, he ordered her to take the tea and get down some meat and prepare the dinner. She quickly set to work. The meat was dirty, but she did not stop to wash it. Dirty and dusty as it was it was soon in a pot over a fire quickly kindled. In a half sulky manner the old man invited the missionary to sit down beside him, and they talked about various things until the dinner was ready, and then together did the missionary and that old conjurer eat and drink. The old fellow said the meat was venison; the missionary thought, and still thinks, it was dog-flesh; but what it was is of very little consequence. The old conjurer was conquered, and not long after burned his fire-bag and bad medicines and became a sincere, earnest Christian. Only twice a year could the missionary visit that distant region; but whether he came by canoe in summer or dog-train in winter no one could give him a more cordial welcome than did the once notoriously wicked conjurer, but now the earnest, consistent Christian. He followed the missionary around like a shadow. He heard every sermon and address. He acted as guide to the different wigwams where personal visitation and talks could influence unconverted ones to decide for Christ. He also took the missionary to the homes of the sick and sorrowing ones, and drank in with avidity the sweet promises of the word of God which were there quoted and the prayers there offered. Sometimes so hungry did he seem for every thing spiritual that he would follow the missionary to the spot where he was about to unroll his camp-bed and rest after the day of this blessed toil. And when he bowed in prayer ere he wrapped himself for sleep the old man would kneel beside him and softly whisper, "Missionary, please pray out loud, and pray in my language, so that I can understand you." And then again at the morning devotions, no matter how early they were, the now dear old saint was there, and again his earnest words were, "Please, missionary, pray out loud, and pray in my language, so that I can understand you." Such genuine conversions repay a thousandfold for all the risks run and privations endured. Very blessed indeed is it to be able to quote Paul's words and say:

> Now thanks be unto God, which always causeth
> us to triumph in Christ, and maketh manifest the
> savour of his knowledge by us in every place.
> (2 Corinthians 2:14)

CHAPTER VIII

VISIT OF A DEPUTATION OF STRANGE INDIANS

LOOKING FOR A MISSIONARY—ABLE TO READ THE GOOD
BOOK—TAUGHT BY OUR CHRISTIAN HUNTERS—OBTAINED
BIBLES, THEN TAUGHT THEIR OWN PEOPLE—LONGING FOR
INSTRUCTION—STORY OF THE ETHIOPIAN EUNUCH HERE
REPEATED—VISIT THEM—HUNGRY FOR THE TRUTH

I WAS sitting in my study one day when noiselessly and quietly there came filing into the room a dozen or more stalwart Indians. I greeted them kindly and bade them welcome. On scanning their faces I observed that they were all entire strangers. Seating them as well as the limited accommodations of my little study would admit, I began a conversation with them. They were a fine-looking lot of men, with characteristic Indian faces. After a few commonplace remarks had passed between us I became anxious to know who they were and what was the special object of their present visit. So, addressing the one who seemed to be the principal man among them, I asked:

"Where do you live?"

"Very far away," he replied.

"How far?" I asked.

"Thirteen nights away," he said.

The Indians compute long distances by the number of nights they spend on their journey. So, to see me, these Indians had, in their birch-bark canoes, traveled fourteen days down great rivers and across stormy lakes.

"What is your object in coming so far?" I asked.

Very decidedly one of them spoke up and said, "We have

come for you!"

"For what purpose do you want me?" I asked, beginning to get interested by the earnestness of these stalwart men.

"Why," they answered, "we have the great book and can read it, but we do not know what it means."

"O, I am delighted to hear that you have the great book and can read it," I said; "and of course you have had a missionary who has taught you to read."

Their answer amazed me: "You are the first missionary we ever saw."

"Then you have had a teacher who has instructed you?"

"What is a teacher?" was the questioning reply. So I explained to them what a teacher was, and to this they said, "We have never seen one as yet."

Becoming intensely interested now in these children of the forest, I replied with a certain amount of inquiry and perhaps incredulity in my voice, "Do you, who have never had a missionary or teacher, pretend to tell me that you can read the great book?"

Quietly they answered, "We can read the great book."

To put them to a test was an easy matter, and so, picking up my Indian Bible—printed in Rev. James Evans's beautiful syllabic characters—I opened it and said to one of them, "Read."

Without any hesitancy he began, and read without making a single mistake. Then I tried another and another, and found, to my great delight, that these Indians from that distant and lonely forest retreat were all able to read in their own tongue the holy word.

"Tell me," I said, "how did you thus learn to read the good book?"

This was their story of how they had come into this great privilege. Would that I could describe the picturesque and dramatic way in which the spokesman of the party told it to me that day in my study! The substance is as follows:

"Missionary, you know hunters roam over a great extent

of country looking for game. So, although our village is many nights away, yet in our winter huntings some of us come up a good many miles this way; and a few of your Indian fur-hunters go many days down toward our country, and so some of them hunt near our hunting-grounds. Well, as we all talk the same language and are at peace with each other, when we have made our little hunting wigwams and set our traps and got every thing ready for catching the wild animals, and then while waiting for them to come into the traps, we often have days when there is nothing to do. These days we would employ visiting other Indians, and among those we visited were some of your Christian Indians from this mission. They always received us very kindly, and we had some pleasant talks. We found that they had with them their Bibles, and, when not busy at their work, they spent a great deal of time in reading them. As we were very ignorant we thought they were very foolish in spending so much time in that way; and so we urged them to shut up their books and gamble with us, as we used to do. But they said: 'Since we have become Christians we have flung all our dice and gambling stones into the fire. We find that we cannot be Christians and gamble; and since we have learned to read this book we find more pleasure in it than we ever did in our old foolish games.' They would read to us out of the great book and we became very much interested, for they read about the creation, and Noah, and Joseph, and David, and Daniel, and Jesus, and many others, until we found ourselves going there every day we could spare from our huntings, even if some of us had many miles to walk on our snow-shoes through the great cold.

"Our hunting season, you know, lasts many months, and so we had time to make many visits. When your Christian people saw that we were so interested in what they read to us they said, 'Would you not like to learn to read for yourselves and of course we said, 'Yes.' So they began teaching us. It seemed strange to us that we, who had thought it was all such foolishness a short time before, should be now seated in their wigwams and hard at work learning a, e, oo, ah; pa, pe, poo, pah; ta, te, too, tah, and all the rest of the characters which your Indians had marked out for us on pieces of birch-bark with a burnt stick. But we had got hungry to know for ourselves, and when we found that 'ma' and 'ni' and 'to' put together meant 'Manito,' 'the Great Spirit,' then indeed we were excited and studied hard to know more. So we worked away, and your good Christian people were kind and so patient with us, and so pleased that our stubbornness was gone, and we were willing to sit at their feet and learn. And very often did they pray with us and tell us of some of the wonderful things that were in the great book besides its stories of warriors and other great men that had at first excited our curiosity. Well, before the snow began to get soft and the time came for us to return to our village with our furs some of us had made such progress in our study that we could slowly read the great book. That spring, as soon as the snow and ice left the great rivers and lakes, a number of us decided to take our furs, as we had been very successful in our huntings, all the way down to York Factory, on the Hudson Bay, as the prices were better there. It took us many days to go, but there was plenty of game and fish, so we had a good trip down. We reached York Factory with our furs, and exchanged them for what we needed for ourselves and families. One day before we returned, the gentleman in charge of the Hudson Bay Company's post said to us: 'There have come out for Mr. Young, the missionary at Norway House, a lot of Indian Bibles from the British and Foreign Bible Society in London. Now, if you Indians could only read, and would try and get some good out of them, I am sure Mr. Young would be glad to have me give you some of these good books.' When we heard this our hearts were glad, and we told him some of us had learned to read the great book and we would be so thankful to get them and would do the best we could with them. When he heard this he said he was pleased we had learned to read, and then he gave us a lot of the books, at which our hearts were made very glad. We carried them safely in our canoes up the great rivers and around the portages until we reached our homes and people. There was great excitement about them. Even some of our oldest people had never seen a Bible before. Some of the old conjurers and medicine-men were angry with us for bringing them, but most of the people were glad, for they had heard from some of our hunters who had not gone with us to York Factory of some of the wonderful stories which had been told them by the Christian Indians. At first we hardly knew what to do with the books. Then we decided that those who, during the winter, had learned to read should each have one, and that they should teach others; and as fast as any one could read, even if only a little, he should get his own book.

"So anxious were our people to learn, and so well did they get on, that the books are all distributed. We are very thankful for them, but we want somebody to teach us what we are reading. We love the book, but we want somebody to make it plain to us. We are like one who has found an instrument which makes music. We get a sweet sound here and another there, but we have never had any teaching, and so we cannot play it aright. So with this great book which we have learned to read and which we have in our midst, we are very ignorant about it, and so we have come all this way to ask you to come to our land and tell us what these things mean about which we are reading."

With mingled feelings of surprise and delight I listened to this marvelous narrative. It was the story of the Ethiopian eunuch over again, but multiplied many fold. Like him they had the word and were interested in it; but how could they understand, never having had any one to guide them? And so they had sent this deputation hundreds of miles through the pathless forest to find out one who could begin at the same Scripture and "preach unto them Jesus." My heart went out to them at once, and I felt that He who had sent the angel unto Philip with the message, "Arise and go toward the south unto the way that goeth down from Jerusalem unto Gaza, which is desert," there to find one man longing after light upon the sacred volume, had surely sent these messengers for me to go on a similar blessed mission.

If these Indians, longing for instruction, had lived in a land of railroads or even ordinary highways, the matter of visiting them could have been easily arranged, but, unfortunately, it was just the reverse. No surveyor had as yet passed through that land. There is not a mile of road laid out in a region of many thousand square miles; and so only by a birch-bark canoe, manned by two Indians, could I visit them in the summer-time, and even then perhaps not be able to travel as rapidly as these experienced men whose lives had been spent in those wild regions.

If I delayed until winter I could find one of those fur-hunters who was acquainted with that distant region of country, perhaps one of the very men who had helped to instruct these Indians in the knowledge of that blessed book which they now had, and which had created such a desire for fuller instruction. I explained to them how my mission field was already over five hundred miles long and proportionately wide. In visiting the different Indian bands on it I had to travel either by canoe or dog-train several thousands of miles each year. I tried to visit each band twice a year, and if possible when present at the different places arranged the date of the next visit, which was generally six months ahead. Through the good providence of God I had been able to keep all of my many engagements, and the Indians, knowing this, often came hundreds of miles by canoe in summer or on their snow-shoes in winter from their distant hunting-grounds to meet me at the place appointed, that they might hear the word of God. Very many were the difficulties and hardships endured in faithfully filling these remote appointments, but many pleasing incidents occurred to compensate for a fixed resolve to be faithful, with divine help, to every promise made, even if we were in "perils oft "from raging floods in summer or the bitter cold in winter.

I remember one summer when going down a broad river in a birch canoe with two Indians, on a long journey of several hundred miles, how we were quickly stopped by the firing of several guns. It was about four o'clock in the morning. We had started so early that the mists had not yet lifted from the shores of the river, which was over half a mile wide. We were well out in the stream, and were availing ourselves of the rapid current to aid us as we were, in unison, plying our paddles. While rapidly hurrying along—for we had had a refreshing rest the night before wrapped in our blankets on a granite rock—we heard coming through the mist from the shore on our left the report of fire-arms. Quickly changing our course, we paddled through the gloom and fog, and found to our surprise a company of Indians, who, having heard several months before that I was to pass that way on one of my half-yearly visits to one of my out-appointments, had come sixty miles from their hunting grounds to intercept me, not for the purpose of getting my scalp, but that they might have a one-day's visit with the missionary and hear from him out of the word of God. Nearly all of them were Christian Indians. There was a young couple to be married, several to be baptized, and all of them were hungry for the bread of life. They were very grateful, and ere we left gave us some choice pieces of venison and dried reindeer tongues, which had been specially prepared for the missionary. So, while I was anxious to go to this new and inviting field which seemed so ripe for the harvest, I dare not break faith with any bands whom I had arranged to visit. The result was I had to inform these Indians, who had come so far for me to go and help them understand what they were reading, that six months must pass away ere I could go and see them. They said they were very much pleased that I would come sometime, but pleaded for an earlier visit, for "who could tell what might happen in all that time?" However, when I explained my work to them they saw how it was and were satisfied. One of them, however, looking out of the study window and seeing the sun which was sinking toward the western horizon and casting toward us a line of golden light on the rippling waves, with the quick poetic Indian temperament said, "Come quickly, missionary, and see us, for your coming will be like that sunlit path upon the waters." We had a long and earnest talk about the truths of the blessed book and the Great Spirit's design in giving it to us that we might know the truth concerning him, and also about ourselves and what we had to do in order to obtain his forgiveness and become his children. Reverently they bowed with me in prayer as upon them we asked the divine blessing in the name of Jesus.

After exchanging some of their furs at the fort for necessary supplies they set off on their return journey to their distant wigwams, thankful that they had got the promise of a visit from a missionary to explain to them the meaning of the great book. In the month of February I began my trip to the land of those Indians who had sent the deputation so far for me to come and visit them. I made every preparation for a long and dangerous journey, and was not disappointed in any way. I took with me two of the best of men, both as regards their genuine piety and their endurance and cleverness as Indian travelers. So many were the peculiar difficulties of the route that all the patience and energy of us all were at times taxed to the utmost. Our trip led us first a hundred and fifty miles down the eastern shore of Lake Winnipeg, and then many days' journey into the wilderness directly east of that great lake. The traveling on Winnipeg was mere child's play to what followed after we had plunged into the forest country. Our way led us over a number of little frozen lakes and streams and through several long, gloomy forest portages. The work of getting through the dense forests was very laborious and often very slow. A little clearing out of the fallen trees and the cutting down of some ere they stand too densely together would have saved both men and dogs a great deal of hardship and our sleds from a great deal of damage, but unfortunately no road-making has as yet been ever attempted in this wild country. Often we had to get down on our hands and knees and crawl under the partly fallen trees, and then all hands were engaged in getting our dogs and sleds over the accumulated fallen ones, that seemed determined to block up our way. Often our sleds would so violently strike against a tree that there was great danger of serious injury being inflicted on our dogs.

Thus on and on we went day after day. Some days we made fairly good progress. This was when we had some frozen lakes or river stretches along which we could travel rapidly. But on the whole, the trip was one of the most difficult I ever undertook. However, as we were in a forest country all the time, we could find good camping-places, and so we were able to rest fairly well after the fatigues and sufferings of the day, although our beds were made in the forest on some evergreen boughs in a hole dug in the snow, with no roof above us but the stars. At length we reached the Indians for whom we were looking. To say that they were delighted to see us seems very cold in comparison with the reality. They had abundance of venison, and so we and our dogs fared well. All that they had said to us about their people being able to read the blessed book, we found to be as they had told us. And so our work was to explain the truths they had for months been reading.

It being the hunting season, and this being their only means of livelihood, many whom we had hoped to meet were far away in their distant hunting-grounds. However, those whom we did meet gave the most earnest heed to our words and drank in the truth with great delight. We felt repaid a thousand-fold for coming to visit them and remained several days among them, during which time we tried to teach and preach unto them Jesus, and many of them were baptized.

Often since, have we thought of and rejoiced at the coming of this deputation to visit us and of the marvelous manner in which they had learned to read the word of God in their own language, without missionary or teacher, and then had imparted that knowledge to others; and then, best of all, there had come into their hearts the earnest desire to understand what they were reading. To satisfy in a measure that longing, it had been given to me to have the great honor of going as the first missionary to visit this interesting people and explain more fully some of the truths of the blessed book.

This was my rejoicing, that:

> [T]he Gentiles should be fellowheirs, and of the same body, and partakers of his promise in Christ by the Gospel: whereof I was made a minister, according to the gift of the grace of God given unto me by the effectual working of his power. Unto me, who am less than the least of all saints, is this grace given, that I should preach among the Gentiles the unsearchable riches of Christ.
>
> (Ephesians 3:6-8)

CHAPTER IX

MISSIONARY ENCOURAGEMENTS

BEAUTIFUL INCIDENTS OF THE GOSPEL'S POWER—SICK INDIAN BROUGHT TWENTY-FIVE MILES TO SEE THE MISSIONARY—CONVICTED INDIAN'S PRAYER, "HERE, LORD, I CAN DO NO MORE. PLEASE TAKE POOR INDIAN TOO"—STORY OF JOE—THE HOT SUNDAY—SIMPLE SERVICE—JOE'S DOUBTS—ACCEPTS CHRIST—THE SMALL-POX—SORROWS AND BEREAVEMENTS IN THE MISSIONARY'S HOME—NONE TO HELP OR SYMPATHIZE WITH THEM—PROVIDENTIAL DELIVERANCE—JOE DYING OF SMALL-POX—HIS MESSAGE—HIS DEATH

MISSIONARY work among the Indians, like that in all lands, has its hours of sadness and discouragement as well as of hope and rejoicing. We look back with thankfulness that it was not only our privilege to go forth weeping, bearing the precious seed, but that in addition the Master of the harvest gave us the joy of the reapers. It was our great happiness to see "many a sheaf both ripe and golden" gathered in. The work was one of peculiar hardships to both Mrs. Young and myself, but the conversion of scores of souls every year amply repaid us for the sufferings and anxieties of that life so isolated and lonely as it must necessarily be in mission fields so far from civilization. Many encouraging incidents were constantly occurring to cheer the hearts of the lonely toilers and to stimulate them to labor on in the blessed work. It is a joy to record some of these trophies won not only through our own feeble instrumentality, but also through the loving, consecrated efforts of our loved brother missionaries. One of these dear brethren, writing, says:

"A young Indian who was very sick had his friends bring him twenty-five miles to the home of the missionary. He wept when he came into his presence, and said he wanted to learn about Jesus before he died. He said, 'I am very wicked, and I want to get a new heart.' When urged to pray he replied, 'I can't pray; I don't know how.' The faithful missionary, with a conscious sense of the nearness and infinite compassion of the Divine One, earnestly pointed him to the Lamb of God. Next day, when the missionary called upon him, the poor sick man, holding out his hand, exclaimed with rapture, 'Jesus has heard my prayer and made my heart good. Now pray for wife also.' He began from that time to recover from his sickness, and a few days later his wife also accepted Christ as her Saviour, and now both are rejoicing in Jesus."

A beautiful story is told by one of our earlier Indian missionaries of a proud and powerful chief who, under the preaching of the Gospel, became deeply convicted of sin. Trembling under a sense of his guilt, he came to the missionary and offered him his much-prized belt of wampum to have his load of guilt removed. When told that the Lord Jesus did not want this offering he went away very sad and depressed in spirit. Soon after he returned and offered his gun and favorite dog. "These are not what Christ wants," said the missionary. Again he went away sorrowful, but after a time he returned and offered his wigwam and family. The faithful missionary, who saw the struggle that was going on in his heart, refused for his Master even these, saying that "the Saviour could not accept even these as a sacrifice for sin." The poor convicted, half-despairing Indian then threw himself down upon the ground, and, lifting up his tearful eyes, exclaimed, "Here, Lord, I can do no more. Please take poor Indian too." The answer of peace and pardon was not long in coming.

Many more delightful instances could be given of the Gospel's power to save even the poor Indian. We give more fully in detail the story of the conversion of Joe. It has been made a blessing to many. We trust the placing it here on record will cause it to be a stimulus and blessing to many more. How true it is that it is not always that the greatest results for God are obtained when the surroundings are most favorable! The crowded, enthusiastic audience does not always yield the greatest number of converts. How often has it been seen by the faithful minister or devoted Sunday-school teacher that their work seemed specially owned of God when under difficulties and discouragements they sacrificed self and personal comfort to be in their place and do their duty!

Many can look back to some cold, wet Sunday or other apparently very unfavorable time, from the human stand-point, when, because they were in their place, precious immortal souls were then influenced by the truth and heartily, believingly accepted Christ as their personal, conscious Saviour. Little did I dream, as I stood up before the little company on that Dakota prairie and preached that short, simple sermon, that it was to be one of the successful sermons of my life.

The last Sunday we spent on the prairies on one of my missionary journeys was the hottest day of which I have any recollection. The fierce sun seemed to beat down upon us with tropical heat, and we all felt more or less prostrated by it. We had been traveling with our horses for nearly thirty days over those wonderful fertile meadows, and as became us, as a party of missionaries, we rested on Sunday, and in rotation held religious service. When we reached this hot Sunday the good minister whose turn it was to officiate was so prostrated by the heat that he declared it was impossible for him to preach. I had conducted the service the previous Sunday, and had the good excuse that it was not my turn. The other good divines also had their excuses, and so it really seemed as though the day would pass by and no service be held. So I volunteered to take the work rather than that it should be neglected. This being announced, the different members of our company, with a few exceptions, gathered round the front of my canvas-covered wagon and seated themselves as comfortably as they could in the prairie grass, improvising sun-shades where they were not the fortunate possessors of umbrellas.

Among the members of our party were two Sioux Indians, who had induced our leader, the Rev. George McDougall, to permit them to join our band. Their wish was to leave their own country and to go and join the Indians on the great plains of the Saskatchewan. And perhaps it was felt best by them to get away, ere a worse evil should befall them; for doubtless they had been seriously mixed up, or implicated in the terrible Sioux Indian war which had raged a short time before, in which hundreds of whites had lost their lives and a large region of country had been desolated. With but one of these Indians we have to do. The only name by which he was known to us was that of Joe. He was a wild-looking fellow, and yet had quite a knowledge of the English language, which doubtless he had picked up in the frontier settlements in times of peace or when he was employed as a guide by hunting-parties on the plains. But he hated the white man's religion, and generally spent Sundays strolling off with his gun on a shooting excursion.

This hot Sunday, however, Joe felt the heat so oppressive that he stretched himself out on the grass on his back, and, with his old hat over his face, tried to sleep. The spot he had selected for his resting-place was only a few yards in front of my wagon, and doubtless he had taken this position from the fact that as I had taken charge of the service the previous Sunday it would be held this day somewhere else, and so he would not be troubled with it. When I stood up to begin Joe partly got up, as though he would depart, but whether it was the prostrating heat or not he dropped down again on the grass, and looked up at me with his glittering coal-black eyes with any thing but friendliness. As I saw him remaining there for the first time at one of the public services the thought came, "Now, may be this is the only opportunity of saying any thing that will reach Joe." So I lifted up my heart and prayed, "Lord, give me a message for the poor Indian warrior and hunter that will reach his heart. Help me to deliver the message with such simplicity and plainness that, even with his little knowledge of English, he may understand it." And with that thought or wish uppermost in my mind I conducted the whole service, and preached the divine word. The service closed as usual, and each did his best to comfortably and restfully pass the remaining hours of the sweltering, oppressive day.

A few days after, our long trip across the prairie was ended. The Territories of Minnesota and Dakota had been crossed, and then, after entering into British territory at Pembina, we traveled on through the French half-breed settlement, until we reached the quaint, old-fashioned, mediæval fortress of Fort Garry. Strangely out of place did it seem to us. As we first looked up at its massive walls and turrets and bastions it seemed as though some freak of nature or magic wand had suddenly transported it from some old historic European nation and dropped it down amid the luxuriant grasses and brilliant flowers of this wild prairie country. For more than a month we had been traveling through the wild, unsettled prairies. For many days we had left behind us all vestiges of civilization. No newspapers or letters had we seen for weeks. The "sound of the church-going bell" or the busy hum of civilized industry had never broken the stillness of those solitudes. The last Anglo-Saxon settler's cabin was hundreds of miles behind us, and now, after being slowly ferried across the Red River of the North, as we climb up the river's bank we are suddenly confronted by massive castellated stone walls, round towers, turrets, port-holes, cannons, and piles of balls! Strangely out of place as it seemed at first, there comes a feeling of regret in these later years that it could not have been allowed to remain, but the "land craze" came, and its site at so much per foot was too much for mere sentiment, and so the old historic Fort Garry had to go down, leaving scarce a wreck behind.

Here our party broke up. Revs. George McDougall and Peter Campbell, with their families, Messrs. Sniders, the teachers, and several others, whites and Indians, pushed on still farther west, a distance of over twelve hundred miles. The Rev. George Young remained in the little settlement that was springing up around Fort Garry to open our first mission for settlers speaking the

English language.

After a few days' delay Mrs. Young and I started off on our journey for our home, four hundred miles directly north. Many were our dangers and startling were some of our adventures, but after a couple of weeks of weary toil we safely reached our humble home in our Indian mission field.

But we must now go back to the party that we saw start off on their twelve-hundred-mile trip. Their first stopping place would be Edmonton, on the great North Saskatchewan River. A few days after they had left Fort Garry, while Joe and one of the young gentlemen, a Mr. Snider, who was going out as a mission teacher, were walking along the trail, Joe began asking some strange questions.

"Mr. Snider," said he.

"Well, Joe, what is it," was the reply.

"Didn't that young missionary tell lies when he preached that sermon that hot Sunday?"

"Why, no, Joe; he told the truth."

"But did he not tell a big lie when he said the Great Spirit loved every body, white man and Indian alike?"

"No, Joe; God is no respecter of persons."

"But did he not tell a great big lie when he said the Great Spirit gave his Son Jesus Christ to die for the Indian as well as for the white man?"

"No," was the answer of the pious young teacher; "Jesus, the Son of God, died for all mankind."

"But—but did he not tell a great big one when he said that the Great Spirit had prepared a fine place for all, Indians and whites, if they would be good and love him?"

"No, Joe; that is all true, and the best thing you can do is to accept it and believe it." Other conversations were held with the Indian, and he said at last, "Well, if I could believe all that that young minister said that hot Sunday was true I would become a Christian."

When they reached the far-off mission station Joe, instead of going to the plains and joining the wild, warlike, horse-stealing bands, settled down at the Christian village. He was thoughtful and interested, and by and by became a decided and thorough Christian man. His life was so changed that all who met him were conscious of the fact. No one seeing him then would ever have imagined he had had such a history and that he had ever been guilty of such crimes as were imputed to him.

A couple of years or so afterward that terrible scourge, the small-pox, broke out among these western Indians. It was supposed to have been brought among them by some traders from Montana. The havoc it wrought can hardly be overestimated. Being to them a strange disease, they did nothing to arrest its ravages, and in sullen despair, without even an effort at isolation, let it literally mow them down by thousands. Whole villages were nearly annihilated. It got into the home of the Rev. George McDougall, and three loved inmates died. It invaded the Hudson Bay Company's trading-post, and the gentleman in charge, Mr. Clarke, was one of its first victims there. And, strange as it may appear, the fact that a few whites died of the disease in all probability saved the remainder from being massacred.

When it got in among the wild Blackfeet Indians they held a tribal council and said, "This is the white man's scourge; he has sent it among us to kill us, and we must have revenge." So they decreed that all the whites in the West should be put to death. They sent out a strong company of well-armed warriors to kill every white man, woman, and child. They started off to carry out their terrible purposes, and the first place they reached was the little Christian mission at which Mr. McDougall lived. When they drew near, Indian like, they acted in their sly, stealthy way. The bulk of the warriors remained some distance off, while a few, under the mask of friendship, visited the mission. They came into the house and looked about and talked to Mr. McDougall; he, never dreaming of what was in their hearts, treated them kindly and told them that this terrible disease, called small-pox, had come into his house, that some were dead and others very bad. They soon hurried away back to their comrades hiding in the tall grass and told them what they had seen. They counseled there together and decided that the missionary was not the one who had brought this strange new disease into their country to kill them, for it was his enemy too, and was killing his loved ones. Then they decided it must have been the traders, and so away they hurried, and many long miles they had to go. When they reached the trading-post they adopted the same plan. The majority hid themselves, while the few went as friends to the post. Imagine their horror to find that even there the mysterious disease had entered and the principal man of the place himself was dead. So they hurried back to their warrior friends in hiding and told them what they had seen. They deliberated, and at length came to the conclusion that they were mistaken—that, instead of this disease having been brought in just to kill the Indians by the white men, its coming was beyond their finding out; but perhaps it was sent by the Great Spirit as a punishment to Indians and whites on account of their sins. So as quietly and as secretly as they had come they hastened back to their own country and told what they had witnessed. Thus, humanly speaking, the death of the few saved the lives of the many.

But how few living amid the blessings of civilization and Christianity can realize all that is included in this simple state-ment: "The small-pox has got into the home of the missionary, George McDougall, and three of his family have died." They were hundreds of miles from the nearest doctor or physician. They had tried to scatter their Indians on the plains so as to save some of them from catching this terribly contagious disease. Of the few remaining at the mission numbers of them were down with the dread pestilence, and the few who escaped were so busy attending to their own sick, or so terror-stricken, that they could afford but little help to the afflicted missionary family. And so there they were, all alone with their dying and their dead; no loving friends near to help; none to come and perform the kindly acts of attendance and helpful care; none to watch with them through the long hours of day or through the sad, gloomy vigils of the night; no loving minister's voice to come in and read the "exceeding great and precious promises," and then at the mercy-seat to invoke the presence of Him who has promised to be his people's comforter and to carry their sorrows. Missionaries and their wives and children are human, and in the hour of sore trial they crave, as other people do, the presence and sympathy and prayers of those whose intercessions avail at the throne.

But in this far-off home, on the banks of the North Saskatchewan, there were none of these visitants to come as angels of mercy to help in mitigating the deep sorrows of those days which cannot be expressed in words. However, there was this blessed consolation: the divine Presence was not missing, and his almighty arms were underneath and round about, and so the survivors were saved from despair. Still, how sad was their condition! Can we look into such a home at such times without realizing that still there are severe trials in connection with missionary life? When the loved ones died, one after another, the father and his son, the beloved Rev. John McDougall, had to saw the boards with a pit-saw to make the coffins, dig the graves, and bury their own dead. When they were lowering into the grave the body of the third loved one there fell from the lips of John a sentence that touched the hearts of thousands of sympathetic Christians and filled their eyes with tears. It was, "Father, it seems so *hard* that we have to bury our own dead."

There are some of us who can, in a measure, sympathize with such sorrow; for the arrow has pierced our own hearts also; and there are grassy mounds under which rests all that was earthly of our own precious ones. But they shall rise again, and so we wipe away the tear and rejoice in our sorrows with glad anticipation that that glorious country in which so much suffering and hardship has been cheerfully endured to win the Indians to Christ has also been in this fuller measure permanently consecrated to him by the laying down of the lives of some of his sanctified ones.

During the sad afflictions at Mr. McDougall's, my good

friend, the teacher, had been stationed many miles away at another mission and was doing good service for Christ among the Indians. He—Mr. Snider—has since fully entered the ministry and is a valued and useful minister. When he heard of the sorrows and calamities that had assailed the missionary's household and the Indians around he hurried down to be, as he was, a help and a blessing. One day somebody came in and told him that there was a poor dying man outside from the Indian wigwams, who wanted to see him and had a message to leave with him. Mr. Snider's sympathetic heart was at once interested, and he hurried out. He went down the path, and just as he was getting over the fence he saw the dying man. His first thought was that the man was dead; but seeing there was still life in him, he said, "Are you the man who sent for me?"

"O, yes, Mr. Snider, I sent for you. I could not die until I left with you a message. They told me you had come, and I was so glad."

"Who are you?" said Mr. Snider, for so terribly had the small-pox seized him that the missionary had not been able to recognize him.

"I am Joe," said the dying man.

"O, Joe, is this you? I am very sorry. Can I do any thing for you? Can I bring you a drink of water or help you back to the wigwam?"

"No," said the poor fellow, "but I want to leave a message with you. I cannot see you, but I can see Jesus, and I shall soon be with him."

"Why, of course I will take your message, Joe. What is it?"

"Well, Mr. Snider, if you ever see that missionary who preached that sermon that hot Sunday will you please tell him for me that that sermon made me a Christian. You remember I thought he was telling lies, but you told me it was all true, and now I have found it to be so. You know I have tried to live right and have given Him my heart, and now I cannot see you, but I see Jesus and shall soon be with him."

And thus he talked, and soon after he died in sweet and simple faith in that Saviour who would light up his pathway through the valley of the shadow of death, though his bodily eyes had gone through the fell disease.

Years passed away ere I heard of Joe's message to me and of his happy, triumphant death, and that he looked back to that simple, plain talk on the beautiful verse, the sixteenth of the third of St. John's gospel, as the time when the good resolution to be a Christian first entered his heart. Doubtless very much was owing to the faithful words which were uttered by Mr. Snider and others. Still there was a time of seed-sowing, and it seemed to have been that day, apparently the most unlikely when any permanent good would be done.

So I give the incident, the latter part, as well as I can recollect it, from the lips of Mr. Snider and also Mr. McDougall. Mr. McDougall was afterward caught in a blizzard storm on one of those wild western plains, and laid down to die.

About fourteen days passed away ere his body was discovered. It was frozen as hard as marble and but little harmed by prowling beasts. The features were as natural as in life. It seems when all hope of reaching home had left him he laid himself down on a snow-drift, folded his arms across his breast, went to sleep, and was not, for God had taken him.

Yea, though I walk through the valley of the shadow of death, I will fear no evil: for thou art with me; thy rod and thy staff they comfort me. Thou preparest a table before me in the presence of mine enemies: thou anointest my head with oil; my cup runneth over. Surely goodness and mercy shall follow me all the days of my life: and I will dwell in the house of the LORD for ever. (Psalm 23:4-6)

A NORTHERN CAMP-FIRE

CHAPTER X

PRESIDENT CLEVELAND
WANTED MORE DOG STORIES

MRS. CLEVELAND'S KIND WORDS FOR THE MISSIONARY'S
WIFE—MY DOGS—ESSENTIAL FOR TRAVELING IN THE
NORTH LAND—ESQUIMAUX—A TRIAL OF PATIENCE—
BITING A DOG'S EAR—A STUBBORN DOG'S END—THE
MEAT-POT OR SOAP KETTLE—THE ECCLESIASTIC'S
EXPEDIENT TO GET ON—THE METHOD OF BREAKING IN
YOUNG DOGS—JACK'S HELP—CUNNING OLD CAESAR—
MY OWN TRAIN—VOYAGEUR, THE MATCHLESS LEADER—
HOW I UNFORTUNATELY BROKE HIS HEART—JACK THE
NOBLEST OF THEM ALL

"THE President said, as we were driving home from church,
'I wished that missionary had told us more about his dogs.'"

The above was said to me by Mrs. Cleveland, the beautiful
and accomplished wife of the then President of the United States,
in the White House at Washington, where I had called with the
Rev. Dr. Sunderland, her pastor, and for whom I had given a
missionary address the previous Sunday, which was attended
by both the President and his wife. My answer to this noble
woman was that it could hardly be expected that on the Lord's
day, and in a pulpit, I could more fully refer to my dogs than
merely to describe their work in taking me on my long journeys
as I wandered through the country carrying the Gospel to the
poor Indians who could be reached in no other way. This reply
was considered satisfactory, and a very delightful and profitable hour was spent in talking about the best methods which
ought to be adopted for the Indian's progress in Christianity

143

and civilization, both in the United States and Canada. As we rose to leave the White House, the palace of the President of the mighty republic, Mrs. Cleveland grasped my hand and with much feeling said: "Mr. Young, give my love to your noble wife. A woman who for the Master's sake, and for the poor Indian's sake, would go through what she has ought to be loved by every Christian woman in the land."

My heart was deeply touched by these kind words from this noble lady, the first in this great land. Would that all in high and exalted stations were as is this Christian lady, full of loving sympathy and busy in tangible efforts for the uplifting of humanity and the bringing in of the kingdom of the Lord Jesus!

As I could not say enough in a missionary sermon about the dogs of the Northwest which play such a prominent part, and aided me so successfully in my work, I am going to say something more about them in this chapter. They deserve to be honorably mentioned. But for them many of my most successful missionary journeys could never have been made, and hundreds of Indians now in the happy possession of an intimate knowledge of the Lord Jesus would never have heard his name. For traveling in the dreary wintry wilds of the vast regions north of the fertile prairies, the dogs are swifter and more enduring than horses, and can go where horses would soon perish. For them no surveyed road or well-beaten trail is required. The skillful guide, with his unerring intelligence, running ahead on his large snowshoes, makes all the road required by the dogs whether the journey leads over the vast frozen morass or through the dense, unbroken forest.

Years ago, when the buffalo roamed in countless herds on the great western prairies, every Indian village and Hudson Bay Company's post swarmed with dogs. This was because meat was so abundant and the dogs could be so cheaply kept. But with the disappearance of the buffalo the dogs are also going, on account of the great expense in feeding them; and now about the only places where they are still used in goodly numbers are in the great northern regions beyond the prairies, where there is

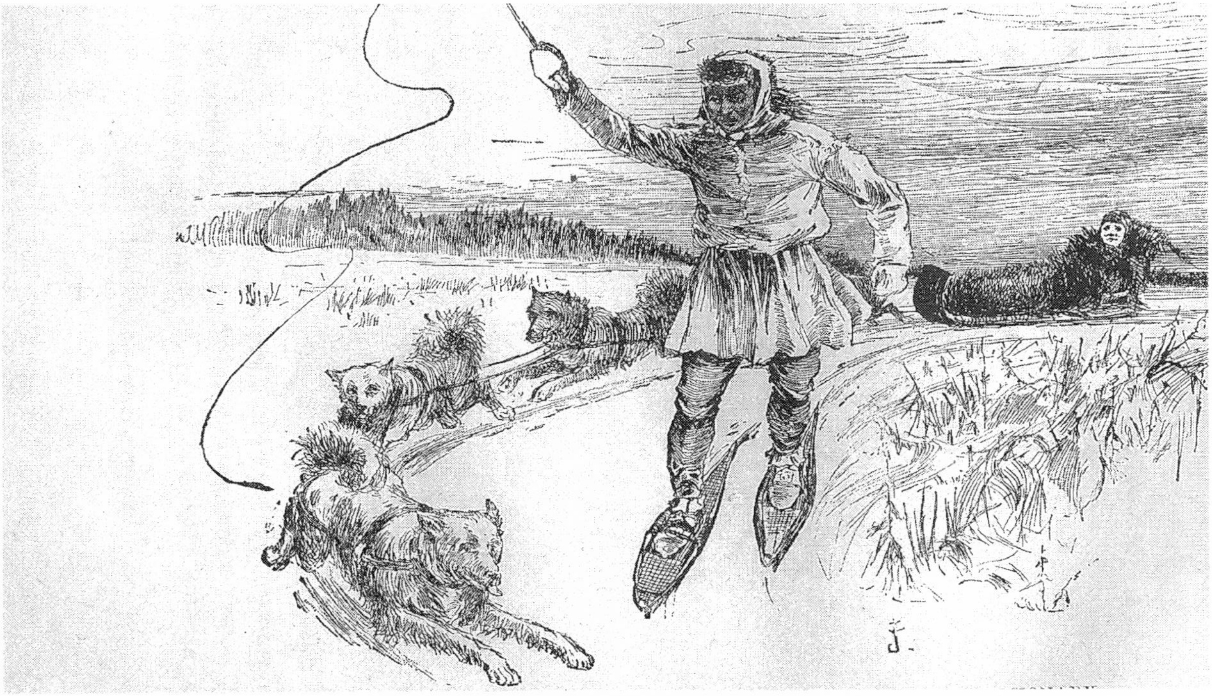

THE DOG-TRAIN OF THE WIFE OF THE MISSIONARY

an abundance of game or fish.

Dogs of various kinds are to be found in the country. The most common ones, however, are of the Esquimau or Huskie breed. They are hardy and enduring. They have a warm, furry coat, curly tails, and are of every color belonging to the dog tribe. They have some very serious defects, perhaps partly owing to their defective education or wolfish origin. Some of the best of them are very treacherous, and with very few exceptions they are persistent and cunning thieves.

PUNISHING A STUBBORN DOG

It is commonly said at some of the posts that to drive successfully these native dogs the driver must be able to swear in English, French, and Indian. But as there are no words in the Indian language in which to swear the native words used are only those of reproach or entreaty.

As with poor obstinate teams of mules or balky horses so it is with badly trained or skulking dogs; there is not much pleasure in driving them. On one of my trips we overtook a French half-breed who, wild with passion, was punishing a stubborn dog in a most extraordinary fashion. After he had whipped him until tired, and kicked him until his moccasined foot was sore, he had thrown him down and, dog-like, was biting his ear. On my remonstrating with him on his ungovernable passion and unseemly conduct he replied, "Missionary, it is no use. You know I have tried to be a Christian, but I give it up, if I have to be a dog-driver."

At Oxford Mission, one of my out-stations, a native family had a dog so stubborn that it seemed impossible to make him voluntarily move when harnessed up. So one day they took him by force a mile or so away from the wigwam and there securely harnessed him to an empty sled. Then they returned home and patiently waited to see how long it would be before he would drag that sled back to the house. He waited only until they were out of sight, and then after cutting off his traces, and eating the greater part of them, deliberately walked home. I forget just now whether that dog's flesh supplied the family that day with a capital dinner or whether they made a pot of soft-soap out of his fat.

A good story is told of a well-known Red River divine who was making an extended winter tour of several hundred miles through his diocese. He noticed that although the dogs attached to his sled were the finest in the party, yet they did not keep up to the other trains. Annoyed at this, and nearly frozen to death, he inquired of Baptiste, his driver, why it was that they kept so falling in the rear and thus apparently delaying all. Baptiste's reply was that his dogs were the best of all, but that they did not care for his whippings unless he also swore at them; but "out of respect to his reverence he had abstained from using strong words." Almost beside himself from the bitter cold, the ecclesiastic ordered him to swear away to his heart's content—to do any thing if they could only get on—and he would give him full absolution at the end of the journey. Out rolled the familiar expletives in turn with the crack of the whip. The dogs sprang to their work, and soon the bishop's train was ahead of all the others.

"There, Baptiste, that is something like traveling," said his grace. "Rush on, Baptiste, and get me out of this cold. Your theological phrases are out of place, but I'll make it all right at the end of the trip. Only push on."

The dogs are generally broken in when about a year old, but are not considered to have reached their prime until the second winter. The breaking-in process is not always very pleasant. Some dogs take to the work naturally, and give very little trouble. Others, however, desperately resist and stubbornly refuse to submit to the loss of their liberty. Kindness and firmness succeed best in training them, yet there are some with whom harsher measures have to be used. I have been amazed at the amount of ferocity and vindictiveness some of them develop when they begin to understand what is required of them. Some of them will not hesitate to bite and cruelly mangle the hand that tries to harness them, even if it is the hand of their own master who has ever treated them kindly.

In breaking in a stubborn young dog the better way is with the aid of a train of experienced old ones. Three of these steady old fellows are harnessed before the one to be conquered, and a good, sagacious, strong one is put behind. The harness must be securely fastened on the young dog to be broken in, for he will make the most desperate efforts to squeeze himself out, and if he once succeeds he will, in all probability, be like a horse that has once run away, apt to try it again, and consequently is never considered perfectly reliable. "When well harnessed the driver shouts, "Marche!" and the three well-trained dogs ahead spring off on the jump. Sometimes the new dog takes to the work naturally and gives no trouble, but as a rule the native dog especially does not surrender so easily. When he finds that he is kept in line by collar and harness he makes the most frantic jumps and springs to escape. Failing in this he will sometimes stiffen out his legs and try to stop to think a little about this novel situation. But the strong dogs ahead of him are not of the same mind just then, and so they jerk him along in spite of his stiff limbs and efforts to the contrary. This not being very pleasant to his feelings, and as he is getting hot and excited, he thinks he will rest a while, and so he throws himself down on the snow; but the steady, powerful dogs in front by their onward progress seem to say to him, "No, you don't!" and he is obliged to keep on the road. Failing in this also, he makes the most desperate attempts to turn somersaults or in some way twist himself out of line, and here, in thwarting all these efforts, the steady dog behind often displays great intelligence.

Some of these old dogs seem to know as well as their masters when they are having the fun of breaking in a new dog, and they enter into the work with great intelligence and zeal. My noble Saint Bernard, Jack, used to render me great service in this not always pleasant or agreeable work. I used to employ him as the strong dog behind the new recruit in the breaking-in process, and very clever indeed was he at his work. Watching carefully the frantic actions of the excited fellow in front of him, he would by slackening or tightening the traces so keep him in bounds that he would soon find out that about all the movements he could make were the forward ones, which were the ones desired.

Sometimes a specially stubborn young dog would so annoy Jack that when the entreaties or even whip of the driver had failed to conquer he would, metaphorically speaking, take a hand in the breaking-in process, and, rushing on the sulky young dog, would bite him in his hind-quarters, and so roar and growl at him that the frightened creature would often yield, and so spring to his work that the three dogs ahead now had all they could do to keep out of his way. Thus faithful Jack quickly conquered several dogs that but for him would have given us trouble for many a day.

Many of these Esquimau dogs are great shirks, and are so cunning about it that it is often hard to find them out. I had one of this class that I had long suspected was not doing his share of work with the rest of the train. He was a large, powerful fellow, and when in the traces would, with tongue out, and apparently with tremendous effort, keep tugging at his work. The trip we were on was a long and heavy one. The other dogs were showing the effects of it, but Caesar was fatter than when we started. For days I watched him, and he watched me. When I shouted to him he would tug away at his collar, and by his puffing and blowing and injured look seem to say, "What more can I do?" Not satisfied with him, and yet not very certain as to my suspicions, I arranged his harness so that in the train he should have his own traces, and even then he acted so cleverly that I was not positive that he was deceiving me. So one day I looped up his traces and tied them with some weak cotton thread. Then I carefully started the train and watched. Caesar acted as though he were drawing the whole of the load. How he seemed to tug and pull and puff, while his tongue hung out of his mouth! He would occasionally look back at me out of the corner of his eye, as though he expected the cheery word of approval for his gallant efforts. I let him go on in this way for quite a distance, while, both amazed and amused, I watched his most consummate hypocrisy, for with all his apparent efforts he did not pull enough to break that cotton thread and straighten out his traces. Well, I straightened him out with a whipping that he remembered, and, realizing that his little trick had been discovered, he never tried to repeat it.

After a few winters' experience and many annoyances with these native dogs, and finding that the grandest part of my work as a pioneer missionary was what I could do in these long journeys through these northern wildernesses, I banished my native dogs, with a few exceptions, and imported, through the aid of dear friends, St. Bernards and Newfoundlands in their place. These had all the good qualities of the Esquimaux and none of their miserable tricks. As soon as I could dispense with a driver, and my muscles, by vigorous toil, had become so hardened that I could endure the hardships and do the work of driving, I had what I was proud to call my own train. Three of my dogs were

St. Bernards, but the fourth was old Voyageur, a long-legged cross-breed, the grandest leader-dog I ever drove. When out of his harness he was a morose, sullen brute, but once captured (and it was not always an easy thing to get our hands on him) he was without a peer as a leader. No horse more readily responded to the touch of the rein than he to the call of his driver. Not only on the great lakes, but even in the dense forests, did he often lead on, when blinding blizzard storms, added to the bitter cold, made it almost impossible for man to face the dreadful gale.

Faithful old Voyageur, I loved thee as one of my dumb companions, even if thy disposition was surly and thou didst ever prefer being let alone to receiving the caresses of friendship which most dogs love so well. It was a sad day for me when I broke thy heart, but it gave me an insight into dog nature such as I never had before. It happened in this way: As Voyageur was getting old, and I had a number of splendid young dogs of my St. Bernard and Newfoundland breed, I thought it best to train some of them as leaders. Not one dog in ten can be trained to the work of being a first-class leader. Many dogs that will do admirably in any other position in the train are not to be depended upon at the head. For example, my noble Jack, the wisest, grandest dog I ever saw, while always as true as steel when harnessed as second or third, if put in as leader was constantly playing pranks. One of his tricks was, if the road happened to be a specially dangerous one, of occasionally turning round, and, of course, bringing the other dogs with him, and coming to the back end of the sled where I was sitting or running, to see how I was getting along. This, of course, was very much appreciated, as showing his affection for his master, but when we were out in the bitter cold, with the thermometer indicating from fifty to sixty below zero, and very anxious to get on, a leader was preferred that would ever keep his eyes to the front and his traces always taut. So in the work of training a dog to be a good leader there is an opportunity for tact and patience and a good deal of knowledge of dog nature.

On the occasion to which I have referred I was out, with Voyageur as usual at the head, when I thought I would see how one of my young St. Bernards would act as a leader. So I harnessed him up and put him before Voyageur, fastening, as we generally do, the traces to the dog behind, as we always drive tandem style. Then I went back to my place at the rear of the sled, and after putting on my fur mitts I shouted "Marche!"—the word we use for "go on."

Imagine my surprise at seeing the young dog dash one side, out of the track, completely severed from the train, while old Voyageur led on the other dogs as though nothing had happened. I quickly stopped the train, and on investigating matters found that during the short time I was arranging my sled and putting on my mitts old Voyageur had resented the harnessing of this young dog before him, and had quickly with his teeth cut off both the traces, which were of moose-skin, thus leaving himself in his right position as leader of the train. I gave him a good scolding, which, of course, he received quietly. Then I caught the young dog and again fastened him at the front. As I saw a wicked look in Voyageur's eyes I took out my whip, and, as I suspected, the instant I turned to go to the rear of the sled, again his sharp teeth were cutting the traces. Turning quickly back, I caught him ere much damage was done and gave him a good whipping. Then straightening out the dogs I started them on the trail, still keeping my eyes on Voyageur. The young dog did well, but Voyageur was indignant, and several times tried to cut him off, and for this I punished him. When he found out that he could not succeed his old proud spirit left him, and with head and tail down he slouched along like a frightened wolf.

He was never the same dog after. His heart was broken. Vainly I tried to pet him, and gave him the warmest bed and best of food, and gave him the lead of my finest dogs, but he was never the same and never forgave me for the insult of putting a mere pup before him to usurp the place he had so long and faithfully filled. I kept him for a year or so, but his spirits were all gone. Gloomily and morosely would he skulk along, grudgingly aiding in dragging home wood or fish. One day, after watching the trains start off upon a journey where he was not required, he set up a dismal howling and then went off and died. Poor old dog! He had not sufficient of the spirit of self-abnegation or equanimity to accept the situation of these utilitarian days, which so rudely push aside, for the crude and untested, the tried and experienced, no matter how grand may have been their labors or how valuable the rich stores of their experiences may be to those who often find themselves sorely in need of them.

Some of my other dogs were Jack, Cuffy, and Muff. Jack was a smooth-haired black St. Bernard. He stood thirty-three inches high at his fore-shoulders, and his hard-working weight was about one hundred and sixty pounds. He could do almost every thing that a dog can do. If the wood-box in the kitchen became empty—and it often did, as we used nothing but wood for fuel in that cold north country—all Mrs. Young had to do was to say, "Why, Jack, I am ashamed of you; do you not see I have no wood?" Instantly would he spring up and with great glee work away carrying the sticks in his mouth from the wood-pile outside and industriously continue at the work until he had filled the large box, which would hold several dozen pieces, although each stick was between two and three feet long and weighed several pounds. He could open doors from either side, and knew the difference between gloves, slippers, moccasins, or other things for which he was often sent. He was the finest dog I ever shot over, and to him we were often indebted for a meal, when perhaps but for him we would have gone hungry.

One day as we rose from a rather poor breakfast, which consisted principally of a piece of cooked wild cat, Mrs. Young said to me, "My dear, that was the last food in the house, and unless you succeed in shooting something for dinner or an Indian hunter happens to bring in some game I am afraid there will be no dinner." As the Indian hunters were at some distant hunting-grounds I knew there was but a slim chance of immediately receiving aid from them, so I took my gun and, calling to Jack, I started off to see what could be obtained. After hunting

JACK AND ALEC

unsuccessfully a while for partridges I went down toward the great lake and was gladdened at seeing a couple of mallard ducks go flying by and alighting among the waves. Creeping cautiously along to the nearest point, with Jack crouching at my heels, I found that the ducks were a long way out, and, what made it worse, a stiff breeze was blowing from the land, making heavy waves. However, I waited patiently behind a clump of willows, and was at length rewarded by seeing the two ducks, which for a time had been swimming about twenty feet apart, so come into line that they both formed a good though distant target. Instantly I fired, and fortunately with the one shot killed them both. "All right, Jack!" I said to my noble dog, who quickly sprang into the seething waters and soon reached the first duck. Seizing it in his mouth he turned for the shore, when I sprang on a rock and shouted to him, "There is another one, Jack." At once he turned around and looked back, but as a wave just then hid the second from him he could not see it, and so again he turned toward the shore. Again I shouted, "There is another duck, Jack. Try and bring them, both, good dog." Once more he turned, and this time he waited until a big crested wave so lifted him up that he was able to see in the trough of the waters the other duck. Instantly he swam out to it, still holding on to the first one. He succeeded in getting both of their necks in his mouth, with their bodies each side of him, and swam to shore. As the ducks were very large ones and he had to swim against the wind and waves he had a hard time of it, but he gallantly persevered, and so we had a good dinner that day.

The only thing at which Jack was a complete failure was rabbit-hunting. He was so large that the rabbits used to dodge all around him, and there were some that lived near the mission which seemed to enjoy his desperate but futile efforts to capture them. Without the use of a whip he was broken in to his work, and for many winters was the sheet anchor of my train. Other dogs might tire out, but Jack never would give in. Master and men and the other dogs might seem to lose heart and become

almost discouraged and despondent after long hours of struggling in the treacherous blizzard or howling gale and bitter cold,
but Jack's head was ever up, and his cheery bark, ringing through
the wintry tempest, gave fresh heart, and nerved to desperate
effort to reach the friendly shelter of distant wigwams or balsam
forest till the fury of the storm was spent.

Faithful Jack! thou wert ever true when in thy place in the
train, not only when dashing along over the emerald ice-fields of
the great frozen lakes at the rate of eighty or ninety miles a day,
but also in the dreary forests where no vestige of a road was seen,
where the snow was deep and the obstruction from logs, rocks,
and dangerous places were constantly opposing our progress and
were so very trying to both dogs and men. And when through
long delays by blizzard storms, or when, alas! our *caches* of food
had been discovered and devoured by prowling wolves, and dogs
as well as their masters were reduced to rations of only half the
usual size, and thy big, pleading eyes looked up and seemed to ask
for more, the empty hands of thy master held up and shown thee
were all that was necessary to make thee submissive to thy lot, while
native dogs had to be chained to the trees around to keep them,
in those days of short supplies, from devouring every thing, even
to our shoes and harness, if they could get their teeth upon them.

Faithful Jack! Dog thou wert, and so short was thy life! After
a few years of toil thy work was ended, and now beneath the old
maple-tree thy worn-out body sleeps in peace. But never can I
forget how, after the days of toilsome traveling in the bitter cold
were ended, thou didst watch so wisely while my wintry camp
was in construction. This camp, which was often but an excava-
tion in the snow with a diminutive barricade of balsam boughs
erected on the windward side to arrest the force of the pitiless
gale, was all the protection which the country could offer to thy
wearied and frost-bitten master. Interested didst thou ever seem
while, with his faithful Indians, thy master ate his frugal meal
and joined with them in their evening devotions, where, instead
of the pealing notes of some glorious old organ sounding forth

FAITHFUL JACK

amid the columns, aisles, and arches of a grand cathedral, we sang our evening songs in unison or discord with the diapasons of the blizzard storms which howled through the gloomy forest of that wild north-land. Then, when my trusty guide had spread out my camp-bed of fur robes and blankets, and had carefully tucked me in with all a mother's love, can I ever forget how thou, as thy master's favorite, didst claim the honor of sleeping at his back and with thy huge body add greatly to his comfort and possibly save him from falling a victim to the terrible Frost King? Noble Jack! thy love never wavered and thy heart never failed.

CHAPTER XI

MORE INDIAN DEPUTATIONS

CAUGHT IN A BLIZZARD STORM ON LAKE WINNIPEG—
ALONE AND BEWILDERED IN THE GALE—EXPEDIENT TO
KEEP FROM BEING LOST—WELCOME WAR-WHOOP—
FAITHFUL INDIANS—A NOISY RECEPTION—CEREMONIOUS
COUNCIL—RELIGIOUS SERVICES—TREATY DISCUSSIONS—
THE INSIDE VIEW OF PAGANISM—WOMAN'S SAD AND
HUMILIATING CONDITION—MY BREACH OF ETIQUETTE
IN KINDLY PREACHING TO THEM—CONTRAST BETWEEN
WOMAN'S CONDITION IN PAGAN AND CHRISTIAN
VILLAGES—INVALID MOTHER CARRIED TO CHURCH.

"AYUM-E-A-OO-KEE-MOU,"* said an Indian lad to me
one day as he came into my study at Norway House, "there is a
band of strange Indians outside who have come to have a talk
with you." When they were brought in I found that they lived
many miles away, and that they had come to have me go and visit
their land to give them advice, and, if necessary, be their spokesman with the government agents, who were soon expected to
come to make a treaty with them. I felt highly honored in having
such confidence reposed in me by a band of pagan Indians who
had known me only by reputation, and who had sent a delegation
so far on, to them, so important a matter. I was also much pleased
at this invitation, as it would give me such a good opportunity
to preach the Gospel in a place where it had as yet never been
heard. As soon as possible I responded to their request. I commenced the trip one beautiful wintry day, accompanied by two

---

* Ayum-e-a-oo-kee-mou literally means "the praying master" and is the
Cree name of the missionary.

159

Indians. We had with us two splendid dog-trains. Our course lay at first down the eastern coast of Lake Winnipeg, and was then directly across its wide expanse to the western shore. The first part of the trip was performed without any unusual incident and occupied us a couple of days in making it. Our last camp ere we crossed the lake was made in a grove of balsam trees. Here, with no walls around us but the primeval forest, and no roof above us but heaven's glorious star-decked canopy, we lay down in our robes and blankets in the snow and slept. The cold was intense, but in spite of it we had a few hours of refreshing sleep, as we were very weary. Before midnight the clouds gathered and there was a heavy fall of snow. This was to us, while we were in our bed, as an extra comforter. While enjoying the additional warmth it gave us, we little imagined the trick it was going to play upon us and the danger we would in a few hours be in on account of it. We arose hours before day, kindled up our fire, cooked our breakfast, packed our sleds, harnessed our dogs, knelt down together and said our morning prayers, and then, after throwing the balsam boughs on which we had slept on the fire, aided by its brightness we wended our way out from the forest gloom on to the frozen surface of the great lake. Winnipeg, which is the Cree word for the sea, is well named, as this great lake is one of the largest and stormiest on the continent. When we started to cross it the stars were shining brightly above us. So much snow had fallen during the recent storm that the traveling was very heavy upon the dogs. The result was that missionary and Indians were all obliged to tie on their snow-shoes, and for hours in this way tramp along ahead to make a temporary road over which our noble dogs might drag their heavy loads. For hours we tramped on. The snow was of such a character that my two Indians and myself had to walk on in single file ahead of our dogs. This beaten trail made the work easier for them, as they gallantly followed us dragging their heavy loaded sleds. As we journeyed on the magnificent Northern Lights flashed and scintillated with a beauty and splendor unknown in more southern regions. Sometimes they formed themselves into a corona at the zenith so dazzlingly beautiful that we could only think of it as a fitting diadem for Him "on whose head are many crowns." After a while the auroras flitted away and the stars paled into oblivion. The eastern sky behind us became crimson and purple, and then the monarch of the day sprang up from his snowy bed. My faithful attendants, rejoicing that the long night was ended, shouted out, "Sagastao! Sagastao!" ("The sun rises! the sun rises!") And the missionary, too, although he had had food for thought in the changing, flitting glories that had adorned the heavens in the nightwatch before the dawn, also rejoiced that the day had come.

The light, fine snow made the traveling very heavy, and we made but slow progress in comparison with trips made on this same lake in other years, when the icy pavement, swept by the winds, was so firm and hard that we have dashed along at the rate of ninety miles a day. When about twelve or fifteen miles from the bold headlands of the western shore, which in that clear atmosphere could be most distinctly seen, I said to my Indians, who could without any trouble travel much faster than I, "Perhaps you had better push on with the dogs to the shore, as time is precious. Make for yonder headland, and, if possible, by the time you have the snow cleared away, the fire built, and dinner cooked I will be with you." To this they gladly assented and quickly struck off at a rapid rate. The dogs also quickened their pace into a swinging trot and closely followed them, although at first some of them, especially my noble St. Bernard Jack, the gift of Senator Sanford, of Hamilton, looked back with wistful regret that his loved master was being so rapidly left behind. The distance between us quickly increased, although I kept steadily tramping on. The fact was, my early education in this essential branch of knowledge for a Northwest missionary had been so sadly neglected that now, in the testing time, I found myself not able to toe the mark or to keep step with my bronzed parishioners. But although being distanced I was not discouraged; I

AN APPROACHING BLIZZARD STORM

remembered an old saying, "Perseverance conquers all things," and so I persevered and kept marching on. The day was a glorious one for such vigorous exercise. Very cold it was, but tramping on snowshoes is warmth-producing work. The sun shone down brightly upon us, and there was something exhilarating in the atmosphere. The trail before me was well marked by my forerunners, and the distant headlands were rapidly becoming more vivid and distinct. And so there was a pleasurable excitement in the long tramp, and I was congratulating myself that after all I was better off than many others. But as I was thus thinking, while I kept marching along, I happened to turn my eyes northward, where the sky and snow seemed to meet, and there was a sight that quickened my pace and rudely broke up the even tenor of my thoughts. Far away northward a blizzard storm was visible, and it was coming southward with a rapidity that could hardly be imagined.

The fine, light, dry snow that had so recently fallen was being lifted up by its power, arid now like a great cloud-like wall it kept looming up larger and denser and was bearing down rapidly upon us. Miles ahead of me I could see my men hurrying on toward the welcome shelter of the forest-covered bluffs, which from them were not far off. I realized my danger and hurried on as quickly as I could run, for I well knew that the instant the storm reached me not a vestige of the well-defined trail of my traveling companions would be seen. The first blast of that gale would obliterate all impressions of snow-shoes and dog-trains. With a deafening roar at length it overwhelmed me, and with a suddenness that was almost bewildering. The bright, cloudless sky was obscured, the brilliant sun seemed annihilated, the trail was destroyed, my Indians and dogs were lost sight of, and I seemed imprisoned in a space so confined that the impression very vividly came that soon there would not be room enough in which to move. So dry and cold was the atmosphere that the vast clouds of snow which were being lifted up from the icy pavement of the great lake were like fine, dry ashes. I was almost overwhelmed in it as it madly swept along. It was so thick in the air that I could literally seize it in handfuls. At times I could not see ten feet around or above me.

Keeping the wind on my right side, as I was traveling west-ward, I hurried on. After a while, knowing by bitter experience the fickle, changing character of these storms, for there are many instances where the wind without abating has been known to change around and blow from almost every point of the compass within the space of twelve hours, I began to be haunted with the idea that the wind had veered and that I had got out of my course, and, instead of now going across I was going northward on the lake. If this surmise or fear were true, a tramp of a hun-dred miles or more would have to be taken ere the northern shore would have been reached. Well knowing the impossibil-ity of being able to accomplish such a task, I began pondering over what had best be done. Judging by the distance traveled since my dogs and men left me I felt certain that I could not be more than six or eight miles from the shore. So this was decided upon, that whatever else happened I must not get any farther from the land. I felt certain that I could keep myself alive for at least twenty-four hours by vigorous exercise, and there was the hope that as the wind was so fierce in that time it would have lifted up and so driven away the late snow-fall, heavy as it was, that the shore would become visible and I could escape. So I decided upon a course of action, and it was this: I would take off one of my snow-shoes and fasten it upright in the hard snow on the ice, and around this I would keep rapidly moving in a small circle. This plan would keep me from wandering out on the lake, and also afford me all the exercise necessary to save me from freezing to death. No sooner thought out than done. But I had hardly got my plan into working order before something better happened. Coming through the gale I heard the "Ho! Ho! Ho-o-o-o-o!" of my faithful Indians, and very musically did that whoop, which has startled many a rival camp and terrified many a frontier settlement as the signal for the massacre and the

LOST IN A BLIZZARD STORM

more dreaded torture, fall upon my ears. I shouted back through the roaring gale as well as possible, and again fastening on my snow-shoe I rushed through the blinding storm, guided by the welcome war-whoop, and in a few minutes the missionary and his faithful Indians were together again.

We hastily piled up the dog-sleds as a little barrier against the gale, then we pulled the hoods of our coats well up over our caps and huddled down together on the lee side of our slight barricade, with our back to the storm and our faces almost between our knees. Our dogs curled themselves up around us and were soon almost invisible in the snow. For hours the storm raged on. Then very gradually the sun and sky appeared. Our horizon slowly extended until at length the distant shore became visible. Every thing above us and in the distance seemed as before, but under us the change was very great. Instead of sinking in several inches of snow we trod once more on the firm, solid, icy pavement. The wind, as if to make amends for having almost buried us in the snow, now seemed to search us most carefully for every particle, which it whirled instantly away. The dogs, which appeared during the fierceness of the storm as if buried in a snowy grave, were now left completely denuded of it and stood shivering on the glaring ice. "We straightened out our trains, tied our snow-shoes to the sleds—for there was now no more use for them—and resumed our journey. In less than an hour we were in the welcome forest and busily engaged in preparing the wintry camp and the evening meal. While under renewed obligations to Him who holds the winds and the waves under his control, I was also profoundly and gratefully impressed with the promptness, courage, and self-sacrifice of my noble Indians, who, although shelter and safety were within their reach, for they could have easily made the shore, yet, at the risk of losing their own lives, had unhesitatingly turned back into the blinding storm to reach and rescue or, if not, to perish with their beloved missionary.

The next morning we continued our journey down the great lake. The day was bright, the ice good, our dogs were in capital spirits, our loads were not very heavy, and so we were able to make good progress. A little after night-fall we reached our destination, and were very cordially received by the Indians, who had long been on the lookout for us, and who were specially adorned with all their finery for the occasion.

After we had been liberally fed on white fish, and had quenched our thirst with some strong tea, and knew that our weary dogs were well cared for, we were escorted to the big square structure known as the council-house. Nearly every Indian village of any pretension has its council tent or house. In them the people frequently assemble. All questions pertaining to the welfare of the inhabitants themselves and their relationship to other villages or tribes are there discussed. In these council-rooms speeches of rare eloquence are sometimes delivered, for the Indian, generally so chary of his words under ordinary circumstances, is very ambitious to excel as a public speaker in the councils of his own people, and to have his name sounded abroad among other tribes as a great orator. The house into which we were ushered was well filled by men, women, and children, all arranged in their own places according to the strict Indian idea of etiquette. As an expected and invited visitor I was given the place of honor, next to the principal chief. His associates were next to him, and I observed with great pleasure a sign that they must be prospering, namely, that so many of the men were well dressed. However, as I was able to take in the whole situation, my heart was saddened as I observed here, as I had seen elsewhere among the pagan Indians, the women were literally "driven to the wall" and clothed in wretched apparel. Very different in appearance were they from the men. Not the least sign was there of any personal adornment. While the men and boys held up their heads most proudly, and by their fearless gaze told of a race not one of whom has ever yet been enslaved, the poor women and girls crouched in the outer circle and drew their old shawls or dirty blankets over their heads, pictures of absolute serfdom. For hours, like bent-up mummies, there they remained, as still and motionless as of the dead.

AN INDIAN WOMAN IN NATIVE DRESS

The calumet, or pipe of peace, was lit and ceremoniously passed around, as is customary on such occasions. The head chief began the speech-making, and for an hour or two he and others had the talking in their own hands. When my turn came, ere I referred to the matter of treaty-making with the government, I called my Christian dog-drivers to my side, and with their aid I held a religious service. My men were good singers, and so for the first time the sweet songs of Zion were heard in that council-room. After reading some portions of the good book and engaging in prayer I gave them an address or sermon. This was the first one that they had ever heard. Great indeed was their interest in what I said, but instead of expressing their approval or dissent to my utterances in words, as had other Indians to whom for the first time I had gone with the message, they got out their pipes and began smoking; and it did appear to me that the more impressed they were the harder they smoked, as though the fumes of tobacco would enable them to better understand. At times it seemed as though every man and most of the larger boys were smoking. I had been longing and praying for the cloud of the divine glory to overshadow us, but, O, humiliating contrast! while with clouds we were surrounded, through which we could but dimly see, they were clouds of vile tobacco-smoke. However, I lifted up my voice, and preached away for a couple of hours, and then requested my godly attendants to tell these wild savages the story of their acceptance of Christ and the blessedness of this new way. When the religious services closed we had a few minutes' delay, and then entered into the discussion of the secular matters about which they were so much interested as to invite me to their land and aid. Many addresses were delivered, and while some of the more ignorant ones launched out into extravagant expressions in reference to the demands they intended to make ere they would sign the treaty with the government, yet on the whole there was really much more common sense in the remarks of the majority than I had looked for. Indian like, they were good talkers at the council-fire, and I was very much interested and pleased with some of the illustrations used and flights of fancy indulged in by some of these natural orators. Some of the speeches were delivered with great energy, and while there was a good deal of diversity of opinion on several matters I could not but be pleased with the courtesy and deference with which each speaker was treated. There were no rude interruptions or noisy sounds of disapproval, no matter how much they might happen to differ from any speaker. In this respect it was a model political meeting, and I was charmed with its spirit, and could not but admire the cleverness and ability of several of its members. If a superficial observer had been present he might have said, "Why trouble this people by offering them the Gospel and schools and civilization? They are well off as they are." And he might justly have added, "See how vastly superior their conduct in transacting their business in reference to their state affairs around their council-fires is to similar political meetings in the so-called civilized and Christian lands."

This is all true, but after all it is only a little polish on the surface of their sinful natures, and before that long night-meeting at that Indian council-fire broke up an incident happened which showed the native savage Indian man in his true character. About midnight the stately decorum of the meeting wore off, and as the set speeches had all been delivered a more conversational character was given to the council. Questions were asked and answered, and a good deal of conversation was going on among the principal men. All at once I noticed a good deal of excitement among the men, and on looking to find out the cause of it I was surprised to observe that it was because an old woman back near the wall had pushed back her blanket from her head and had said something in quiet tones to another woman near her. Such a breach of council decorum was dreadful in their eyes, and so one of the "braves" was sent to inflict instant and severe punishment. He rushed over to the spot where the old woman was, and, although she had soon become aware of her error and had again covered up her head and crouched down to the ground, he rudely jerked the blanket from her and gave her three severe blows with his hand on the side of her head. My indignation was aroused at once, and, springing from my seat, I rushed over to the spot, and ere he could strike her again I fairly shouted at him, "You miserable wretch, to so strike a woman! I am ashamed of you, you great coward! Get out of this!" I added, as I pushed myself in between him and the poor trembling old woman.

The big rascal at first was so amazed at my decided action and strong words that he stood there in silence. Then, finding his tongue, he said, "Women should not speak in a council"; and then he quickly went back to his place. Hardly noticing the flashing eyes of chiefs and "braves," for my conduct had now been a great breach of decorum, I turned to the poor old woman, who, crouched down with her face to the ground, was sobbing at my feet. Reaching down my hand, I put it under her forehead, and, as with gentle force I raised up her head, I said, "Mother, look up at me. I have some good news to tell you." I had to use a good deal of persuasion to get her to sit back and look up at me. When she did so, I found that she was an old woman of at least seventy years. As I looked into that poor old wrinkled face, and saw there in its lines of sorrow and suffering the story of woman's treatment, so harsh and cruel, by these haughty tyrants, who think in their pagan state that it is a sign of weakness to say a kind word or do a noble, generous thing for a woman, my sympathies were aroused, and then and there I resolved to break through all Indian rules and try and say something to cheer and comfort those poor creatures who were huddled around where I was now standing.

So, lifting up my voice, I said, "Women, listen to my words. My heart is full of sorrow at what I have seen done to one of your number. I feel very sorry for her and for you all. The Great Spirit never gave your fathers or husbands or brothers or sons the right to strike you like that. In his sight all are the same. He loves you women as well as he does the men. You have good ears and my voice is strong, and you heard me when I spoke from the good book about the love of the Great Spirit in the gift of his Son. You heard all I said. It is all for you. Take it into your hearts. It will comfort you to receive it. I know you have many sorrows, but here is the happiness you want." In this strain I went on speaking to those poor women, who, as much as they dared, pushed back their old shawls or blankets from their faces and looked up at me.

In the meantime the men, who at first seemed confounded at my audacity and had looked on in astonishment, now in quite a number gathered around the chief and engaged in an excited talk. So interested had I become in talking to the poor women that for a time I neither cared for nor tried to catch any of their words. But once, when I stopped speaking for a moment, I overheard one of the principal men say something like this: "Did you ever hear of anything like that? Why, that missionary is preaching to the women! He had better go and preach to the dogs next!"

This incident gives us the true picture of paganism. The fine speeches and etiquette and decorum of the council fires are all very well in their place, but the man brutally striking the woman—and I found out next day it was *a son who struck his own mother*—gives us the correct idea of savage Indian life and the great need there is for the Gospel of the Son of God, which is the Gospel of gentleness and love. Marvelous were the changes wrought among these Indians when they became Christians. And in no way was the change greater or more visible than in the improved condition of woman. In paganism she has not the life of a dog.

She is kicked and cuffed and maltreated continually. She is the beast of burden and has to do all the heavy work. If her husband shoots a deer anywhere within several miles of the wigwam he comes marching in, carrying his gun, and orders his wife to go and bring in the game, which may weigh anywhere from a hundred and forty to two hundred pounds. This she has to carry on her back all that distance, unless it happens to be in the winter. Then she drags it on a little sled. Very quickly after they become Christians does all this change. Then happy homes begin. Mother and wife and sister and daughter are loved and kindly cared for. When they become aged and feeble the warmest place in the little home is assigned to them, and the choicest fish and the daintiest piece of game is given them.

When standing up in my pulpit in some of my mission churches, about to begin the service, I have seen what must have made angels rejoice. Anyway, my own eyes were dimmed with tears of joy. I have seen the big Indian sexton suddenly throw open the double doors of the church, and, while I was wondering who so large was coming in as to require two doors I saw that it was two stalwart Indian men carrying their invalid mother. With their four hands they had formed a chair, and over this and their two shoulders a blanket had been thrown, and there, seated on their hands, with one arm around the neck of one son and the other around the neck of the other, was the poor sick woman being tenderly and lovingly carried into the house of God, that once again she might worship with his people in his sanctuary. Carefully did they put her down and do all they could to make her comfortable, and when the service ended with equal care and tenderness did they bear her away so lovingly to their home. Christianity made them do this. In their old state they would rather have died than thus carry an old woman. Now it is a labor of love. Surely missions are not failures when such transformations are taking place.

OUT IN THE BITTER COLD

CHAPTER XII

OUT IN THE BITTER COLD

THE MISSIONARY'S CAMP-FIRE STORY OF HIS BITTEREST
EXPERIENCE FROM THE EXTREME COLD—TRYING TO
MEND THE BROKEN HARNESS—HANDS FREEZING—
SERAPHIC MUSIC—GORGEOUS COLORS—SNOW-SHOE
TRACKS TRANSFORMED INTO LUXURIOUS COUCHES—
THE WARNING VOICE—THE ROUGH TRIP—RETURNING
VITALITY—THE NARROW ESCAPE FROM FREEZING TO
DEATH—SIMILAR EXPERIENCES OF ARCTIC EXPLORERS AND
OTHER NORTHERN TRAVELERS WHO HAVE BEEN NEARLY
FROZEN TO DEATH—A NECESSARY BUFFETING

TELL us, missionary, when you suffered most intensely from the
cold?" This question was asked me by one of my dog-drivers as we
sat shivering around a camp-fire in the dense forest on the shores
of Oxford Lake one very cold wintry day. I had been visiting the
noble Christian Indians at our mission at Oxford House, and
was now on the journey home. A blizzard storm had struck us,
and so terrible was the cold that accompanied it that we froze
every part of our faces exposed to its pitiless fury. Both Jack and
Cuffy froze their feet, and some native dogs perished in the cold.
My nose, lips, and even eye-brows were badly frost-bitten, and
every one of my Indian dog-drivers suffered almost as much as
did the white man. Some Hudson Bay Company officials and
servants had joined us with the intention of traveling to Norway
House. They were well supplied with brandy and rum and freely
used the intoxicants. At first they were inclined to scoff at the
persistent refusal of my Christian Indians and myself to take a
drop of their spirituous liquors. But to me it was no trouble to
refuse, as I had ever been a total abstainer, and in addition my

own observations had taught me that he who used these things when battling with the terrible blizzard storms, or in any way exposed to the pitiless cold, did it to his own hurt and put his life in additional jeopardy.

It is true there might perhaps for a little time be a glow of warmth and a short stimulus of energy, but these soon vanished and the quick reaction came, and then the poor victim fell far below the average traveler, who in quiet, persistent endurance toiled on against the storm, with no stronger drink than an occasional cup of tea, made where a little camp-fire could be lit in some sheltered spot in the forest or in a hole dug in the snow down to the surface of the frozen earth.

It was at one of these improvised camp-fires among some dense balsam trees where we had fled for refuge, and had made a fire, cooked some fat meat, and had prepared our kettle of tea, of which we were partaking when the question at the beginning of the chapter was asked. I was at first almost unable to say when I had most suffered, for during several winters past I had been out for weeks on these long, cold, dangerous trips with my dogs and Indians, and several times the hardships and sufferings seemed as though we could never survive them. However, there was one experience that I passed through that rose up vividly before me, and while we drank our hot tea and ate our fat meat I tried to describe it to them.

"I think I was nearer freezing to death last January, when returning from Nelson River, than I ever was on any other occasion. I had three trains of my own dogs, and was attended by three Indians, the guide and two dog-drivers. The route we had taken was so very wild and rough that the guide had to go on ahead the whole distance of three hundred miles and break the way with his snowshoes. I drove my favorite train, and the other Indians had charge of the other trains. We succeeded in getting down to Kelson River all right, although it took us seven days. The snow was deep and we had to open the trail all the way.

"At the Wolfs Cave, as we were about to go down the steep

wall-like precipice, the guide said I had better ride down, and he would, by holding on to the ropes of the sled, try to steady it and keep it from running over the dogs. The dogs were in the highest spirits and eager to go, especially as a black fox had for a moment been visible before us and had then quickly disappeared over a hill in the direction we were going. Although the snow was deep, yet as our route was down hill there was nothing to prevent our dogs from going down at full speed. Just as we reached the steepest place the rope, which was in the hands of the guide, who was endeavoring to hold back the sled, which had been running at full speed, suddenly broke. The instant the rope separated he fell on his back in the snow, but as he did so he shouted out to me, 'Mind your eyes, missionary!' And there was great need for, and wisdom in, his advice, for the moment the rope broke, which in his hand had been as a brake, away dashed the sled at a fearful rate. Over the dogs we rushed like a small avalanche, mixing them in strange confusion and winding them up in the traces of their harness. So steep was the precipice that there was no possibility of stopping until we had reached the bottom, and there in the deep snow we plunged; missionary, dogs, sled, ropes, and blankets were mixed in one strangely tangled mass. Fortunately, nobody was hurt, and the Indians who had hurried to our rescue as they dragged us out of the deep drift laughed heartily at our rapid descent of the famous Wolf's Cave.

"We had a joyous welcome and a very pleasant and profitable visit among the Nelson River Indians, a goodly number of whom had but lately renounced their old paganism and had heartily accepted of Christianity. They listened with the greatest respect to the word, and their anxiety and eagerness to hear all they could of the essential truths of salvation repaid me a thousand-fold for the sufferings and hardships of the journey to their land. Nothing of very special importance occurred during the first day or two of the return journey, although the weather was intensely cold, but fortunately without any blizzard storms."

"That is always the case," said one of my Indian listeners.

"We have found that the coldest weather occurs when not a breath of air is stirring and often when the sun is brightly shining. It may seem more painful to face the blizzard or any other wintry storm, but the cold of a dead calm is more to be feared than even a fierce headwind."

"Well said," I replied; "and so it is in a Christian's life. Many a one has perished in a dead calm who would have lived and thrived in the stormy head-wind of persecution."

"Tell us the rest of your story, missionary," said the youngest Indian of our party; "the ice has formed on the top of my cup of tea while I have been holding it here in the cold and listening to you."

At this not uncommon occurrence there was a laugh at his expense, and so after he and the rest of us had filled up our tin cups from the copper kettle which was kept boiling on the fire I proceeded with my story:

"It was the third morning, I think, of the return trip when I passed through my strange experience. We had risen up very early in our wintry camp, for the cold was so great that we could not sleep. We fortunately were where there was lots of good wood, and so we made a glorious fire and cooked our breakfast. But we noticed that even when standing with our backs as closely as possible to the fire the moisture on our whiskers and fur hoods froze into solid ice. All of our dogs shivered, and some cried out like children in pain. We let them huddle on our blankets and robes before the fire, and we put on their dog-shoes to save their feet from freezing.

"When the sun arose it shone down upon us from a cloudless sky, but there was not a particle of warmth in its rays. When we got on the way we traveled just as fast as we possibly could, as the vigorous exercise seemed the only thing that would keep us alive. On we went until about ten o'clock, when in the crooked forest trail the head of my dogsled struck so vigorously against a tree that my harness was badly broken on account of the suddenness with which my dogs were brought to a stop. The Indians at once offered to remain and help me, but I foolishly thought it was best for them to go on with the other two trains for an hour or two longer until they found a suitable place for dinner, and there build a fire and get it ready. So on they pushed, leaving me and my train behind. I got out my awl and deer-skin twine and began at once to repair the damage done to my harness. Of course I had to take my hands out of my big fur mitts when trying to sew the leather, and they were soon numbed by the cold. I did all I could to warm them up so that I could get on with my work, but I had a hard time of it. Soon my whole body was shivering, and I got so cold that I could have cried out in my agony. I had run every step of the way since we left the last night's camp, and so in spite of the cold I had sweat a good deal and my under-flannels were quite damp; but now I felt the cold had reached them and they were freezing like armor around me. It was a fortunate thing I had my harness so mended by this time that I could proceed on my journey. I should have started at once, but a strange sensation came over me. It began by a singing in my ears which seemed to change to the most exquisite music that ever fell on mortal ears. I was entranced by it and seemed rooted to the spot. Then there flitted before my eyes the most delightful forms and colors. On the bare branches of the trees around me were gathered all the hues of the rainbow. It seemed as though great numbers of prisms were before me and every thing visible danced and flitted in ever-changing yet gorgeous beauty. Then my eyes happened to fall upon the trail before me, which was well marked by the snow-shoe tracks of my Indians, who had but lately gone on ahead. But what a transformation! These long snow-shoe tracks now seemed like the most luxurious couches and divans; and, as though they had a voice, they seemed to say, 'You are tired and weary; come and rest a while upon us ere you continue your journey.'

"Every pang of suffering or twinge of pain had now left me, and a strange sweet languor seemed to take possession of me. While music the most ravishing, sights the most gorgeous were mine to enjoy to an extent unknown under ordinary circumstances, I seemed to rapturously live in an Elysium of bliss.

"How many seconds I was in this state I know not, but I am certain they were but few, for I suppose my experience was like that of a person when drowning, where events pass through the mind with marvelous rapidity. I can remember that I had taken up the line of my dog-sled at the beginning and there was nothing for me to do but to shout, 'Marche!' and my eager dogs would have dashed off, when the almost seraphic music and the vision of beauty arrested my movements. Before me still lay in tantalizing luxury the imaginary couches inviting me to repose upon them that I might not only rest but the more thoroughly enjoy the wondrous melodies and the beautiful and gorgeous sights. All at once I felt my will-power leaving me and I was looking at these different couches to see upon which one I would rest for a little while, when suddenly a little inward voice of warning was heard saying to me, 'You are freezing to death! Don't you know that what you are now experiencing is what you heard those arctic explorers who went up in search of Sir John Franklin describe as the sensations that precede freezing to death? Arouse yourself or you are doomed!' With an effort which seemed to tax to the utmost all the powers I had of mind and body I managed to fasten the end of the sled-rope which I held in my hand to my sash-belt, which was tied tightly around my moose-skin coat, and then as well as possible I cried, 'Marche!' to my dogs. Fortunate indeed it was for me that they were eager to be off and overtake the other trains, which were now miles ahead. With a bound they sprang to their work, and we were off. But I fared rather roughly. I could not walk a step, but the rope was strong, and so I was rapidly jerked along; sometimes I was down on my side or back at right angles to the sled, and then, as well as I could make out in my dazed condition, I was being dragged at times feet foremost, and then it seemed as though with my head foremost. I was plowing through the snow in that undignified manner at a great rate. It was a good thing for me that the snow was deep, or I would have had some bones broken or my brains dashed out. As it was, this vigorous although involuntary and at first almost unconscious exercise saved my life. How far the dogs dragged me over that rough, uneven road or against how many trees I struck as they jerked me along I know not, but this I do remember, that this violent exercise sent the blood tingling through my body and brought me back to a state of consciousness that at first was painful in the extreme.

"When I was able to scramble to my feet and then throw myself, although in a dazed, semi-conscious condition, on my dog-sled I experienced the most painful sensations. The prickling sensations felt when a foot is said to have gone asleep were felt all over the body, but magnified a hundredfold. It was more like being pierced by awls than tickled with needles. This must have lasted for several minutes. A cold sweat then seemed to burst out upon me, followed by shivering, and then I felt I was again getting chilled to the bones. As full consciousness had returned I had sense enough to be warned in time against allowing the dangerous experiment of the last hour to be repeated; and although I was so weak that I had some difficulty in getting on my feet I by soothing words checked the speed of my dogs, who had the advantage of the trail made by the other two trains which had preceded us, and clinging to the rope I reeled and staggered along behind until in a short time we reached the camp-fire, where my Indians had a good fire burning and dinner ready. A few cups of good black tea put fresh life and warmth into me, but for weeks I felt the effects of this strange adventure."

With the greatest interest the traders and Indians listened to my story, and then several of them related some of their experiences. A few of them had been so cold that they had heard musical sounds ringing in their ears, others had noticed the beautiful colors dance before them, and nearly all of them had experienced that strange and almost luxurious languor come over them accompanied by a great desire to lie down in the snow and have a rest. One told of a party with whom he once traveled where one of their number was so resolved to stop and sleep a while in the snow that when entreaties failed they had to use their dog-whips upon him. When under this vigorous treatment he got a little better, but he was so angry at them that he wanted to fight. As something like this was just what they wanted him to do a stalwart member of their party accepted his challenge and "at it" they went as hard as they could. They cuffed and pounded each other as they flew around in the snow until the poor fellow got warm with the exercise, and then at once realized his position and laughed as heartily as any one at the plans wisely used to save him from freezing to death, which undoubtedly would have occurred if he had been allowed his own way.

CHAPTER XIII

CAMPFIRE STORIES

BAPTISTE'S STORY OF THE BATTLE BETWEEN TWO BUFFALO BULLS AND A GRIZZLY BEAR—SAMMO'S STORY OF BEING CHASED BY A GRIZZLY BEAR THAT ROBBED HIM OF HIS ANTELOPE MEAT—SANDY BAR—THE STORY OF THE PLUM-PUDDING AND THE HAPPY INDIANS

So large are some of the great lakes in the wild North land, and so terrible and treacherous are the storms that frequently occur, that many and tedious were the delays we at times experienced. Very clever were our Indian boatmen, but a birch-bark canoe is only a frail craft, and so there were times when for days together we had to wait as patiently as we could for the head-winds to lull or the storm to cease. And even in winter sometimes the blizzard would blow with such blinding power that we were often driven into a winter camp in some dense balsam grove and there kept shivering around the camp-fire until the blizzard's fury was spent and the sun or stars shone out again and it was safe for us to venture out and on our way. As the delays were sometimes from three to ten days they became very wearisome, and we had to resort to various expedients to pleasantly and profitably put in the time. Sometimes it rained so incessantly in summer, and the snow fell or was blown in upon us so constantly in winter, that it was almost impossible to read. However, the ancient custom of story-telling was always popular, and some of these Indians of mine were capital fellows at it. The following was one told to us by a stalwart Indian, who, having been among the French half-breeds a good deal, had received from them the French name of Baptiste. He had been a great wanderer in his day, and had had many strange adventures with white men and natives. He had hunted much in the broken prairie country as well as in the Rocky Mountains and also in the forest regions of the far North. This story was told us as we were huddled round a camp-fire in the dense forest on the eastern side of Lake Winnipeg, from which we and our dogs had been driven by a bitter, blinding blizzard storm. He said:

"One summer, long ago, I was with a large party of Indians. We were making a long journey over the rolling prairies from one place to another. That we might have plenty of meat to eat, two of us were appointed to keep about two days' journey ahead of the company, to hunt and to kill all the game we could. The reason why we kept so far apart was because we had dogs and babies and women in our party, and you know they will all make much noise, so they would scare the animals far away.

"Well, we two hunters kept well ahead. Some days we had good luck and killed a great deal, and then other days we did not kill much. What we got we cached so that the party could easily find it by the sign we gave them when they came along. We always put it near the trail for them. Then we would push on, looking for more.

"In the rolling prairies the hills are like the great waves of the sea, only some of the hills are about a mile apart, with the valleys between. When we were coming to the top of one of these swells or hills we would creep up very carefully in the long grass and look over down into the valley on the other side. Sometimes we would see game to shoot and often there was nothing at all. When there was no sign of any thing worth stopping to shoot, as we were after big game, having many mouths to feed, we would hurry across to the next hill-top and carefully look over into the next valley.

"One day as we had passed several valleys and had seen nothing that was worth our stopping to shoot we came to the top of a pretty large hill and cautiously looked over. There we saw a sight that we shall never forget. Right down before us, within gun-shot, was a very large grizzly bear and two big buffalo bulls. Well for us, the wind was blowing from them to us. They were very angry-looking and were preparing for a big fight. The buffaloes seemed to know that the bear was an ugly customer, and he looked as though he did not know how to manage the two of them at once. For quite a while they kept up what you might call a pretense of battle. The bulls would paw the ground and kept up a constant roaring. This only made the bear the more angry, and if there had only been one he would soon have got his big paws upon him, but there being two made him cautious.

"After a while both of the bulls suddenly lowered their heads, and together they charged the bear. As they rushed at him he quickly rose up on his haunches, and as they closed in upon him he seized one of them by the head and neck, and with a sudden jerk so quickly broke his neck that he fell down as dead as a stone. The other buffalo, which had charged at the same time, gave the bear a fearful thrust with his sharp horns, one of which pierced him between his ribs, causing an ugly wound from which the blood soon began to flow. The bear, having killed the other buffalo, tried to seize hold of this one also; but he, having given the bear the ugly wound, quickly sprang back out of his reach. He ran off for a little distance, but as the bear did not follow him he came back again. There they stood looking at each other, both very angry but both very cautious. As they kept moving round it seemed to us as though the buffalo had so come round on the windward side of the bear that he caught the scent of the blood from the wound. The smell of blood always excites these animals to fury, and so, lowering his head, he furiously charged at his wounded yet still savage enemy. The bear rose up on his hind quarters to receive him, and, seizing him as he did the other, killed him on the spot.

"Imagine, if you can," said Baptiste, while his eyes flashed at the recollection of this royal battle, "how excited we were as we lay there in the long grass and watched this great fight. Then we thought, 'Now, if we can only kill that wounded bear we will

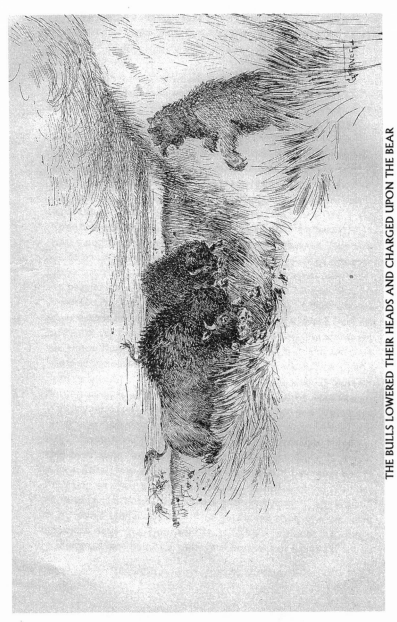

THE BULLS LOWERED THEIR HEADS AND CHARGED UPON THE BEAR

have plenty of meat for the whole camp for a good while.' But, although we had our guns, we were none too anxious to begin the battle with such a bear as that one; so we crouched low and watched him. It was very fortunate that the wind, which was quite a breeze, blew as it did. He never seemed to suspect that other foes were near. We saw him go from one buffalo to another and smell them both, but he did not offer to tear or eat either.

"We could see that he was very badly wounded from the way he kept twitching his side, from which the blood was running. It was an ugly wound, and he was a very sick bear, and so, as he looked so cross, we were not in a hurry to let him know any thing about us. After a while he went off a little distance and lay down in the long grass, which rose up so high around him that we could not see him. We waited long for him to get up, but as he did not, and we could not stay there all day, we prepared for a big fight with him. We put our knives where we could instantly draw them, and carefully examined our guns to see that they were all right. Then we began to crawl down carefully through the grass toward him. My, how our hearts did beat! and how every second we expected that he would hear us and the fight would begin for life or death! We got very close to him, although not near enough to see him. Then, as we heard no sound, we made a little noise to attract his attention. We wanted him to get up so we could have a better chance to shoot him. But he did not stir. So with our fingers on the triggers of our guns we called out, 'Mr. Bear, here are enemies, ready for another battle!' Still there was no stir, and so we got up and went to him and found him as dead as were the buffaloes. So, without firing a shot, we had a great quantity of meat."

The recital of this story had brought the whole so vividly before Baptiste that he had become very much excited, and he finished with, "What would you not have given to have seen that battle? And what would I not give to see another like it?"

We shivered around the miserable fire and listened to the blizzard's fierce howlings which then and at other times reminded me of Niagara's roar when under the sheet of water on the Canada side. Vainly we hoped that it would at least so abate that we could venture on. As there seemed no present prospect of this it was decided we must have another story.

"Now, Sammo, it is your turn to tell us something about grizzlies," I said, as we turned to an Indian who had come down from the North Saskatchewan River country the previous summer, and was now of our party. Who he was, and what was his history, none of us knew. He was very reserved and non-communicative when any one tried to find out his past record. There was even an uncertainty as to the tribe to which he belonged, although he had let slip the fact that he had been much with the Blackfeet, and had hunted grizzlies with them in the mountains. He talked Cree fluently and it was in that language we heard him on this occasion. He, like the rest of us, had been very much interested in Baptiste's story, told with so much dramatic power.

"After that," said he, "I have nothing worth telling." But we all urged him to go on and give us the best he could remember. Like all Western Indians in whose hunting grounds the grizzlies are found, he considered a fair battle with a grizzly equal to a stand-up fight with an armed warrior of another tribe. And a necklace of grizzlies' claws thus won is considered equal in value to the scalp of an enemy, and gives the owner a place of honor in the tribe.

"A queer animal is the grizzly," said Sammo, by way of introduction. "Although he can pull down the biggest buffalo or horse if he can once get his paws upon him, he is ever looking after small food, like worms and grubs and berries. To get the slugs and worms he will turn over rocks and old trunks of trees so large and heavy that you would think it would have required a double team of horses to have done it. He sometimes breaks off his claws among the rocks when at this work, and if he is getting old they do not always grow out again. Once I was out shooting antelope. They were scarce and shy. I did not have very good success, and so I went on farther and farther from the camp until I got in among the foot-hills of the Rockies. I had with me a red cloth which I would fix upon my ramrod or over some sagebush to attract the antelope near, while I hid myself as well as I could so as to shoot them if they came within range. These animals have a great deal of curiosity, and are especially attracted by any thing red. So, if the scent of the hunter is not caught by them, the shy creatures will often come up very near. After a while I saw a couple of them in the distance, and so, as soon as I had found out how the wind blew, to keep them from scenting me, I quietly set up my red cloth and hid myself near it. I had to crouch down in such a poor place that when they came in range and I fired I only succeeded in breaking the leg of one of them. He limped off with his comrade at a great rate, and I after him. It surprised me how he got over the ground, and so he led me a long chase before I got another shot at him, which brought him down. As it was near night now and I was a long way from camp, I very quickly skinned him, and, cutting out the best pieces of the meat, I made a pack and started back for the camp. I was among the hills, and I saw it would be best to keep my eyes open, and ears too, for this seemed to me to be a fine place for the wild animals, like grizzlies or cinnamon bears. I gripped hard my gun and hurried on, and soon I was about half-way through the hills, when I heard a snort and a growl that made me feel almost as cold that hot day as it is here in this cold, miserable camp. With a jump I was off, for I well knew it was a grizzly, although I did not at first see him. Although I had a ball in my gun I had not much fight in my heart just then, and, [he added, with a little dry humor] you know those at the camp wanted the meat I had on my back for supper.

"Well, I ran as fast as I could, but I was in a bad fix. Grizzlies can run faster than men, and there was no tree near that I could climb. If there had been I would have been all right, for these bears do not climb trees like the black bears do. Soon I could hear him behind me. I was afraid to turn and fire for fear I would only wound him, and that would make him worse. I hated to give up

WITH A JUMP I WAS OFF

my meat, as that meant going without my supper. But I felt he was gaining on me, and something must be done. So with one hand I unloosened the pack and dropped a piece of the meat. I was very much more frightened when I found he had passed it and was still coming on. So I dropped another piece, and that did not suit him. I had to think very fast then, and it came to me that perhaps the red cloth would stop him. So I wrapped a piece of meat in it while I was running and dropped it with the antelope-skin. There was, fortunately for me, still light enough for him to see the bright color, and it seemed to astonish him. Anyway, it caused him to stop, and I reached the camp with one small piece, which I had fastened to my belt when the rest had to go. It made but a small supper for us. We got ready to fight the old fellow if he should come on. But whether it was the fire, or that he thought it best to be satisfied with what there was along the trail, we never knew; he did not show himself within range, and we never saw him afterward."

"Have something more now," we said to Sammo, "to make up for what you lost then." And he was nothing loath to respond. But Tom, the guide, who went out to the lake to see how things looked, has returned with the welcome news that although the wind is as fierce as ever it has driven all the loose snow from the lake. The stars are to be seen, and we can go on without much danger. This is good news. We quickly make up a fresh kettle of hot tea, eat some more supper, harness up our dogs, pack up our sleds, and are off. All night long through the fierce wind and the bitter cold we travel. We suffer severely, but ere the sun rises we are seventy miles from that wintry camp.

After another day's journey we reached the Indian village at Sandy Bar. Here I was to remain for several days, preaching and teaching the people, scores of whom had accepted the truth and were very anxious for farther instruction. We met with a cordial welcome from the Indians, and to me was assigned a corner in one of the best houses in the place. It was a log house, about twenty feet square, and consisted of one room. My dog-drivers had another corner, and there was an Indian family in each of the others. My men only remained for a day and then went on to lower Fort Garry for supplies, while I remained attending to my missionary duties until their return. The little house had a stove in the middle and was furnished with benches and boxes. Our beds were rolled up during the day and spread out at night, as in the winter camp. All the disrobement I indulged in was to change my moccasins and unfasten my shirt-collar so I could breathe a little more easily when sleeping.

These Christian Indians informed us that they had not as yet been very fortunate in killing deer, but that they had abundance of white-fish. With these they gladly supplied us. Several were soon cooked, and with some strong tea were very much relished by us. Hunger is a good sauce. As we sat there in that little home and partook of that homely meal we were thankful for white-fish and black tea. So cordial was the welcome, and as these Indians were some of my own people, we passed a pleasant, joyous evening in bright and happy converse and closed with religious worship. When I got up in the morning I found a little tin basin of water and a cotton cloth, as a substitute for a towel, on a little box near me. I hastily washed myself and got ready for breakfast, which one of the good women had already prepared. She drew out from near the wall a little box, and using the cotton cloth which had served me as a towel for a table-cloth she placed upon it my fish and tea. I remained in this house about ten days, and that cloth served as my towel and tablecloth every day. As it was not once washed it looked sadly demoralized toward the end.

I was very busy and happy in my work, teaching the children and holding daily services. Of course, I would not have objected to a change in my "bill of fare," for it was fish and tea every time with one or two exceptions, when we had snared rabbits. When ten days had passed I accepted the urgent invitation of another house-holder and became his guest or boarder. There we had the same diet without any variation.

On the evening of December 24, as I was wandering around, I went into the house of the Indian with whom I had first stopped. All the light they had was that which came from a poor fish-oil lamp. When I could discover what was going on I was surprised to see the owner of the house seated cross-legged on the floor on one end of an empty flour-bag, the other end of which was opened out before him. As he was kneading away at a great rate my curiosity was excited, and I said, "What are you doing, William?"

He replied, while he continued industriously working away, "I am making a plum-pudding."

"A plum-pudding!" I replied. "Where in the world did you get the material for a plum-pudding?"

"Why," said he, "I visited my traps and I found in them some fine minks, and I skinned them and sold the furs to some traders I saw going up the lake for some flour and some plums."

These people call a coarse kind of raisins plums. These the traders sell to them about Christmas-time at a very high price.

I AM MAKING A PLUM-PUDDING

"Have you any grease or fat in your pudding?" I asked.

"No," he replied; "I have not killed a bear for a long time, so I have only water and flour and plums in it."

"William," I said, "I tell you what it is, I can improve that pudding for you, for I have got some sugar yet; so wait a minute."

Away I hurried to the other house, and soon returned with a large tin cup full of sugar. Great was the joy of the happy wife and the dancing children as I slowly shook the sugar in while William kept kneading away. After a good deal of solid work upon it William thought it would do, and then he asked his wife to try to get him a pudding-cloth. She flew around and looked through her limited wardrobe, but without success. Happening to look up, her eyes flashed with delight as she espied, hanging on a pole overhead, the identical cotton cloth which had served me as a towel and table-cloth for ten days and had not yet been washed. It was quickly jerked down and in it the pudding was wrapped.

"Where is there a pudding-cloth string?" he next asked. Again the good wife busied herself to find what was wanted, but with poor success.

"O, never mind," he said, "this will do;" and, stooping over to one of his moccasined feet, he cut off part of one of the strings, which had been wound round his ankle. With this he tied up the pudding in genuine style and put it in the fish-kettle, which was ready for it.

The next morning was Christmas. While I was at my breakfast in the other house there was a knock at the door. This was very unusual, as the Indians dislike to knock or ring a bell. They prefer to quietly come in without any fuss. But here was a clear, distinct knock. What could it mean? So I said, "Astum!" (English, "Come in!") and in walked a bright, beautiful Indian girl about twelve years old. She was nicely dressed, her face was clean, and her jet-black hair was well oiled and braided. She had in her hand a tin plate and on it about a third of that identical pudding. As she came into the room and the contents of the plate were seen by the family, there was great excitement. But she heeded them not. Her message was to me, and so she came at once to the spot where I was sitting. Handing me the plate on which was the pudding, she thus addressed me:

"Missionary, my father and mother send this to you with their compliments and best wishes, and told me also to say that they wish you a very merry Christmas."

So up I got and accepted the gift with many expressions of gratitude for their thoughtful remembrance. Then going to my box I took out a quantity of tea and sugar and gave them to the maiden and told her to take them to her father and mother with my kindest regards, and to say to them that I, too, wished them a very merry Christmas. She took the little gift with gratitude and retired. I was very much amused in watching the company as they eyed that pudding, especially the children. "Pudding!

pudding!" they shouted, and then, with all the candor of little folks, they said one to another, "And our kind-hearted missionary will share with us."

"Tapwa" (English, "Verily"). Yes, indeed, verily, of course he would. Had he not seen how that pudding was made, and did he not know all about the cloth in which it had been boiled, and the string with which it was tied? Yes, verily, of course he would divide it all round! Who could be selfish enough to want it all under such circumstances, and especially as this was Christmas day? So, with a good deal of display, the company was counted and it was found that there were just eight of us. Then, taking out my big hunting-knife, I attacked the pudding and succeeded in cutting it into eight pieces. I took good care to so cut it that there was at least one piece that had no original outside to it—a piece that had not come in contact with that wonderful pudding-cloth. The pieces were distributed all round, and there was much rejoicing thereat in that little log house by that Indian family on that cold Christmas day on the western side of Lake Winnipeg.

CHAPTER XIV

EXPLORING NEW FIELDS

DANGERS IN THE WAY—DOG-TRAVELING BY NIGHT—
BREAKING THROUGH THE ICE—SAGACIOUS DOGS—
SCANT SUPPLIES AND HUNGRY INDIANS—INDIAN
HOSPITALITIES—A SUCCESSFUL BEAR-HUNTER—PRIMITIVE
METHODS OF EATING—A DINNER UNDER PECULIAR
CIRCUMSTANCES—ATTENTIVE HEARERS OF THE WORD—
ICE-RAFTS—THE SUCCESSFUL WILD-CAT HUNTER—
PREACHING THE WORD AS WE JOURNEY ON—SLEEPING
TWENTY-THREE STRONG IN A SMALL WIGWAM—A
TROUBLESOME DOG—HITTING OOJIBETOOS BY MISTAKE—
AN ALMOST TRAGEDY TURNED INTO A COMEDY—"ALL'S
WELL THAT ENDS WELL."

NOVEL and exciting were some of the adventures that happened to me one winter when on one of my long pioneering
missionary journeys in the interior of the country which lies
between Lake Winnipeg and Hudson Bay. The Indians there
residing are of the Saulteaux tribe, a wild, passionate people,
against whom many bitter things have been said by their enemies,
and yet if rightly handled, a noble race, full of generous impulses
and capable of warm friendship. Deputation after deputation
of them had come to see me, and had urged and begged me to
come and visit them in their far-off homes and explain to them
the truths of the good book, about which they had heard from
the adventurous hunter or canoe-man who had occasionally
penetrated into their country. So one winter, when I could,
without neglecting any of my other outposts, go and visit them,
I took with me two zealous Christian Indians and two dog-trains

and started off to see them in their native wilds. As that part of the country is exceedingly rough and unbroken our sleds were extra strong. They were made of oak boards an inch thick, sixteen inches wide, and twelve feet long. Each sled had attached to it four of my finest dogs harnessed up in tandem style.

As the trip was to be one of great hardship I selected as my Indian companions two stalwart men, true as steel and full of endurance; and what was better, they were genuine Christians, the converts of our own mission, and anxious that the blessed Gospel which was now such a joy to them should be heard and accepted by their countrymen who were still living in the darkness of a degrading paganism. Such was the character of the country, being very rough, with an entire absence of all roads, that the duty of one of the Indians was to run on ahead on his snow-shoes, thus indicating the best and safest way, although there was not a vestige of a track or landmark before him at times for scores of miles. As closely behind him as possible I followed with my favorite train of dogs. The way was crooked and often very dangerous. Close behind me was the second dog-train, driven by the other Indian.

As we were not able to begin this trip until the month of April it was getting very late in the season for dog-traveling. We found, much to our regret, that, owing to the winter being so far advanced, we were not going to travel as fast as we had anticipated, and we also soon realized that if the journey was to be made at all the greater part of it would have to be performed at night. This was owing to the fact that as it was now April the sun's rays were sufficiently powerful to make the snow so soft that but little progress could be made through it. Then, in addition, the sun's rays were reflected with such brilliancy from the great snowy wastes over which at times our route lay that the painful disease called snow-blindness was liable at any hour to lay us up disabled and helpless. Our only course then was to reverse the usual order of things and travel by night, starting as soon as a crust was formed on the snow strong enough to bear us up on our snow-shoes.

In this way we journeyed on all through the lonely watches of
the night and on through the morning hours, until the frozen crust
of snow, softening by the warmth of day, would no longer bear us
up. Then we hastily prepared a camp in some balsam or spruce
grove similar to those elsewhere described. Here we cooked and
ate our breakfast, fed our dogs, and then, after prayers, wrapped
ourselves up in our robes and blankets and slept until the evening
hours, when, after supper, the journey would be resumed.

We began this adventurous trip by leaving our little mission
home as soon after sunset as possible. It is surprising how quickly
the snow that has been softened by the sun's rays during the
day hardens into a firm crust after the sun has gone down. For
many miles we traveled upon the still frozen surface of Beren's
River, except where its windings were so great that we could save
time by making portages across the points through the forests.
At the rapids and numerous falls where the frost, in spite of its
power, had been unable to bridge over the rushing river, or the
spring freshets had already opened wide chasms, our progress
in the star-lit nights was necessarily slow and not without some
elements of excitement and danger. Sometimes we made portages
around these falls; at others of them, so bold and precipitous
were the rocky shores, this was an impossibility, and so we had
to carefully and cautiously feel our way on the narrow ledge of
ice along the shore which shelved over the dark, boiling, rushing
stream. In some places the ice, under the influence of the warm
sun during the day, had begun to give, so that it sloped down
dangerously from the shore. As a natural result it sometimes
happened as we moved along on some of these dangerous slant-
ing icy ledges the rear end of our sleds would whirl around and
even project a little over the edge of the black, rushing river. But
dogs are sure footed and sagacious and know well how to act
in such emergencies, and so in these times of peril they quickly
sprang ahead, and, keeping as closely as possible to the rocks,
they managed to save themselves and us.

Such was the character of the roads that there was but little riding for me except where we happened to strike a stretch of smooth ice. The result was that most of the time I had to strap on my snow-shoes and walk or run as best I could. Our sleds were heavily loaded, as I was trying to take up sufficient supplies to last us for the whole trip, so as not to be burdensome on the people who are so wretchedly poor. One of the great disadvantages of traveling in this country is the uncertainty of the food supplies. We did sometimes come across Indians with abundance of venison or other meat, but this was the exception. We generally found them very badly off for food, even in some of the best fur producing regions of the country, and so, instead of their being able to render us assistance, we felt several times that we dare not conscientiously pass them by unaided. It did seem such a mockery to offer the "bread of life" to poor, hungry, gaunt, half-starved men and women and little children, some of whom were so weak for the want of food that they could hardly stand. I tried it a few times and then gave it up for the better way of sharing my limited supplies with some of these poor sheep in the wilderness, and then, when the wolfish, famished look had left their eyes and there was a comfortable dinner under their belts, it was astonishing how much better they listened and how much greater was their confidence in me and the message of salvation which I brought them.

Hunger is a terrible thing, as I know by personal experience, having been for three days without a mouthful; and so, although I have received more than one official intimation that "Your work is not to feed the hungry the bread of this life, but to present to him the Gospel," I have preferred to follow the feelings of my own heart and what I thought was the more Christly way, even if on more than one occasion it left my faithful Indians and myself where in lieu of our own suppers we had to tighten up our belts ere we tried to go to sleep on the granite rock or in the forest nook which happened to be our bed. So, after having suffered several times where we had hoped to be able to obtain food on the way and failed, we adopted the plan of carrying with us, if possible, sufficient food, and some to spare, for the whole journey. This, of course, with our bedding, kettles, axes, clothing, fish for our dogs, and other essentials, made our loads very heavy, and as a natural result where the roads were bad I had to walk or run.

Two or three times during the night journeys we stopped in some suitable place, kindled a fire, and made ourselves a good cup of tea and had something to eat. Once during the first night's journey I had to stop and change my clothes, as in spite of all my caution I broke through the ice and went down to my neck in the cold, rapid river. This experiment of changing my wet clothes for dry ones—which fortunately I had with me—out in the cold, wintry forest was not a very pleasant experience. However, although it made me shiver, no unpleasant consequences resulted from it.

Thus on we went, traveling night after night and resting as well as we could through the hours of sunshine. At one place we met an Indian hunter who had found a bears' den in which were three large bears. He bravely went in among them armed only with his ax. It was a fortunate thing for him that they were quite stupid and drowsy, for to us it seemed a very foolhardy thing for a man armed only with an ax to go into the den of such monsters. As it was so late in the winter season, and consequently the bears had been there for several months, this Indian only found in each of them a small quantity of oil or grease in the sack near the heart, which often in the fall of the year, when the bears are about retiring to their dens, has in it several quarts. This oil is the fuel or food on which the animal lives during the long winter months when they remain in a state of torpor. He kindly gave us some of the meat, which had the taste of young pork, with the addition of a strong gamy flavor. For his kindness we gave him what he desired, namely, some ammunition, tea, and tobacco, and then hurried on.

After a number of days, or rather nights, traveling in this way we at length succeeded in finding the first village of the Indians for whom we were seeking. They gave us a most cordial reception; some even, as at Nelson River, when I first visited that place, seemed determined to kiss me. However, I succeeded in putting the most of them off with a kind word and a cordial grip of the hand, and was then taken into one of the wigwams to rest while dinner was being prepared for us in the tent of the principal Indian of the place. With considerable ceremony I was escorted to the place where I was to dine. The dinner consisted of the head of a moosedeer, which had been cut up into large pieces and then boiled. These were brought before us in a large pan and placed on the ground, around which we gathered in a circle. A tin cup full of strong tea was then given to each one of us. Thus meat and tea constituted our dinner, and it was considered a very good one, as the head of the moose-deer is accounted one of the three great luxuries of the country. The other two are bears' paws and beavers' tails. After I had said grace, which to them was a great surprise, we each reached out and helped ourselves to a piece of the meat. With our hunting-knives in our right hand we cut and carved and then ate the meat as well as we could. Such things as plates or forks were then unknown among them, and although I had my own on my dog-sled, yet as I was their guest it would have been considered a very great insult if I had brought them out and used them at this feast. However, as I had a good appetite and was anxious to secure their goodwill, that I might be the more able to do them good, I attacked my piece of meat as promptly as the rest assailed theirs, and succeeded in cutting off some savory morsels and was making out quite a dinner. Not very far from me was a big Indian who had been exceedingly friendly, but during the meal he adopted a method of showing his goodwill toward me that I could easily have dispensed with. His hands were very dirty, and he had great strong teeth. Like the rest of us, he had taken up a piece of meat, and from it he cut and ate at a great rate. Sometimes he dispensed with his knife, and, holding his meat in both of his dirty hands, he tore off with his teeth large pieces and swallowed them with great satisfaction. Suddenly he stopped, and, looking at his piece of meat, he then scrutinized mine, and before I knew what he was about he quickly exchanged our pieces, saying, as he did so, that mine was not a very good piece, while his was very fine. This is considered a great act of friendship, and although I would have preferred refusing, yet, knowing their sensitiveness, I accepted it in the spirit in which it was done, and from his half-eaten piece I made out a hearty dinner. Upon another occasion, I was thus honored by a chieftainess, who exchanged with me pieces of the head of a reindeer which had been similarly prepared.

Being very thirsty, I drank my first cup of tea as soon as it was cool and then placed my empty cup at my side. Another Indian observing this, and wishing to show his kindness by filling it up for me, did it in a novel way. Of course we had no such luxuries as tea-pots. Our tea was made on the fire in a copper kettle into which the cups were dipped. My Indian friend, instead of taking my cup and filling it up in the usual way, adopted another method, which doubtless he thought was much more polite. Taking up his own cup, which was almost half full, he poured the contents into mine, and then, filling it up from the kettle, he added to mine the other half; then, refilling his own, he sat down again in his place in the circle on the ground very much pleased at the service he had been able to render the missionary.

After this primitive dinner, which was much enjoyed, we had a long afternoon service. Very attentive were they, and deeply interested did they become as I read to them from the good book and talked to them of sacred things. For hours they sat on the ground and listened to these most blessed and important of all truths, which were new to the majority of them. There is a pure, rapturous joy in the heart of the missionary when he finds a willing audience eager for the truth among a people who have never before seen a copy of the word of God or heard the glad story of redeeming love. Physical sufferings and "perils oft" are all forgotten in the joy of being permitted to preach the Gospel in the "regions beyond," where up to that hour Christ's name had never been heard.

After the long address we had a more social service, as was our custom. My Christian Indian dog-drivers spoke, dwelling a good deal on their own experience and conversion. There is a wondrous power in the testimony of the genuine convert. Then we had our usual hymns and endeavored to teach these Saulteaux to sing, but with indifferent success, as they do not seem to have as musical voices as the Crees.

I questioned the people about their wishes and feelings, and found out that they had long been dissatisfied with their old pagan ways and were longing for something better. Summing up what they said, it was, "We are like travelers who have lost the trail in the darkness of the deep valley, and long have we been wishing for some light, that we might get our feet in the right way. Your words seem very good. Now we have some hopes that the daylight is coming and that we shall get out of this dark place where we and our fathers have so long groped, and over the great hill of our ignorance into the light that is beyond."

We adjourned this most fascinating and blessed service for a short time that we might have our suppers, which consisted of boiled fish and tea. Then we again assembled, and there around the fire which burned brightly on the ground in the center of an improvised sort of a camp wigwam we sung and prayed and read from the blessed book and talked and had them talk. This service lasted well on into the night. Then as the snow had sufficiently hardened we bade good-bye to these friendly, hospitable Indians, and, harnessing up our dogs, we pushed on by the light of the stars still farther into the interior of this vast country. The journey was beset with perils and strange adventures. At some places where broad rivers had to be crossed and the ice had gone, except where in great masses or fields it skirted the shores, the plan we adopted so as to safely get across was this: First we cut a few long poles, and then, getting our dogs and sleds with ourselves on a great solid piece of ice many yards square, we set to work with our axes and cut it off from the shore as a great raft. Then by the aid of our long poles we managed to reach the other side of the river. Sometimes we had a good deal of difficulty, as the current was generally rapid and an ice-raft is an awkward, unwieldy thing, with a tendency to crack in pieces at very critical moments in the passage.

At one place we came across the hunting-lodge of an Indian hunter whom we had seen at our mission home the previous autumn. Among other things I had shown him my little garden, where I had succeeded for the first time in the history of that place in raising several kinds of vegetables. No effort had ever been made before in this line. These Indians for generations lived solely by fishing and hunting. I was somewhat surprised to notice that my Indian visitor became very much interested in my bed of onions, the peculiar odor of which he was quick to detect and which he called "the bad-smelling grass." Before he left to return to his hunting-grounds he asked me for all the onions I could spare. I gave him quite a number, but could not then find out for what purpose he wanted them; but now that we were with him in his own hunting-lodge the reason was plain. By their aid he had been able to trap an unusually large number of wild cats. He had never seen onions before his visit to my house, but as soon as he became acquainted with their pungent odors, and knowing how the lynx or wild cats are attracted by such things, he shrewdly thought they would be helpful to him in capturing them. So with all an Indian's secretiveness he kept his thoughts to himself, while he pleaded with such earnestness for the onions that he got them. His method of work, which he described to us, was as follows: When he found a forest where the tracks of these animals were numerous he would set his traps and make his "deadfalls" in some central place. Then crushing the onions with his ax he would smear the soles of his moccasins with the juice and then walk along paths that he had made, all radiating from the place where he had set his traps. The wild cats prowling about through the forests soon came across these paths, and, attracted by the scent, at once began to follow them up and soon found themselves in the trap. I congratulated the hunter on his success and admired the acuteness and cleverness which he had displayed.

We had a little talk about the great salvation, and then bowed down in prayer and asked God's blessing upon him and his family. Thus on and on we went, occasionally meeting the lonely hunters and becoming at times very much interested in them and their work. For them all we had some kind words, as they were all friendly, and were very much pleased to have the monotony of their quiet, lonely lives broken by the appearance of the missionary. When we could arrange it or happened to find the hunting-lodge on our trail it was very pleasant to visit them and hold religious worship with the few inmates. They listened attentively while we tried to tell them how they could live true and happy lives and be the friends and children of the Great Spirit through his divine Son. Sometimes we met quite a number of them together, but never very many, as there are no large villages in this vast section of the country. However, when we met even a few families who for society's sake had clustered together we generally spent a day or two with them, teaching and preaching as opportunity offered.

At one place a strange adventure happened which might have had a tragic ending. We had reached a place where quite a number of wigwams were clustered together, and had been most cordially received. To my words the greatest attention had been given and every thing was going on most pleasantly. After the evening service, when the time had arrived to retire, I was informed that I and my two men were to sleep in the wigwam of a tall Indian whose name was Oojibetoos. We immediately went with him to his wigwam, but when we saw its limited dimensions and the crowd who were to share it with us we would much have preferred to have made our usual wintry camp outside and there have passed the night as had been our custom. But, having accepted the invitation, and not wishing to give offense, we resolved to stand by it. The wigwam was not over sixteen feet in diameter. When we entered a bright wood fire was burning in the center of the ground floor, the smoke from which was supposed to find its way out of the top, where the poles, which were the frame-work of the wigwam, were tied together. When arranged in our places in the circle around the fire I found that my position was next to Oojibetoos, on his left. Next to me, on my left, were my two Indians. On Oojibetoos's right, in the circle, was his wife, and beyond her were their children. Then next to them was another Skwew, and beyond her was her husband. Who constituted the rest of the circle I do not now recollect, but this I do distinctly remember, that there were twenty-three persons, young and old, male and female, to spend the night in that little birchbark wigwam.

As it was late and we were very tired I said a few words about family prayers and then conducted the first ever held in that tent. Soon after my guide, who had brought in my blankets, quickly arranged them in order and tucked me up in them. I was so placed that while my feet were toward the fire my head was close to the birch-bark covering of the rude wigwam. The rest of the company quickly arranged themselves in order, and when this was accomplished as we lay there we looked like the spokes of a wagonwheel, while the fire represented the hub. Some of the Indians, as is their custom, smoked away even after they had wrapped themselves up in their blankets. A little hum of conversation continued for a time, and then all was still. The native dogs had all been driven outside, owing to the crowded state of the wigwam; but now, when all was quiet, one of them pushed himself in under the door, which was nothing more than a deerskin hung between two poles. After jumping over a number of the prostrate persons on the ground, and only stopping at one place where he could lick the fish-kettles clean for the cooking of the next morning's breakfast, he continued moving around the circle until he jumped over me and then quickly curled himself down at his master's back between us. The space was very limited, but I quietly said, "If you behave yourself and keep still you may stay there; if not, you shall go out." For a little while he was very still, and I was trying to go to sleep, when suddenly the dog began a vigorous scratching of his ear with one of his forefeet. Such was his position that the part of his leg corresponding to the elbow began to beat most vigorously against my ribs. This was not conducive to sleep, and although I am a great admirer of fine dogs I could not stand this treatment, and so I gave him a vigorous blow, which sent him howling out of the tent in a hurry. Several times during the night did that dog return, and as many times as he began his scratching did I thus decidedly drive him out. At length he seemed to get discouraged by such treatment and decided to remain outside, and I at length fell into a sound sleep.

Oojibetoos had gone to sleep with his back toward me, but owing to the small space he had between the fire and the sloping bark-wall of the wigwam he had to lie with his knees well drawn up, so as to keep his feet out of the fire. During the night he seemed to have become tired sleeping on his right side, and so he turned over toward me, on his left side. So close together were we in the limited space allowed us that when he rolled over his knees touched me with sufficient force to make me in my dreaming or semi-conscious state imagine that that miserable dog was there again. Quick as a flash I drew up my left hand, and, striking out vigorously from the shoulder, I gave my big Indian host a blow in the ribs that fairly made him howl. There was trouble at once. Oojibetoos was a wild Saulteaux, and for such a man to be thus struck, and in his own wigwam, too, was a mortal insult. So up he sprang, and, seizing his gun, he yelled out his war-whoops and made his direful threats. At the first yell he gave, of course, every body was aroused. Papooses cried, women screamed, and all were excited. My own men were alarmed at seeing a great big Indian with a loaded gun standing over me. I too had now become wide awake, and quickly did I realize the trouble into which I had placed myself. I saw at once there was no time for explanation, but like a flash there came into my mind the remembrance of the power of tobacco over the Indian, and so without saying a word I quietly reached over to the fire-bag of my Indian guide, and taking from it a large piece I quickly reached up and put it on the hand of my angry, excited Indian friend. His gun quickly dropped from him when he felt the touch of the tobacco, and while he pulled out his pipe and began filling it some one put some more wood on the fire which had nearly burned out, and soon the wigwam was bright again. Oojibetoos passed the large piece of tobacco on to the other men, who, when they had filled their pipes, all began smoking, although not a word had been said since the angry man had ceased his fierce, threatening words. When all were smoking I drew myself out of my blankets, and standing up before them I told the story of the dog and of how I had been annoyed by him during the earlier part of the night repeatedly coming in and disturbing me, but that at length he had decided to remain outside and I had gone to sleep. Then I showed how Oojibetoos had been sleeping, and explained his turning over and touching me with his knees near where the dog had annoyed me, and how that in the stupidity and foolishness of sleep I had imagined it was the dog again, and in my half-waking state I had struck out so vigorously and hit my friend by mistake. "For doing this," I said, "I am very sorry, and I sincerely ask his pardon, for there is no quarrel between us. The whole trouble was owing to the dog and my own stupidity when half asleep." Of course I was freely forgiven, and great was the merriment of the people at my mistake. Oojibetoos came in for a good deal of good-natured banter, which he took in capital spirit. He visited me several times in the years following and eventually became a good Christian. We often used to laugh over, our first night together in his wigwam. As he had a thorough knowledge of that wild country I used to employ him as my guide on some of my trips in the winter-time. When arranging our sleeping-places in the wintry camp Oojibetoos would never sleep next to me, although as guide he was expected to take that position. When rallied about his refusing to sleep there he used to laughingly say, "Once I tried it and the missionary mistook me for a dog and gave me a crack that made my ribs ache, and who knows what he might do again?"

CHAPTER XV

COURTSHIP AND MARRIAGE

RAPID CHANGES—DIFFERENT TRIBAL CUSTOMS—
FLUCTUATING PRICES PAID FOR WIVES—MARRIAGE OF
OLD JA-KOOS—WEDDING-FEAST—NERVOUS ATTEMPTS
AT CIVILIZED COURTSHIP—SEEKING ASSISTANCE—YOUNG
MAIDENS ANTICIPATING LEAP-YEAR PRIVILEGES—BARKIS-
LIKE, SHE WAS "QUITE WILLING."

So rapidly are the old habits and customs of the Indians passing away that it is necessary to quickly gather up all the knowledge of them we can, as the indications are that these will soon only exist in tradition. In these days, when governments are adopting the plan of placing them on reservations, under the influences of agents, school-masters, and missionaries, and constant observance of the ways of the dominant race, such transitions are taking place that the old Indian will soon only have an existence in the past. Would that every change might be for the better!

Among these changes, amounting almost to a revolution, those pertaining to courtship and marriage are very marked. Once, among some of the tribes, when the young men wanted wives they had to purchase them from the parents, the young damsels themselves having nothing to say about the bargain, but were expected to quietly submit to the arrangement. Among some of the other tribes the young expectant bridegroom had to go through a sort of ceremony in order to obtain the good will of the young Indian maiden ere he purchased her from her father. He was obliged to go early in the morning to the door of her father's wigwam, and there, wrapped up in his blanket, to sit during all the hours of the day. It was considered the highest etiquette not to take the slightest notice of him. Day after day he would come and remain in the same quiet position. After a week or more had passed, if he was considered an agreeable suitor for the damsel he wished, his patience was at length rewarded and he was invited into the wigwam and food was set before him. Then his friends appeared and brought forward the presents he was willing to give for the girl of his choice. Days and even weeks were sometimes spent in discussion and bargaining ere all the parties were satisfied. Often the maiden was held at too high a price, and so the disconsolate lover had to seek a bride at another wigwam where the price was not so high.

Among the Choctaws when a young Indian saw a fair maiden whom he wished to wed he would watch for an opportunity to find her alone. Then he quietly advanced, and, in passing, dropped a little pebble at her feet. If he was agreeable to her she quietly let him know that she thought well of him. If otherwise, a scornful look or a repelling word caused him to beat a retreat as soon as possible. When both parties were satisfied and the marriage arranged, time and place were soon agreed upon by the relatives. When the time arrived the friends of the young people met at the homes of each and from thence escorted them toward the marriage-ground. Both parties halted at a distance from the selected spot. Then the brothers or some of the nearest male relatives of the bride approached the other party and, escorting the bridegroom forward, seated him upon a blanket spread out upon the ground. The sisters or, if none, the near young female relatives of the bridegroom then went over to the other party and brought forward the bride. It was expected of her that she would break loose from them and run away. Great was the excitement, but the fleet youngsters of both sexes joined in the chase, and soon she was pursued and captured and brought back in triumph and seated by the side of the bridegroom. Circles of friends then formed around the young couple. A bag of bread was brought forward by the woman's relatives and given to the bride, a significant symbol that the woman should hoe the corn and make the bread. The man's relatives brought a bag of meat to him, indicative of the hope that he would be a good hunter and keep the house well furnished with game. Then presents of various kinds were given to the young couple, and the whole ceremony ended up with a feast.

Among the different tribes the price of a wife varies considerably. Once when I was marrying a young couple of Christian Indians in a church, crowded as they usually are upon these occasions in all lands, an old pagan Saulteaux, who had come in early and taken a seat on the floor, after witnessing the affair and hearing the responses of the different parties, spoke out so loudly that I heard him saying at the close of the ceremony, "When I wanted a wife I did not have to go through all that trouble to get her."

"How did you get your wife?" I asked.

"I bought this old wife," was his quick reply, as he poked an old woman who was sitting on the floor beside him in the ribs with the end of his long pipe.

"How much did you give for her?" I asked.

"A blanket and a gun," he answered.

"Were you never married with a book?" which is the way of expressing Christian marriage.

"No, indeed," he replied.

"Well," I said, "I think it is about time you were."

The other couple had departed, yet hundreds of the people remained to see if a second wedding was coming off; so I said, "Bring your wife and come here and I will marry you."

The old fellow, who was a great favorite, although still a pagan, entered into the spirit of the hour, and seeing where he could get even with me quickly sprang up, and, bringing his old wife with him, stood up before me, amid the merriment of the crowd. We added the name of William to his Indian name of Ja-Koos, and gave her the name of Mary. I put them through the translated ceremony of the marriage service, and he heartily responded to all the promises to love and cherish therein recorded. When the ceremony was ended and they were receiving the profuse congratulations of every body the old woman of over seventy years, who had been his wife for over fifty, looked up into his face and said, "William, that is the first time you ever took my hand in yours and said you loved me."

The crowd laughed, but to me there was a volume of meaning in her words. In paganism these Indian men think it is a sign of weakness to say a kind word to a woman. Christianity marvelously changes these things.

William winced a little under her words but made no reply. He was thinking about something else, and so, turning again to me, he said, "Now, missionary, you know a wedding is not complete without a big feast, and as you got up this wedding of course you will furnish the feast."

As there was some force in what he said we did not disappoint him; but the appetite he had was simply marvelous, while the number of his relatives who seemed to think they had a right to all the privileges of that marriage-feast was amazing, especially as before the event it seemed as though he had but few.

Very amusing are some of the attempts at courtship of some of these Indians, as, dressed up in the Hudson Bay store clothes, they, like young white men, start off on their adventures. In some cases so completely do the bashful young fellows fail either in their attempts to muster up courage to ask the dusky damsels to be their wives or to win their notice that often do they wish the old custom was back again and they could without any of this fuss of courting go and purchase from their fathers those who had taken their fancy and then at once take possession of them. In their perplexities and troubles we have had them come to us to aid them in this very important crisis. Some of them, even when feeling quite certain that the object of their affections would not say them nay, had not the courage to ask the important question upon which so much depended; and so it was no very uncommon occurrence in our routine of duties to have some fine young fellow come into our mission home and, after hemming and hawing about various things, with much trepidation, in a roundabout way begin something like this:

"Say, please, missionary, you know I have built a nice new house?"

"Yes, I am glad you have a nice house."

"And, missionary, I have a large potato field all ready."

"Yes? That is a good thing."

"And I have some nets and traps."

"All very good," I replied.

"And I have thirty pounds to my credit in the company's books." (This was equal to about one hundred and fifty dollars.)

"I am delighted to hear that. It shows that you have been prudent and careful."

Then, as the nervous fellow could go on no farther, I said, "I am pleased to hear all these things; but why have you come to-day to tell them to me?"

"O, because I was thinking it was time I should get married," he said.

"A capital idea," I replied. "How old are you?"

"Twenty-eight," I remember one young fellow said.

"Twenty-eight and not married yet? Why, of course it is time you got a wife."

As he waited for me to go on I continued: "Who is the fortunate girl you have selected as your bride?"

With a good deal of blushing and hesitancy he said, "Kitty is the one I want."

As Kitty, to whom he referred, was a good, industrious, Christian girl, I congratulated him on his choice and inquired when the wedding was to come off.

"O," he explained, "we have not got as far as that yet."

"Well, how far have you got?" I laughingly replied.

"Why, I have not asked her yet," was his answer; "but I think she is the nicest of the girls, and I want to get her if I can."

For my reply I said, "Do you not think that you had better hurry up? For you know Kitty is a great favorite, and some other young fellow may get up courage and ask her before you."

This seemed to throw him into a great state of excitement, and at once drew from him the reason of his visit to us; and so in a way that was pathetic as well as ludicrous he pleaded that either Mrs. Young or I should go and ask Kitty if she would be his wife, and to tell her how great his love was for her, and how hard he had worked to get his little home ready for her, and that he had the thirty pounds ahead with which to make the biggest wedding-feast ever known in the village. We laughed heartily over the young fellow's timidity in this matter. He was one of our bravest hunters, and nothing would give him greater delight than, armed only with his hunting-knife, to meet the biggest bear in the woods; but here, when it came to the matter of asking a pretty black-eyed, blushing Indian maiden to be his bride, his courage all left him, and to us he came to help him out of his troubles. As we much respected him for his sterling worth, and the match was in every way desirable, and it was soon found out that the young lady was looking in the same direction, every thing was quickly and happily arranged, to his great delight, and there was a wedding-feast of such dimensions that the memory of it still lingers among them.

The change from the old style of things has even affected the maidens themselves, and knowing now that they are not to be bought from their fathers as was the custom in the old pagan times, and so in their shrewdness having an idea that some of the young men are a little shy and fearful about declaring themselves, they are at times not unwilling to let their preferences be known. Not that they are bold and forward, which is not the case, for we ever found that the Indian women, both young and old, of the different tribes among whom we lived were modest and retiring to a degree that could safely be imitated by many others of a whiter skin who have despised them as inferiors.

Still, as it is with their white sisters, there are times when a bashful lover needs a little encouragement to help him declare his intentions, and as these Indian girls have not yet been initiated into leap-year privileges they think there are times when in some way or other they should be permitted to make their preferences known.

Take this for an illustration: While Mrs. Young and myself were busily engaged in our work there came into our house one Monday morning a young maiden without ceremony, and, demurely seating herself, began a conversation with us. Indians, young and old, never knock at the door or ring the bell, but quietly and noiselessly come in when they think they have any thing to say. As this young woman had her shawl well drawn over her face and moved nervously about on her chair, and I was engrossed in some study that needed all my thoughts, I said to Mrs. Young, "That girl has something she wants to talk about; please find out what it is and let her go." As soon as the girl heard this she turned to me and said, very earnestly: "Benjamin was looking at me in church last Sunday." I was inclined to laugh, but of course it would never do, I thought, and so, trying to frown at her, I said, "Shame on you! You ought to have been looking at the preacher and listening to the words from the great book instead of looking at the young men."

"O, but he was looking at me," she said with great serious-ness. In this church the men are seated on one side and the women on the other, with a broad aisle between them.

"Looking at you?" I answered. "How could you have seen him looking at you if you had not been looking at him?"

Not to be thwarted, she sturdily replied, "Well, I felt he was looking at me, and so every time I turned and looked at him, sure enough, there he was, looking at me."

Feeling that her conduct was not that which ought to be en-couraged, and yet amused at her candor, I said as sternly as I could under the circumstances, "Well, suppose he was looking at you; what has that to do with you, and why do you come here to tell us?"

Gathering her shawl over her face so that not even one of her black eyes was visible, she said in a half-roguish, half seri-ous way, "Why, I have come to see you because we girls know that Benjamin had built a house, and we had heard that he was thinking about getting married." And then she started for the door, and as she fled out she said, "As he was looking so much at me in church I thought perhaps I was the one he wanted, and if it is so you can tell him I am quite willing."

IN THE INDIAN COUNTRY

CHAPTER XVI

INDIAN WIT AND HUMOR

THE DISH OF HORSE-RADISH—GENERAL CUSTER'S STORY OF THE CHIEF WHO SURRENDERED BECAUSE A WHOLE MULE WAS FIRED AT HIM—QUAINT STORIES OF JOHN SUNDAY—HIS FABLE OF THE BLACK-SNAKE AND THE FROG—HOW JOHN SILENCED THE MORMON PREACHER—HOW NEAR HE CAME TO GETTING A D.D.— HIS QUAINT MISSIONARY APPEAL TO MR. GOLD—OLD THICKFOOT—THE STOLID, HUMOROUS CHIEF'S IDEA OF SIN—AN INDIAN'S SHREWDNESS IN CARRYING CIDER IN A BASKET—A SENSIBLE REPLY TO A CHALLENGE TO FIGHT A DUEL—THE INDIAN MAGISTRATE WHO FINED BOTH PLAINTIFF AND DEFENDANT—THE STRANGE VERDICT— MAN AFRAID-OF-NOTHING

I have filled up this chapter with a number of stories illustrative of what with a certain amount of latitude may be called Indian humor. As a general thing, however, these red men are very much behind many other races in the possession of this characteristic. The elderly men are naturally grave and sedate in private life, and in their public addresses, amid their flights of fancy, while they are quick to grasp the subject under consideration or to observe the weak points in an opponent's speech, very seldom indulge in banter or strive to be humorous or witty. Still, they were not all so solemn or stoical. I was well acquainted with many who were just the reverse.

On my long journeys by canoe or dog-train, where some-times we were delayed for days on some rocky isle or point, or in some wintry camp, I was often amused by the bright repartee and ready, clever replies of my Indian attendants, some of whom seemed never to lose their vivacity or become disheartened amid our disagreeable surroundings. In our darkest hours they ever seemed able to find something ludicrous at which to create a laugh and thus brighten up the dreary hours through which we had to wait until the storm abated and we were able to push on.

The Chiefs and the Horse-Radish

THE following incident, with its witty retort, occurred at Washington. Two prominent Indian chiefs, who were part of a deputation which had come to the city on business, were taken home to dine by a large-hearted gentleman with his family. The dinner was a grand affair, and there was a great variety of dishes provided. The chiefs, Indian-like, had a curiosity to taste every thing on the table. Among other things provided was a dish of horse-radish. The chief nearest it, not knowing any thing of its fiery nature, took a spoonful of it and quickly swallowed it. As a natural result the tears were soon running down his face, although by a great effort he was able to conceal every other effect it had upon him.

The other chief, on observing his tears, with much concern said, "Why do you weep, my brother?"

As soon as the victimized man could control himself enough to speak calmly, he replied, "I am weeping as I think of my ancestors who were slain in battle."

The subject was then dropped and the dinner proceeded. After a while the horse-radish was moved round to the other side of the table and the second chief helped himself to a spoonful of it with the same result. Observing him weeping, his comrade, with a great apparent show of sympathy, put to him the same question, "Why do you weep, my brother?"

As quickly as possible came back the witty retort, "I weep with vexation because you were not slain with your ancestors in battle." He was quite indignant that his brother-chief had not given him timely warning against the fiery dish.

General Custer's Story

A few months before General Custer was killed at the battle of Rosebud by Sitting Bull I spent three days with him. We had many talks and some discussions about the Indians and the different methods of dealing with them. In one of our conversations he told me the following story, which showed that one Indian, at least, was not entirely destitute of a kind of grim humor.

General Custer said he had been following up a band of hostile Indians, and when night overtook him had driven them well up into some ravines and mountains. He rested his troops a few hours, and then, as he had a number of capital scouts or guides who knew the country well, he resumed the march very early in the morning, and the scouts discovered the Indians on a bluff before them, beginning to make preparation for their breakfast. General Custer immediately sent a part of his force by a circuitous path around in the morning twilight to try and head off the enemy when he would make the attack. When he thought all was ready the signal of attack was sounded, and with his troops he dashed into their midst. The Indians were so completely taken off their guard—for they had never dreamed of being followed up through the night—that they made but little defense, and, seizing only their weapons, rapidly disappeared over the precipitous bluff. Such was the wild character of the country, and the intimate acquaintance that these Indians had of every part of it, that Custer had but little hopes of shooting or capturing any number of them.

Having a small howitzer or mountain cannon, which was carried upon the back of a large mule, Custer ordered it, while still fastened to the mule, to be quickly loaded and fired down the side of the steep bluff where he had observed the greatest number of the enemy to disappear. From some cause or other the mule, generally so reliable, perhaps upset by the concussion, lost her footing on the edge of the bluff and went crashing down the mountain-side and disappeared in the dense underbrush and trees at the foot many hundreds of yards below. So precipitous was the place that no effort could be made to recover either the poor mule's equipment or the cannon. With that part of his regiment which was with him he breakfasted where the hostile Indians a short time before had made all preparations for the same morning meal, but from which they had been so unceremoniously driven. After a few hours' waiting he was joined by the rest of his troops, who had been sent on ahead to try if possible and intercept the retreating Indians. To Custer's surprise his troops had secured quite a number of prisoners, and among them one of the most warlike and cunning chiefs of the hostile tribe.

When the stiffness of the surrender had worn off, and the general had heard the reports of his subordinate officers and the conversation had become general, Custer asked the chief for his version of how it was that he was captured. His answer was characteristic and unexpected:

"General," said he, "I am not afraid to fight men armed with bows and arrows or with spears and tomahawks, and I love the battle with your soldiers armed with carbines or rifles, and you know I have not often been whipped, and I have often heard the roar of your big guns and have not been afraid; but, general," he continued, with a little bit of a twinkle in his eye, *"when I found you were able to fire a whole mule at me I made up my mind it was time to surrender."*

It seems he had been among the crowd, when the attack was made upon them, who had slipped over that side of the bluff down which the howitzer was fired and were hiding at the bottom in fancied security when the mule came tumbling into their midst. This new method of warfare seemed to so impress them that they decided on an immediate surrender, although their hiding-place in all probability would not have been discovered.

The Fable of the Black-Snake and the Frog

THE Rev. John Sunday, a full-blooded Canadian-Indian missionary, was full of wit and shrewdness. For many years he was a favorite speaker in all the cities and towns of Canada, and never failed to charm and delight as well as profit his large audiences.

As a missionary among his own people he was very successful in his work. As pastor and general adviser his good judgment and tact gave him great influence over them for good. His methods of work and schemes to overcome the difficulties showed him to be a man of no mean ability. Here is the plan adopted to prevent a couple of his people on one of his missions from going to law to settle a dispute about the exact location of the boundary-fence between their respective farms.

John Sunday was a great admirer of *Aesop's Fables*, and so when he found out that his two parishioners were resolved to imitate the whites and go to law about the fence rather than submit to arbitration in the presence of some wise people, he told them this fable:

"Once upon a time an Indian was walking on the shore of Rice Lake when he saw a great big black-snake out looking for his breakfast. He looked here and he looked there, under this log and in that dense bush, until at length near a marshy place he saw a great big bull-frog. At him he rushed, and at length he managed to catch him by the hind legs and at once began to swallow him. The frog was a very large one and resisted with all his might. He struggled and pulled and jumped this way and that way, and tried to shake off the snake, but he could not succeed. But in his struggles he managed to make the snake's body fly around like a whiplash until the tail came so near that the frog was able to catch hold of it in his forefeet. Holding on tightly to it, the frog at once began to swallow it while the snake was hard at work swallowing him from the other end. And thus," added the missionary, gravely, "they went on swallowing each other until there was nothing left of either of them."

The story was so ludicrous, and yet so suggestive, that the would-be litigants saw its drift and the object of their faithful missionary in giving them this fable, and then and there shook hands and quickly settled the matter in dispute without any more trouble.

The Mormon Preacher Silenced by John Sunday

LONG years ago, when the Mormon excitement prevailed both in the New England States and Canada, a Mormon preacher came to the Bay of Quinte County, in the Province of Ontario, and held a series of meetings with the object of making proselytes for the western Mormon country. But shortly before this a number of Indians had become Christians, and hearing of these Mormon services, but not knowing their character, some of them attended. Great was their sorrow at hearing the Bible which they had learned to love so belittled and despised, and the Book of Mormon, which he said had been dug up out of the ground, highly extolled above it. When the Mormon had finished his discourse about the book he gave permission for any of the congregation to say any thing they desired about what he had said. All sat still, and as no white man was found brave enough to get up and defend the old book John Sunday at length arose and asked if an Indian might speak. The desired permission having been given by the Mormon, the pious Indian replied as follows:

"A great many winters ago the Great Spirit gave his good book, the Bible, to the white man over the great waters. He took it and read it, and it made his heart all over very glad. By and by white man came over to this country and brought the good book with him. He gave it to poor Indian. He hear it and understand it, and it make his heart very glad too. But when the Great Spirit gave his good book to the white man the evil spirit, the Muche-Maneto, try to make a book, too, and he try to make it like the Good Spirit made his, but he could not, and then he got so ashamed of it that he go in the woods and dig a hole in the ground, and there he hide his book. After lying there for many winters, Joe Smith go and dig it up. This is the book this preacher has been talking about. I hold fast to the good old Bible, which has made my heart so happy. I will have nothing to do with the devil's book."

This quaint speech ended that Mormon's career in that neighborhood. Would that in other lands and places there had risen up true men like this brave John Sunday to silence and stamp out the pestilent impostors who have done so much evil on this American continent.

His Appeal to Mr. Gold

AT a great missionary meeting held in the old Adelaide Street Church, Toronto, among the speakers on the platform with John Sunday was a doctor of divinity, who had, on this his first public appearance after getting his D. D., to receive a good deal of friendly banter from his brethren, especially as the recipient of the honor had never had other than an exceedingly limited education. John Sunday listened to all that was said in his quiet way, and when called on to speak convulsed the audience by saying in his own droll way, "Mr. Chairman, I never went to school but two weeks in my life. If I had gone four weeks I would have had D. D. too." When the laughter had subsided he gave a most admirable address, appealing to the vast audience for his poor Indian brethren in their wretched wigwams. His closing sentences of appeal for financial help were characteristically quaint and original. Here are his words:

"There is a gentleman I suppose now in this house. He is a very fine gentleman, but he is very, very modest. He does not like to show himself. I do not know how long it is now since I saw him, he comes out so little. I am very much afraid he sleeps a great deal of his time when he ought to be going about doing good. His name is Mr. Gold. Mr. Gold, are you here to-night? or are you sleeping in your iron chest?

"Come out, Mr. Gold! Come out and help us to do this great work to preach the Gospel to every creature. Ah, Mr. Gold, you ought to be ashamed of yourself to sleep so much in your iron chest! Look at your white brother, Mr. Silver; he does a great deal of good in the world while you are sleeping. Come out, Mr. Gold, from your iron chest and fly around like your active brother, Mr. Silver. And then, Mr. Gold, just think of your active little brother, Mr. Copper. Why, he is every -where. He is flying about doing all the good he can. Be active, like him! Come out, Mr. Gold! Do come and help us in this good work, and if you really cannot come yourself, well, do the next best thing you can—that is, send us your shirt, that is, a bank-note."

Thickfoot's Idea of Sin

ON the shores of Lake Winnipeg we had a comical old chief by the name of Thickfoot. He had such a dry, humorous way about him, and such skill in getting a laugh out of the most serious conversation, that while I ceased not to have a great interest in him, and neglected no opportunity of trying to benefit him, I confess I had lost confidence in my persuasive powers over him. One winter, when traveling with my dog-trains in company with a brother-missionary, we stopped for the night at Thickfoot's village. He welcomed us courteously and invited us to spend the night in his wigwam, which he knew, of course, would mean a liberal supply of tea and tobacco to himself. We gladly accepted his offer, and, as was always our custom, had him invite in as many Indians as his wigwam would hold to an evening service. We had a very pleasant evening, and all seemed much interested in the service, even old Thickfoot himself. After the audience had dispersed I quietly asked my brother-missionary to tackle the old chief about his belief and urge him to renounce his paganism and become a Christian. My zealous brother was always ready for this congenial work, and when there was a suitable opportunity immediately began. Very interesting was the conversation, and Thickfoot by his candor and straightforward answers made me think that at length something was going to be made out of him. My brother-missionary became much interested and encouraged. At length the conversation turned to the subject of sin and its consequences if unforgiven. Thickfoot seemed to be absorbed in the subject.

"Have you not felt yourself to be a great sinner, Thickfoot?" asked the missionary. "Do there not come times to you when you feel full of remorse and sorrow for some of the great sins and crimes of which you have been guilty, and for which your conscience tells you you ought to seek for pardon and forgiveness?"

The chief, whose face was grave and devout, took his calumet from his mouth, looked up in the face of the missionary, and replied, "O, yes, I feel that I am a great sinner."

"Ah," replied the missionary, "I thought you must feel this

way and at times mourn over your past conduct."

"Yes," said Thickfoot, "and there is one great sin that rises up before me like the bold, high cliff, and over it I often mourn."

"If it is not asking too much," said the exultant missionary, "I should so like to have you tell me what that great crime is that you so mourn over."

"Well," said Thickfoot, while his face was as grave as the Sphinx, "long years ago I and my people were fighting against the Sioux. I had plenty of ammunition, and I found myself fighting against six who were out of powder. I only killed two of them when I might have killed them all. In a weak moment my heart said it is unmanly to kill unarmed men, and so I let the rest escape. It was a great sin that I did so, and I have never forgiven myself for having been such a great sinner. O, yes," he added, "I am a great sinner for so acting, and need forgiveness."

This answer quite discouraged my good brother. But Thickfoot has since accepted the truth, and has become a good earnest Christian.

An Indian's Shrewdness

ONE cold, wintry day an Indian basket-maker with a couple of large baskets called at the house of a Canadian farmer and tried to sell him one of them. Not succeeding, for the farmer had a notorious character for miserliness, the Indian, knowing he had abundance of cider, asked for a glass to warm him that cold day. This the farmer refused, but while the Indian was gathering up his baskets he jocularly added, "For one of your baskets I will give you all the cider you can carry away in the other."

The Indian gravely handed him one of them and, taking up the other, went out to where a spring of water bubbled up out of the earth. In this he dipped his basket, and then, taking it out, waited patiently until the severe frost—for the temperature of the air was many degrees below freezing—had changed the water into ice. Again and again he repeated the process until the basket was entirely covered with an icy coat which completely filled up all the interstices between the pieces of thin ashwood of which the basket was made. Then going to the farmer he demanded the fulfilment of his promise, and so kept him to it that he went away with several gallons of the coveted liquid.

An Indian's Reply to a Challenge

A good deal of common sense is to be found in the following reply which was sent by an Indian to an angry white man who had challenged him to fight a duel with him:

"I have two objections to this duel affair. One is lest I should hurt you, and the other is lest you should hurt me. I do not see any good that it would do me to put a bullet through your body. I could not make any use of you when dead, but I could of a rabbit or turkey. As to myself, I think it more wise to avoid than put myself in the way of harm. I am under apprehension that you might hit me. That being the case, I think it advisable to keep my distance. If you want to try your pistols, take some object, say a tree or any thing about my size, and if you hit that send me word and I shall acknowledge that if I had been there you might have hit me."

Double-Handed Justice

AT one of our Indian villages where the old habits and customs are rapidly giving place to the new order of things, the people resolved to so far imitate the whites as to have a magistrate of their own. They resolved that no longer would they settle their disputes at their council-fire, but would adopt the white man's mode of procedure. So a big Indian accepted the situation and went in several hundreds of miles to see the governor of the young Province of Manitoba and to get his commission. After an absence of several weeks he returned much pleased with his reception by the governor and full of the importance of his new office. He was anxious for something to do in his official capacity, but the people were so honest and peaceful that weeks passed away ere he had any thing to demand official action. One day, however, there came to him a man who had a formal complaint to make. His story was that, having been out in the woods several hundred yards back of his own house cutting wood, when night came down he left his ax where he had been at work leaning against a log near the trail, and when he returned in the morning it was not there. Somebody had most assuredly stolen his ax. His story very much interested the magistrate, who saw at once that here was something calling for the exercise of his official duties. But of course the first thing was to find out who was the thief who had taken the ax.

Said the magistrate to the young man, "You get the old women of the village to keep their eyes open and look around, and it is likely they will soon find who has your ax. Just as soon as it is known come and let me know."

Sure enough, in a short time it became known that a young man had possession of the lost ax, The magistrate sent some of his young braves after the transgressor, and he was brought without much ceremony into the presence of the official magnate.

The court opened with much mock dignity, and the offender was asked what defense he had to make for having in his possession another man's ax. He stated briefly that, having been out hunting for several days in the forest, he was returning home to the village, and coming along the trail he noticed the ax there beside the path, leaning up against a log, and so, without being thoroughly conscious of what he was doing, he picked it up and put it on his shoulder and carried it home. He supposed he should not have touched it.

After the magistrate had listened to his story he called up the owner of the ax and questioned him. First he said, "Did you say that you left your ax leaning against a log near the trail?"

"Yes," replied the owner.

"And that you did not cover it over with snow or hide it in the branches of the balsam tree, or put it out of sight in some way?" said the magistrate.

"No, I did not put it out of sight; I just left it as I told you," the man replied.

"You did!" said the magistrate with a growl of disapproval, which meant somebody was going to get hurt.

After asking a few more questions of both parties he very deliberately gave his decision, which was as follows:

"I fine the man who stole the ax five dollars. He knew it was not his and that he had no right to take it." Then turning to the owner of the ax he said, "I will also fine you five dollars, too, for putting temptation in the man's way. You ought to have either brought your ax home with you when your day's work was done or else to have so hid it out of sight that no one would have been tempted to take it."

This punishing both plaintiff and defendant showed his practical, common-sense character, but it made the people so shy of his administration that up to the time I last heard of him he had had no additional case.

The Strange Verdict

THIS willingness to give up the old tradition and customs and "do as the whites do" had another very amusing illustration years ago in a tribe that was located near to a white settlement. One of their number, a poor slave to drink, had been found frozen to death. At first the Indians were perplexed as to what ought to be done. Some of them, however, had learned about the white people holding "inquests" over unfortunates who had perished in this or other ways, and so they resolved to do the same in this case. So a jury was called, and after hearing all the evidence they, after gravely consulting together, brought in the verdict that "the deceased came to his death from the freezing of a great quantity of water inside of him, which they were of the opinion he had drunk for rum."

I have sometimes wondered whether it was humor or conscientiousness that made the man feel that he dare no longer bear a name which now was not all the truth, and caused the Indian, whose name literally meant Man-afraid-of-nothing, shortly after his marriage to a wife with a bit of a temper, to petition the council to allow him to have his name changed.

CHAPTER XVII

INDIAN ORATORY

THE GIFT HIGHLY PRIZED AND CULTIVATED—ADMIRED BY EMINENT WRITERS—CHARLEVOIX'S OPINION—DR. PUNSHON'S TESTIMONY TO SALASSALTON—SPECIMENS GATHERED FROM VARIOUS SOURCES—LOGAN'S SPEECH—TECUMSEH'S CHARACTER AND ADDRESSES—HIS HAUGHTY REPLY TO GENERAL HARRISON—ORATIONS AT PEACE COUNCILS—HIGHEST STYLE OF ORATORY AMONG THEM—PATHETIC WORDS OF PUSH-MA-TA-HA—SIMMO'S BEAUTIFUL ADDRESS—A CHIEF'S SPEECH AT THE CEREMONY OF THE BURIAL OF THE TOMAHAWK—WEATHERFORD'S ELOQUENT AND BRAVE ADDRESS TO GENERAL JACKSON—THE ANNIHILATION OF SUCH A PEOPLE TO BE REGRETTED

CONSIDERING from the civilized stand-point the Indians' lack of educational advantages, they are gifted with an ability to utter their sentiments and views in their public gatherings or around their council-fires in a more elevated and impressive style and with greater force and flexibility than is possessed by any other uncivilized people. The talent for public speaking or the gift of oratory has ever been prized and cultivated among them. The interested student in these things has often been surprised by the lofty style of their thoughts and their capacity to rise above mere individual or tribal selfishness and give expression to sentiments as sublime and comprehensive as any that live in the tradition or records of any uncivilized people. It is to be regretted that some of the best specimens of their oratory are now only remembered in tradition. Under the most favorable conditions it is difficult for interpreters to grasp and correctly follow some of their lofty flights and their sustained and often complicated expressions when delivering some of their finest orations. That a people untaught in the schools and so depressed and harassed by dissension within and wars without should in such a marked degree be so gifted is indeed both surprising and interesting. These oratorical gifts attracted the attention of the early writers on the American continent. From only one among a great many need we here quote. Charlevoix says:

"The beauty of their imagination equals its vivacity, which appears in all their discourses. They are very quick at repartee, and their harangues are full of shining passages which would have been applauded at Rome or Athens. Their eloquence has a strength, depth, and pathos which no art can give and which the Greeks so much admired in the barbarians."

The Rev. Dr. Punshon, himself one of England's greatest orators, after listening to a speech of Salassalton, an Indian in British Columbia, said: "I have heard all the best orators in Europe and America, but a more perfect oration than that of this uncultured Indian I never heard in my life."

We have thought it best to gather up some of the authentic reports of some of these Indian orations that have been preserved. They are at best but fragments, but in them are golden nuggets of truth as well as evidences of true oratory.

Logan's speech is perhaps most widely known. He was a Mingo chief, and like many others had been treacherously and cruelly dealt with. Crushed down by his disasters, he had retired to his cabin and refused to respond to the summons of Lord Dunmore, the governor, that he should come to the place appointed for the making of a treaty. So important a personage as Logan could not be overlooked, and so a special deputation was sent to him urging his attendance at the council. Although still refusing to go, he, however, consented to address the deputation. After referring to the butchery of all his relatives, he pronounced this remarkable speech:

"I appeal to any white to say if ever he entered Logan's cabin hungry and he gave him no meat; if ever he came cold and naked, and he clothed him not.

"During the course of the last long bloody war Logan remained idle in his cabin an advocate for peace. Such was my love for the whites that my countrymen pointed as they passed and said, 'Logan is the friend of the white man!'

"I had even thought to have lived with you, but for the injuries of one man, Colonel Cresass, who last spring in cold blood, and unprovoked, murdered all the relatives of Logan, not even sparing my women and children.

"There runs not a drop of my blood in the veins of any living creature. This calls on me for revenge. I have sought it, I have killed many, I have fully glutted my revenge. For my country I rejoice at the beams of peace. But do not harbor a thought that mine is the joy of fear. Logan never felt fear. He will not turn on his heel to save his life. "Who is there to mourn for Logan? Not one!"

Tecumseh was one of the greatest Indian warriors as well as an eloquent orator. He devised a great scheme, worthy of Napoleon, which was to unite all the Indian tribes into one great confederacy, from the Gulf of Mexico to the great lakes. They were to unite their forces in an army that would be able to meet and drive back the white people, who were continually advancing on the Indian tribes and forcing them westward toward the Rocky Mountains. This great scheme was maturing with marvelous rapidity when the premature death of Tecumseh put a sudden end to it.

Of his great orations but little that is reliable has been preserved. The following is his indignant address when he met General Harrison to discuss the sale of some land which had been made by some of the tribe in the absence of Tecumseh, and at which he was justly indignant and displeased:

"It is true I am a Shawnee. My forefathers were warriors. Their son is a warrior. From them I take only my existence; from my tribe I take nothing. I am the maker of my own fortune; and O that I could make that of my red people and of my country as great as the conceptions of my mind when I think of the Great Spirit that rules the universe! I would not then come to

General Harrison to ask him to tear the treaty and to obliterate the land-mark. But I would say to him, Sir, you have liberty to return to your own country. The voice within me, communing with past ages, tells me that once, nor until lately, there was no white man on this continent; that it then all belonged to the red man, children of the same parents, placed on it by the Great Spirit that made them to keep it, to traverse it, to enjoy its productions and to fill it with the same race once a happy race, but since made miserable by the white people, who are never contented but are always encroaching.

"The way and the only way to check and stop this evil is for all the red men to unite in claiming a common and equal right in the land, as it was at first and should be yet; for it was the gift of the Great Spirit to us all, and never was divided, and therefore by the few could not be ceded away forever. Backward have the Americans driven us from the sea-coast, and on toward the lakes are we being forced; but now we will yield no further, but here make our stand."

Vain indeed were all the efforts of the governor to get this truly patriotic chief to consent to the ceding of his domains to the whites. When asked if he was resolved to make war if his terms were not complied with he bravely replied, "It is my determination, nor will I give rest to my feet until I have united all the red men in this determination." Then began on his part those extraordinary and resolute exertions to unite all the tribes west of the Mississippi as well as those around Lake Superior in one great confederacy against the whites. No romance ever abounded in more startling adventures than were his, but his death at the battle of Moraviantown, on the Thames, put a stop to all his great schemes.

The following incident will give an additional insight into the character of this remarkable man. At one of the many meetings held with the white commissioners to try and arrange a peace, after Tecumseh had made a speech, and was about to seat himself in a chair, he observed that none had been placed for him. One was immediately ordered for him by the governor, and as the interpreter handed it to him he said, "Your father requests you to take a chair."

"My Father!" said Tecumseh with great indignation. "The sun is my father, and the earth is my mother, and on her bosom only will I repose," and immediately seated himself in the Indian manner on the ground.

When an Indian of high rank died embassies were frequently sent from even distant tribes to sympathize with the relatives. The message of condolence was delivered with great solemnity, and the tears were said to be wiped away with the acceptable presents which were brought. With the presentation of the gift the mourners were often addressed in the following manner: "We bury the remains of the deceased and cover the grave with bark, that neither the dew of heaven nor rain may fall upon it. We wipe off the tears from your eyes, and take all sorrow from your heart. We put your hearts in good order and make them cheerful again."

When a chief was in mourning he attended to no business, neither was his advice or counsel asked in reference to any of the affairs of state. When a chief of great repute died embassies of the tribes with whom his nation was at peace were sent to assure his mourning people that they shared with them in this great loss. Long ago, when the Cherokees sent a large and influential embassy to the Delawares to renew their peace alliance with them, they learned ere they reached their country that Ne-ta-wat-wees, the most influential chief of the Delawares, was dead. The ambassadors therefore halted about two miles below the town and sent word that they had arrived this far. The next day some of the influential captains of the Delawares went down to meet these Cherokees and bid them welcome. Among the beautiful things they said to them on this occasion were these:

"We extract the thorns from your feet which you have got on the journey. We take away the sand and gravel from between your toes. With balsamic oil we anoint the wounds and bruises made by the briers and brushwood. We wipe the sweat from your weary bodies, the dust out of your eyes, and cleanse your ears, throats, and hearts from all evil which you have seen or heard by the way or which has entered into your hearts."

On the conclusion of this address a string of white wampum, emblematical of peace and friendship, having been delivered in confirmation of it, the captains conducted the visiting ambassadors to the town. On entering the Cherokees saluted the inhabitants by firing off their guns, which was answered in a similar manner by the Delawares. Then the most influential member of the visiting embassy began a song, during which they were conducted to the council-room, which was elaborately prepared for their reception. All being seated, the first ambassador of the Cherokees expressed his sorrow at the death of the Delaware chief and the share he took in the national mourning. He said: "Tenderly I wrap up his remains in a cloth; I bury them and cover his grave with bark; I wipe the tears off the eyes of the weeping nation that again they may look up into the sunshine; I clear their ears of the sounds of mourning and their throats of the choking sensation of grief, and I take away all sorrow from their hearts."

In confirmation of this speech a string of wampum was delivered by him to the principal chief. The calumet was then smoked, after which there was a feast. On the following day the subject of the embassy was taken into consideration.

It has always been a matter of surprise and admiration to see with what cleverness and power these wild orators can handle their different languages, which are so poor in themselves. Yet so vivid and varied are their powers that their best addresses are full of apt illustrations, of elegant phrases, of poetic beauty, and are fraught with convincing logic and sound sense.

An Indian orator when speaking on some great occasion as the voice of his tribe is one of the highest ideals of dignity, wisdom, and eloquence. Untrammeled by any of the artificial rules of the schools of oratory, but with Nature as his only mistress in this fascinating art, he becomes an apt student. To his susceptible, sensitive soul she is ever an open book. From her he derives his beautiful pictures and choicest illustrations. In all her varying moods he enters, and so he can speak in the sweet, soft notes of her zephyr breeze or thunder out in tones that are not unlike her wildest storms. Gifted with intelligence and good judgment, possessing memories that in many instances are perfectly marvelous, and cultivating all his gifts in the most natural and effective school, he becomes possessed with an energy and fluency of expression, as well as a power of imagery, sometimes so exquisitely delicate and then of such soaring sublimity that he is able to rival the finest efforts of an ancient or modern orator.

Very impressive and never to be forgotten are the scenes and incidents of an Indian council-room when some subject of deep and exciting interest is being discussed. The sacred fire is burning in its place, the chiefs and warriors are ranged according to precedence, the calumet, or pipe of peace, is being gravely smoked, and an air of quiet dignity and decorum prevails. Speech follows speech in quick succession, but there is never any interruption or contradiction. Every man, no matter how divergent or peculiar may be his views, is allowed to give them without being molested. But now the orator of the tribe is rising to speak, and there is a hush of the most intense interest. He is a battle-scarred veteran, with all his wounds in front, everyone of which has its exciting story and gives him additional influence over the people. He seems to impress us as he begins. The dignified stature, the quiet, easy repose of limb, the graceful gesture, the dark, expressive eye at once captivate his auditors. Then, as he kindles with his subject and the genius of his eloquence bursts forth, the apparent apathy in which the Indian generally encases himself is here cast aside, and we see him as he is at his best, natural, legible, human. We are captivated by his eloquence. His gorgeous and apposite metaphors, numerous from the very poverty of his language, charm us by their quaintness and force. We listen to the story of his complaints and hear the recital of his people's wrongs and oppressions by the pale-face until our blood boils and our hearts get hot within us, even if we are of the oppressor's race. He conquers us, charms us, and throws around us that spell of fascinating power which comes so seldom in a life-time, and then only under the spell of the true orator. Very pathetic as well as felicitous were the closing words of the speech of the aged Push-ma-ta-ha, a venerable chief of a distant tribe, who traveled many hundreds of miles to attend a council where he strongly and eloquently pleaded for a lasting peace. In alluding to his great age and to the probability that he might not live to complete the long and arduous journey back to his own tribe he said:

"My children will walk through the forest and the Great Spirit's voice will be heard in the tree-tops. The flowers will spring up in the hunters' trail, and the birds will sing in the branches, but Push-ma-ta-ha will hear them not, neither will he see the flowers any more. He will be gone, his spirit will have fled. Then when he returns not, his people will know that he is not among the living—that he is dead. The news will come to their ears as the sound of the fall of a mighty oak in the stillness of the woods."

Where can we find any thing more beautiful than this commencement of a speech made by a chief called Simmo, to the English governor, Dudley, who had sent for the Indians to come and conclude a treaty of peace with him during the early French war? He said: "We thank you, good brother, for having come so far to speak with us. It is a great favor. The clouds are hovering in the air and are becoming dark; but still we sing with love the songs of peace. Believe my words, as far as the sun is from the earth so far are my thoughts from war and even from the slightest rupture between us."

Some of their finest addresses, like that of Sirnmo's, were at the ceremonious councils where peace was made, often after long and bloody wars. A good deal of preliminary negotiation was often necessary before the opposing parties met for the closing ceremonies. The final embassy of peace generally consisted of several of their most influential chiefs, including the best ora-tors among them. They carried the calumet, or pipe of peace, which was generally elaborately carved out of the famous red sandstone and fitted with a handsome stem often over four feet long, and also beautifully carved and decorated. So great is the respect which is ever associated with the calumet of peace and its bearers that any insult offered to them while on the message of peace, even if passing through a hostile country, is denounced as the most serious of crimes, which will most certainly and swiftly be visited by the abhorrence and vengeance of the Great Spirit.

If the negotiations are successful and peace is concluded a tomahawk or Indian hatchet, which perhaps had been the instrument in the murder of many, is made sharp and glittering, and then, being decorated with wampum or bright ribbons, is buried, with its edge down, with great ceremony and speech-making. Then often on the spot where it is buried a thrifty young tree is planted. The following is a good specimen of the addresses given on these peace-making occasions. The reader must add the singularly natural and yet animated gestures and beautifully modulated voice of this son of the forest. It is the address of one of the chiefs of the confederacy of tribes which were called the Five Nations, on the occasion of the making of a treaty of peace with Great Britain, which was long maintained:

"We are happy in having buried under ground the red ax that has so often been dyed with the blood of our brethren. Now in this spot we inter the ax and plant the tree of peace. We plant the tree whose top will reach high up into the sunlight, and its branches will soon spread abroad, that it shall be seen afar off. May its growth never be stifled and choked, but may it continue to flourish until it shades both your country and ours with its leaves. Let us make fast its roots and extend them to the utmost of your settlements. If enemies should come to shake this tree we would know it by the motion of its roots reaching into your country. May the Great Spirit allow us to rest in tranquillity upon our mats beneath its shade, and never again may the ax be dug up to cut down this tree of peace. Let the earth be trod hard over this ax which we have buried on its edge, so that if ever it moves it may only sink down the deeper. Let a strong stream like that which rushes by wash the evil thoughts and deeds of war out of our sight and remembrance. The war-fire that has so long burned is now extinguished. The bloody bed on which our wounded tossed, breathing vengeance, is now washed clean as are their hearts, and the tears are wiped from their eyes. Brothers, we now renew the covenant chain of friendship. Let it be kept bright and clean as silver, and never again may its beauty be tarnished by contact with any rust. As now it unites us in the bonds of friendship may not any one pull away his arms from it."

Weatherford was one of the most celebrated chiefs of the Creek tribe. He defeated the American troops in several pitched battles and was the leader on the attack on Fort Mimms, where nearly all the white soldiers were massacred. Some time after the Americans, under General Jackson, took a terrible revenge upon these Indians, and the majority of the Creeks were put to death or made prisoners. Wishing to test the fidelity of some of the surviving chiefs who had made their submission, General Jackson ordered them to bring to him their redoubtable warrior, Chief Weatherford, bound hand and foot. When these chiefs informed him of the general's demand Weatherford, to save himself and them from such a humiliation, at once resolved on presenting himself to the American general. The latter was naturally much surprised when the Indian warrior, for whose head a price had been offered, should in this way appear before him. He said: "I am Weatherford, who commanded at the taking of Fort Mimms, and who wishes for peace for my people. I come to ask for it."

On hearing this bold speech Jackson said: "I am surprised that you have dared to appear before me after your conduct, which deserves death; and if you had been brought in the way I had ordered I know how I would have treated you."

To this, Weatherford bravely replied: "I am in your power; do with me whatever you please. I am a soldier. I have done the whites all the harm I could. I fought against them, and I have fought bravely. If I had an army I would fight again; I would fight to the last; but I have one no longer. My people are no more. I can only weep over the misfortunes of my nation."

General Jackson was deeply moved by this chief's courageous conduct and noble address in this hour of his people's calamities. So, addressing him in reply, he said that although he had him in his power he would take no advantage of it, and that he allowed him to choose between submission without condition or liberty with war, but without quarter or pity. In response to these hard terms the brave but unfortunate chief replied in the following dignified but indignant words:

"You can with all security offer me such conditions. There was a time when I could have answered you differently; there was a time when I might have had a choice. Now I have none. I have even no hope. Formerly I could encourage my warriors to combat; but I cannot animate the dead. My warriors can no longer hear my voice; their bones rest at Talladega, Tellushatches, Emuakpan, and Tohopekon. I have not given myself up without reflection. Whenever I had the slightest chance of success I never quitted my post nor asked for peace. But my people are gone, and if I sue for peace it is for those who yet live, but not for myself. I look upon the past with profound sorrow, and I desire to avoid greater calamities. Your people have destroyed my nation. You are a brave man, and I rely on your generosity. You will only demand of a conquered people such terms as they should accede to. Whatever they may be it would now be madness and folly to oppose them. If they are opposed you shall find me among the sternest enforcers of obedience. Those who would still hold out can be influenced only by a mean spirit of revenge. To this spirit they must not and shall not sacrifice the last remnant of their country. You have told our nation that they might go with all security, no matter where, and be safe. This is good talk, and they ought to listen to it. They must listen to it. They will listen to it."

Such an address is almost above all criticism. True dignity and a lofty spirit of resignation under his nation's misfortunes breathe in every sentence uttered by this brave but beaten chief. In this pathetic address we get a good idea of Indian eloquence, and where, even in the civilized world, at the close of a disastrous campaign can we find the vanquished addressing their conquerors in nobler sentiments or greater elevation of thoughts?

Weatherford had been visited by Tecumseh, and had entered heartily into his great design of forming a mighty confederacy against the ever-advancing whites. With all his Indian impetuosity and bravery did he fight, but the forces against him were irresistible, and under them he went down. But what a pity and an everlasting disgrace that a people who could produce such men of such powers should not have been earlier understood and more honorably dealt with by the powerful and dominant white man!

It is a cause of thankfulness that there is now, both in the United States and in Canada, a disposition to deal honorably with the Indians. Unfortunately, it has not always been so, for the record of the white man's conduct toward these red men has, with few exceptions, been one of dishonor and disgrace. Treaties have been made and solemnly ratified with the most emphatic assertions that they were to continue as long as "the sun would shine or waters run." Yet, just as soon as the selfish interest of the whites seemed to call for their abrogation, they were ignored and broken without the slightest regard for the interests of the Indians who had faithfully remained true to their promises. Then time after time have peaceful Indian tribes been driven violently out from their homes into regions that they knew not of. And it is also a well-known fact that tribes after having been placed on reservations by the government, and who were living quiet, harmless lives, have, because the dominant race has looked with greedy eyes upon their lands, been, without their consent being asked, or adequate compensation granted, forcibly removed hundreds of miles farther west.

The following expressive lines, written by Mrs. Catherine Walker, are not only applicable to the case of the tribe for whom

she wrote them, but they could be applied to many others, some
of whom suffered even more than did these. These were written
on the occasion of the forcible removal of the Wyandot Indians
from their native land to the far western Indian Territory.

INDIAN WRONGS

Go, fated Indians, to the farthest verge
Of earth's remotest shore:
There let the night-bird sing thy dirge
When thy weary wandering's o'er.

Go sit upon the ocean's brink,
And in its solemn moan,
Fit music for thy broken heart,
Forget thy distant home.

But the white man's foot is on thy track
As the blood-hound seeks the hare;
Then arise and scale some barren rock,
For the white man will not spare.

Go dwell upon some craggy peak
Where the eagle makes her nest,
And eternal snows are drifting down
There thy weary foot may rest.

Away from where thy kindred sleep,
Beneath a frigid sky,
Where the wintry blasts will freeze thy tears
There lay thee down and die.

Cast not a look to thy native land,
But to that blissful shore
Where oppression's sigh is never heard
And thou shalt weep no more.

CHAPTER XVIII

THE MEDICINE-MEN OR CONJURERS

DESCRIPTION—AMONG ALL THE TRIBES—POWER THEY EXERCISE—KNOWLEDGE OF SOME MEDICINES—RELY PRINCIPALLY ON THEIR IMAGINARY SUPERNATURAL POWER TO RETAIN THEIR INFLUENCE—SHREWD OBSERVERS OF NATURE—RAIN-MAKERS—CHARMS—GOOD MEDICINE—GENERAL CUSTER—TEST OF SKILL BETWEEN RIVAL MEDICINE-MEN—JESUIT PRIEST—MOUNTAIN SHEEP KILLED BY THE CONJURER'S WORD—WILD GOOSE KILLED BY MAGIC—CONJURERS BLACKMAILERS—POWER OF SUPERSTITIONS—FRIGHTENED TO DEATH—SUCCESSFUL CONJURER AT NORWAY HOUSE—FAILURE OF A BOASTFUL MEDICINE-MAN—NOT INVULNERABLE AGAINST FIRE OR BULLETS—THE RED-HOT POKER TOO MUCH FOR HIM—SOME OF THEM CONVERTED—"CALL ME DANIEL"

THE medicine-men, or conjurers, are to be found among all the Indian tribes. They are a kind of priest, doctor, and charlatan combined. Many of them have a fair knowledge of the medicinal properties of some roots and herbs, and are skillful in managing some diseases and in dressing wounds; yet they rely principally upon their pretended supernatural powers to overawe their dupes. With them disease is only a tangible evidence of the presence of the bad god, whom they called Muche-Maneto. If he only can be exorcised by their incantations and medicines, health will return, and greater far will be the influence and power of the medicine-man over his patient, whom he ever tries to convince that it was his supernatural power rather than the medicine given that wrought the cure.

They profess to be able to foretell future events and to explain all the unusual phenomena that may occur. They profess to be under the guidance of their familiar spirits, from whom they declare they often receive direct communications. Before they are able to obtain a commanding influence over the people they have to pass through a long series of rigorous acts of self-mortification and suffering. They must submit to long fasting, and among some tribes to personal mutilation. So prolonged and intense are some of these ordeals that death often prematurely intervenes. In many other cases, as the result of the physical pain and anguish, the mind becomes partially disordered, and the medicine-men thus acquire additional sacredness and influence among these very superstitious people. Very great indeed is the power which many of these medicine-men exert over the tribes. They preside over all the religious ceremonies, and have a voice and vote in every thing that goes on.

As a general thing the amount of influence they have over the people is according to the fear or terror they are able to inspire in the minds of their dupes. Like their ancient congeners, they pretend to observe the flight of birds, the movements of the clouds, and other meteorological phenomena, and from these they prognosticate events which they say will happen. They give great attention to dreams, and are elated and pleased at what they consider good ones, and are correspondingly depressed at what are called bad ones. They are very cunning and cautious in the display of their power, as they well know that frequent failures mean the lessening of their influence and emoluments.

Among the more southern tribes, where a portion of the soil was cultivated, the conjurers were also called the rainmakers, and were expected to keep the right supply on hand for use when required. Loud were the clamorings of the people, and often dire were their threatenings if a long drought seemed likely to destroy the maize or burn up the grass. To the importunate pleading of the people for rain the cunning impostor, knowing the disastrous effects that would follow if he failed, generally delayed the public commencement of the ceremony until a change in the atmosphere, bringing up the black clouds, made it almost a certainty that his efforts would be crowned with success. When his sharp eyes saw indications favorable to the venture, he left the interior of his lodge, where he had been keeping up an incessant drumming, and, armed with his shield and bow and quiver of arrows, he climbed the roof of the sacred medicine-lodge and delivered boastful orations to the people, who rapidly assembled to welcome the long-looked-for rain, which he was to produce. He recounted his dreams, which indicated that he was the favorite of Heaven, and that the Good Spirit had made his arrows so powerful that they would pierce the clouds and bring down the refreshing showers. Keenly watching the gathering clouds, he limited or prolonged his oration until the favorable time arrived. Then, when the muttering thunders were heard and the big drops began to fall, with all his strength he shot his arrows into the clouds above him. If the refreshing showers really did fall he was the hero of the hour, and was well rewarded. If no rain or but little fell he was overwhelmed with ridicule, and had for the time being to hide himself from the people as a discredited and unrewarded man, as among those tribes the medicine-men or rain-makers were only rewarded in proportion to their success.

The word "medicine" among the Indians means much more than is generally understood by it. To them it has a much deeper meaning than mere healing remedies or curative practices. While there were those who had devoted all their time and were called the conjurers, or medicine-men, yet every body was supposed to have his good or bad medicine. When specially fortunate in hunting or warfare or in more quiet duties of life he was said to be under the influence of "good medicine." When misfortune overtook him in any of his affairs his "bad medicine" was said to be the cause. A man specially fortunate in war, and one who had escaped the bullets of his enemies, was under the influence of "good medicine." In battle one so noted often escaped because, his enemies thinking him bullet-proof, they would not waste their bullets by firing at him. There was an impression among the Sioux that General Custer had such good medicine that it was foolishness to fire at him. He had so often escaped from their bullets that he was almost the last man shot in the disastrous battle in which he and his gallant regiment were all cut off. Survivors of the fight informed me that when Custer dashed upon them with his troops he had his bridle-reins in his teeth and a revolver in each hand. With unerring accuracy he shot down several Indians, and then something went wrong with one of his revolvers; the Indians, observing this, although in the heat of the terrible fury, shouted out, "He has lost his good medicine," and at once fired at him. One bullet pierced him through the brain and another passed through his body as he fell a corpse.

While from motives of selfish policy the old professional medicine-men generally live in peace with each other, still there are times when the bitterest hostility exists between them, and there have been trials of their skill that perplexed and astonished those who were witnesses of the strange conflict. The following is an account of a trial of skill of this kind between two celebrated medicine-men that is worthy of record.

Black Snake was the name of one of these medicine-men. He lived on a northern branch of the Saskatchewan River, and so must have been a Cree or Mountain Stoney. He lived a solitary life, was dreaded and feared by the Indians, who firmly believed that the spirit of the evil gods dwelt in him. Yet although he kept himself much aloof from the people, he was vain and ambitious as well as haughty and contemptuous. The report of the skill of a great rival filled him with wrath, and so it was arranged that there should be a trial of their power.

The rival medicine-men, each furnished with his medicine-bag, his amulets, and other professional paraphernalia, arrayed in full dress and covered with war-paint, met in the presence of a great concourse. Both had prepared for the encounter by long fasting and conjurations. After the pipe, which precedes all important councils, had been smoked the medicine-men sat down opposite to each other a few feet apart. The trial of power seems to have been conducted on principles of animal magnetism, and lasted a long while without decided advantage on either side, until Black Snake, concerting all his power, or "gathering his medicine," in a loud voice commanded his opponent to die. Strange as it may appear, the unfortunate conjurer succumbed, and in a few minutes was dead.

This remarkable encounter was mentioned to a priest of the Jesuit order who had been for over twenty years laboring in the wildest parts on the western slopes of the Rocky Mountains, and who had in those long years obtained an intimate knowledge of the doings and power of these medicine men. Instead of seeming incredulous or astonished at the recital of the strange contest he said: "I have seen many exhibitions of power which my philosophy cannot explain. I have known predictions of events far in the future to be literally fulfilled, and have seen 'medicine' tested in the most conclusive ways. I once saw a Kootenai Indian (known as Skookum-tam-aherewos from his extraordinary power) command a mountain sheep to fall dead, and the animal then leaping among the rocks of the mountain-side fell instantly lifeless. This I saw with my own eyes, and I ate of the animal afterward. It was unwounded, healthy, and perfectly wild." This priest always firmly believed that these old medicine-men were in league with and derived a great deal of supernatural power from the evil one, and as a natural consequence he preferred to keep as clear of them as possible.

A circumstance almost similar occurred at Nelson River one spring while I was there. An old conjurer came to the Hudson Bay Company's trading-post and in rather saucy words demanded food of the gentleman then in charge of the place.

Mr. Flett, not admiring the tones in which the conjurer asked for aid, and knowing well that there was abundance of game, as the wild ducks and geese were then passing by in great numbers, rather sternly said to him, "I'll not encourage you in your laziness. Go out and shoot ducks and geese like other people."

A few sharp words passed between them, and at length the medicine-man retorted, "I can get geese if I like without shooting them."

Mr. Flett, who had heard of this old fellow's power, and wishing to see it, retorted, "I don't believe you!"

"Come and see," replied the angry old man as he walked out of the house, followed by Mr. Flett and several members of his family. Soon a flock of wild geese appeared flying from the south, as it was in the spring-time. The old medicine-man called on his familiar spirits, and then imitated the well-known cry of the wild goose, at which all these Indians are expert. Strange to say, a large, splendid goose dropped from the flock and fell dead at the feet of the old fellow, who, coolly picking it up, said to Mr. Flett as he walked off, "You see, now I can get geese if I want to without shooting them."

Very shortly after Mr. Flett and his family told me this strange story, which had made a deep impression upon them. We tried to explain its mystery away, but we have given it just as it happened. Marvelous is the power through fear which these medicine-men exert over the rest of the people. Except in what belonged to their vocation, they always seemed to me to be incorrigibly lazy. Yet they lived on the best that was obtainable, and ever had abundance. Their plan was a system of blackmailing. From the deer-hunters they demanded so much venison as the price of success in hunting the deer; so with the beaver-hunters and others. If any demurred from these exactions they were instantly threatened with dire calamities: "I'll conjure so you will lose your health, your boy will die, your gun will not shoot straight, or the animals will not go into your traps." And the poor deluded fools will believe that they have all this pretended power, and will tamely submit to be thus robbed and swindled.

Poor slaves of superstition! I used to pity them, and nothing gave me greater joy than to see these chains broken from their minds and the people rising up in their spiritual emancipation and boldly defying the medicine-men to do their worst, unless it was to see, as it was my joy in several instances, these old conjurers publicly renouncing their old sinful life and abominable practices and becoming honest, industrious men and consistent Christians.

To those who have not personally been among a people under the power of superstition, fear, and terror such as these notorious medicine-men can inspire, some of the stories that can be told must seem almost incredible. Yet it is well known by us missionaries that there have been cases where apparently healthy men have succumbed under the witchery of these wretches. These conjurers, having had their auger aroused by some act of opposition to their will, have cast such a spell over their victims by telling them they must die within such a time that they have laid themselves down and within that period, without any apparent disease, have died.

One of the best-known medicine-men of my acquaintance was a Cree or Kunista. Of him this happened while I was living at Norway House: One summer when the Hudson Bay Council was sitting at Norway House the private secretary of the governor, a Mr. H., was very anxious to hear about the arrival of the "proofs" of a book he had written and which was being published in London, England. So, without letting any one into the secret, he induced old Tapastanum to conjure and find out what he wanted and where it was. Tapastanum was an ignorant, unintellectual person, and destitute, when sober, of those fierce traits which are generally supposed to be part of the make-up of the dreaded conjurer. After a good deal of reluctance, at length he was induced to comply with the wish of Mr. H., and, erecting a conjurer's tent, he went into it with nothing but his magic drum and medicine-bag. After beating his drum incessantly for hours, and working himself up into a kind of frenzy in calling upon his totems or familiar spirits, he said that he had found out that there had arrived on such a day from across the great sea, and was now in Fort Garry, a parcel the size of which he accurately described. Several weeks after, when Mr. H. returned to the Red

River Settlement, he found that his parcel of "proofs" which he had been anxious about had arrived on the day mentioned by the conjurer, and was exactly the size described by him.

This incident caused a good deal of talk and some excitement. Mr. H. himself was as much surprised as any one else, as he had been very skeptical about the old conjurer's powers, and had only put the old fellow to the test for a little amusement. But he had to admit that here was something that confounded his philosophy.

The Hudson Bay Company's officials, who have lived in various parts of the country for many years, and are frequently coming in contact with these old conjurers of different tribes, are very much divided in their views about them. Some most firmly believe that they have some supernatural power or are in league with evil spirits, and through these agencies are at times able to do things almost incredible. But the great majority of the officers, like myself, believe that they are only clever impostors, shrewd students of human nature, and, perhaps, possessed in some instances of an extra amount of animal magnetism or mesmeric power.

They did not always succeed as in the last incident. Another old medicine-man was constantly boasting that he could so put himself under the power of his familiar spirits that fire could not burn him nor bullets pierce him. So arrogant did he get and boastful in his utterances that the gentleman in charge of the fort, a Mr. Hamilton, offered to take him at his word and test his skill. The cunning old medicine-man, who had an eye to business, offered to accept the challenge on condition that so many pounds of tobacco and tea should be forthcoming. This being arranged to his satisfaction, the ordeal began. The old fellow spent several hours in carefully preparing his conjurer's tent, which he made by bending over, like half-hoops, a number of limber green poles, the ends of which he stuck firmly in the ground. Then over this light frame-work he threw a covering made by sewing together a number of deer-skins, from which the hair had been scraped. The whole tent when thus finished was only about seven feet in diameter and hardly six feet high. Then divesting himself of all his clothing but one garment, which left most of his bronzed limbs bare, and taking his sacred medicine-bag and drum with him, he disappeared under the tent, which had neither door nor window.

Soon the monotonous drumming was heard, and then shortly after there issued from the little tent sounds as though most of the wild beasts of these northern woods had there been gathered. Bears and wolverines growled, wolves howled, foxes barked, wild cats shrieked, and other discordant sounds were heard amid the incessant drumming. Then the little tent began to shake and swing as though exposed to a western cyclone. Above these various discordant sounds the voice of the old medicine-man was heard repeating over and over, "Soon fire will not burn me nor bullets pierce me!"

In the meantime my friend, Mr. Hamilton, had put the long six-foot iron poker into a good fire and was much interested in getting it so heated that he might practically test the amount of protection his satanic majesty could put on the naked legs of his servant, the conjurer. For perhaps an hour the wild medley of sounds came from the tent, while it shivered and shook in a way that threatened any moment to bring it to the ground. Then the old fellow inside seemed to have so wrought himself up into a frenzy that his courage or madness enabled him to leave off all doubts, and he fairly screamed out his challenge, "No fire can burn me, no bullets can pierce me!"

"Are you sure of that?" shouted Mr. Hamilton, above the din and noise.

Back came the answer: "Ho, ho! Fire can't burn me, no bullets can pierce me!"

Quickly seizing the cold end of the long iron poker, Mr. Hamilton, who was a large, powerful man, suddenly raised one side of the leather tent a couple of feet, and inserting the other end of the poker, which was red-hot, he rapidly and vigorously moved it around and pressed it up against any thing within his reach inside. Very abruptly all the queer sounds to which we had been listening ceased, and there quickly burst out a succession of yells of fury and groans of pain. Then the tent suddenly seemed to collapse, and from it there rushed out on the opposite side a severely burned and thoroughly frightened Indian, who made for the woods as quickly as possible, and was not till months after seen again in that vicinity.

In spite of all that has been written disparagingly about those old conjurers it is a matter of great thankfulness that we can report the thorough conversion of several of them. One genuine case was that of an old man who was one of the Wood Cree Indians that lived beyond Norway House. He renounced his old life and habits, burned his medicine bag, and gave himself to the Saviour. Great and marvelous was the change produced in him. When he came to the church for baptism, in answer to my question, "Name this man," he promptly said, "Call me Daniel."

"Why Daniel?" I asked.

"Because," he replied, "I heard you preach about Daniel, and you told about his being delivered from the lions. It was a great deliverance, but not as great as mine from my sins."

Then, lifting up his right hand and looking intently at it, he said in a voice that almost startled us all: "Missionary, that hand has mixed the poisons that have killed fourteen people. I have been a very wicked man, but I have heard the Great Spirit's voice. I have come to him and he has saved me, and my deliverance is greater than that of Daniel, for I was in a deeper, darker place, but he has brought me out into the light."

So, amid the hushed excitement of the audience, we baptized him Daniel.

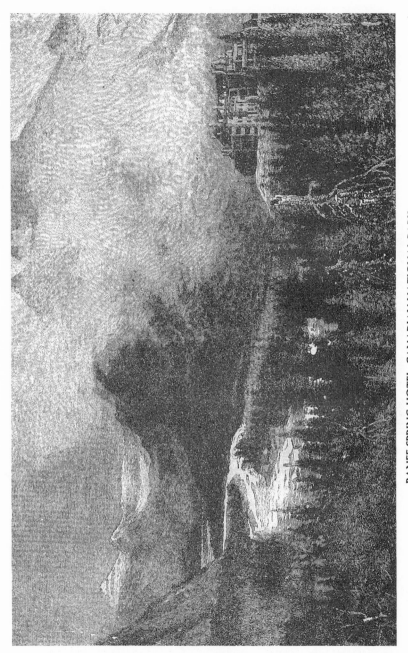

BANFF SPRING HOTEL, CANADIAN NATIONAL PARK

CHAPTER XIX

THE HUDSON BAY COMPANY

ENORMOUS EXTENT OF ITS OPERATIONS—VASTNESS
OF THE COUNTRY—FROM OCEAN TO OCEAN—WORLD
LONG KEPT IN IGNORANCE OF THE POSSIBILITIES OF THE
CANADIAN NORTH-WEST—MARVELOUS CHANGES—
CANADIAN PACIFIC RAILROAD—COMING GREATNESS OF
CANADA—BRYANT—HUDSON BAY TRADERS—TRADING-
POST—METHODS OF BARTER—STORY OF THE INDIAN AND
HIS LOST MONEY—BEAVER-SKIN STANDARD—MAILS BUT
ONCE OR TWICE A YEAR—A DAILY PAPER—JOHN AND
HIS MASTER—THE PEA-SOUP—SECURING THE COMPANY'S
GOOD-WILL—VISITS TO THE LONELY POSTS—GRATEFUL
WHITES AS WELL AS INDIANS—"ALL THINGS TO ALL MEN
THAT WE MIGHT WIN SOME"

To many it may be interesting news to hear that there is in
the Dominion of Canada a mighty commercial firm, employing
millions of dollars of capital, that has been in continuous existence since the reign of Charles I, a period of over two hundred
years. For over two centuries the Hudson Bay Company has
been the wealthiest corporation of, and has exercised almost
despotic powers in, the great Northwest. The charter which it
received from Charles I was only surrendered a few years ago
to the government of the Dominion of Canada. For it the directors received one million five hundred thousand dollars in
cash, and also immense grants of land. This great company has
its head-quarters in London, England. The directors, until very
lately, have preferred to keep the world in ignorance of their
operations, and hence but very little information was given to
the public. The company's shares were at one time of very great

INDIAN FAMILY ON THE MOVE

value, and almost sacredly kept in certain families. Reports tell of almost fabulous dividends and fortunes speedily realized by the fortunate holders of its stock. But those days seem to be over, and now the company's stock is quoted like that of other corporations, with all the incidental fluctuations.

Since the Dominion government has extinguished the exclusive trading privileges of the Hudson Bay Company the glory of that institution has, in a measure, departed; yet the company is still the greatest fur-trading establishment in the world, with forts or trading-posts scattered through the northern part of this American continent from the Atlantic to the Pacific. The company's ships, laden with goods, still leave their London docks and return freighted with cargoes of the richest furs. So persevering were the hardy adventurers in their efforts to advance the company's interests and increase the "returns" that they had, even before the days of Astor, established trading-posts in Oregon, where they did a flourishing business with the Indians of that land.

From the great Mackenzie River traders pushed on westward until they had entered and organized some most successful posts in Alaska. From these northern places they obtained immense returns, and I well remember the vexation of some of them when the sale of that country by Russia to the United States made it necessary for those fur-traders to withdraw. They used to talk of the mighty Yukon River and the gold-mines that are in that northern land in addition to its valuable fur-bearing animals.

It is an almost impossible task to give any very clear idea of the vastness of the country over which the sway of this mighty trading company extended, and in which they have planted their lonely trading-posts in different places between the Atlantic and Pacific Oceans and from the United States boundary to within the arctic circle. Some of them were hundreds of miles from their nearest neighbors. Over this vast country roamed the wild Indians of many tribes, some of them as fierce and warlike as any others on the whole continent; yet the employees of this great trading corporation managed to get along with them so harmoniously and peaceably that robberies or murders very seldom occurred. Their jurisdiction until a few years ago not only extended over the wilder rocky regions of the far north, where only Indians and the rich fur-bearing animals can live, but they also claimed authority over the vast fertile prairies which extend from the Red River to the foot-hills of the Rocky Mountains, into which thousands of settlers have since gone and where many millions of bushels of the finest wheat are being raised, and where vast droves of cattle have taken the places of countless herds of buffaloes that roamed these fertile plains not a generation ago.

The possibilities of the Canadian Northwest are still among the uncertainties; still enough has been demonstrated to show that there is room and capabilities for scores of millions of people to live on its vast fertile prairies, which are greater in extent than France, Germany, and Austria combined. The opening up of the country by the building of the Canadian Pacific Railroad has done much to make these romantic mountain regions better known to the outside world, and to attract from overcrowded lands thousands, who are but the beginning of the vast multitudes who will yet come into its fertile plains, and who are creating for themselves happy and comfortable homes.

Marvelous indeed are the changes which a few years have made. Where the Indians roamed and hunted, or moved from place to place in their own picturesque primitive style—often with all their worldly goods which were not on the backs of their Skwews fastened on two poles, one end of each tied to the side of a horse while the other dragged on the ground—now are to be found thousands of comfortable homes of industrious settlers whose prolific wheat-fields yield the largest average per acre of any in this whole round globe of ours. Where the long trains of creaking, greaseless Red River carts slowly crawled along over the trails with their loads of buffalo robes and dried meat there now dash the well-equipped trains of the longest railroad in the world. Where, up the rivers, over the portages, and across the lakes, in rude native-made boats manned by human muscles,

ROMANTIC MOUNTAIN REGIONS

magnificent though they were, the limited traffic of the country passed, now steam-boats and branch railroads are to be found, laughing in their giant strength with derision at the puny work and crude methods which they have supplanted. Their shrieks and shrill whistles have awakened the echoes amid the solitudes of centuries, and now every thing in that land seems to feel the throbbing pulse of a new and active life.

And all this has come about within a very short time. A few years ago but little more was known about the northern part of the American continent than about the heart of Africa. The great selfish company whose charter made them the despotic rulers over it thought it was to their interest to keep the outside world in ignorance as to its capabilities, and to belittle it to any inquisitive individual or parliamentary committee that endeavored to find out the truth concerning it. And so for two centuries they held it, and in their own way ruled it, and made enormous fortunes out of it. A large proportion of the colossal fortune devoted to the building of homes for the London poor by Peabody, the philanthropist, was stock in this wealthy company. But the days of exclusive fur-trade in this land are ended, and multitudes, as the earnest of what is yet to be, have entered into the goodly land.

Often as over its beautiful prairies I wandered and saw the long procession of brave men and hopeful women coming in and taking possession, and tried to realize the developments of coming years, nothing that I could think of seemed more appropriate, or half so beautiful, as the lines of that sweet poet, William Cullen Bryant:

> I listen long, and think I hear
> The sound of that advancing multitude
> Which soon shall fill these deserts. From the ground
> Comes up the laugh of children, the soft voice
> Of maidens, and the sweet and solemn hymn
> Of Sabbath worshipers. The low of herds
> Blends with the rustling of the heavy grain
> Over the dark-brown furrows.

But we must return to our narrative of doings in the country in the years gone by when with the exception of a few missionaries the fur-traders were the only white people in the land, and some of them were located in places so remote that they received but one mail annually, and were for many years separated from all civilized society. To an outsider, life must have seemed dreary and monotonous in the extreme at these isolated inland trading-posts. Yet the officers and employees in some instances become so attached to it that there are many cases on record where some of these gentlemen, after having acquired a fortune and returned to civilization, have found life there so uncongenial that they have voluntarily and gladly gone back to these lonely places and there ended their days in peace and contentment. For them those sylvan solitudes and the companionship of the Indian hunters had more charms than all the blessings and privileges of civilization. Perhaps it was in the mouth of one with such preferences that Shakespeare put these expressive words:

Hath not old custom made this life more sweet
Than that of painted pomp? Are not these woods
More free from peril than the envious court?
Here feel we but the penalty of Adam,
The seasons' difference; as, the icy fang,
And churlish chiding of the winter's wind;

Which when it bites and blows upon my body,
Even till I shrink with cold, I smile and say,
This is no flattery: these are counselors
That feelingly persuade me what I am.
Sweet are the uses of adversity,

Which, like the toad, ugly and venomous,
Wears yet a precious jewel in his head;
And this our life, exempt from public haunt,
Finds tongues in trees, books in the running brooks,
Sermons in stones, and good in every thing.

The methods of trade with the Indians were novel and primitive. As until very lately such a thing as money was unknown among them, the trade was carried on altogether by barter. So little did some of the Indians at first know of the use of money that the story is told of one who, when the agent at the first treaty gave him his share, went and hid it somewhere in the forest. After a time he thought he would like to go and look at it. Forgetting where the hollow tree was in which he had hid it, he had a long and unsuccessful search, in which he became tired and very much annoyed at himself. While searching for it a happy thought came to him which he uttered aloud: "Why, it is all right; if I cannot find it, no one else can." And so he returned to his wigwam happy and contented.

In the traffic by barter with the Indians, before the introduction of money, the beaver was adopted as the standard fur, and the value of all others was estimated according to it. For

ESTIMATING THE VALUE OF FURS

example, silver and black foxes, which are among the most valuable of furs, were reckoned as equal to thirty beaver skins. A good otter was equal to four beavers, and so also was a good black bear-skin. Of the inferior furs they said it took so many to make one beaver. For example, ten muskrats were one beaver, two red fox-skins were also but one beaver. So the plan pursued, when a, successful Indian hunter came in with his valuable pack of furs to trade, was something like this: The trader carefully looked over his large bundle, which in all probability contained several varieties of foxes, bears, otters, beavers, minks, martens, ermines, musk-rats, and other valuable furs of the country. Although, perhaps, in the pack there were only thirty beaver-skins, yet, by adopting the plan to which we have referred, of bringing all to the standard value of the beaver, the trader would say to him, "You have three hundred beavers here." If this agreed with the Indian's tally—and they are very shrewd at estimating their furs' value—the trader gave the hunter three hundred quills for the furs, and then, both going into the store, the exchange of quills for goods began. Each article of goods was marked so many beavers, or quills, and so the transfer of quills was soon made for blankets, clothing, kettles, tea, knives, ammunition, tobacco, beads, and various other things, until the purchasing medium—that is, the quills—ran out. And this often happened long before the poor fellows had obtained half of what they really needed for themselves and their families.

In the days of the monopoly of the trade the prices given by the company for the furs were apparently very low, and our sympathies were with the poor Indians, who had to endure many hardships in capturing the various animals in the dreary wintry forests.

Still, there is this to be said for the Hudson Bay Company, that every thing they furnished the Indians was of the best materials, and their expenses in carrying the trade were very great. The cost of freightage alone on many things was often more than ten times the original price of the articles; and then there was the fact to which we have alluded, that, owing to the remoteness of some of the posts from the sea-board, years elapsed ere there could be cash returns for the goods sent in. Since the surrender of the company's exclusive rights to the trade in furs, there has been a good deal of what is called free-trade. Small companies and individual traders have endeavored to secure a share of the trade at different places in the country, but only with indifferent success. So wealthy and so strongly intrenched is the old company in the country that it is almost impossible to compete with it. Any attempt to set up a rival trading-post is looked upon with a jealous eye and at once creates the most unrelenting hostility. To crush out the intruders at any price is the motto of the old and wealthy company, and so the battle begins. At first the Indians were pleased to have the free-traders come and traffic among them, but as in the end they became the sufferers by these rivalries, they changed very much in their views.

Owing to the remoteness and isolation of some of these posts from railroads or the sea-board, communication is obtained with the outside world but once or twice a year. It is quite evident that the daily papers are not there received every morning. Yet at one of these places a plan was adopted by which the gentleman in charge was supplied with his daily paper. He ordered out from London a complete set of the *London Daily Times*, for the full year past, up to the date of the sailing of the ship. After several months' journeying over land and sea, and across many portages and up several rivers, his precious box of papers at length reached him. Every morning when summoned to breakfast by his faithful servant, John, he found beside his plate his daily paper. This he carefully perused while John cooked his fish.

But one copy a day only was taken from that box. No matter how exciting might be the events recorded, or how great the suspense which the half-finished information of to-day's copy might cause the reader, all curiosity was curbed and the result was not known until at the regular hour the next day, when the next copy of the paper was read.

A good story is told of this same old Hudson Bay officer which will forcibly illustrate the strict discipline and formal and almost military routine of even the smaller trading-posts of this great company.

One year, owing to the very early setting in of winter, the supply boat taking up the provisions to this place was caught by the frost several hundreds of miles from its destination. This meant that all the employees living there would be obliged to subsist on fish and game, unless they were fortunate to have some of the supplies of the previous year left over. All this old officer had on hand was a quantity of peas. So the following scene used to occur between the master and his faithful henchman: A knock would be heard at the door of the office. In his loud, military voice the master would shout out, "Come!" In response to this John would open the door and with uncovered head would enter.

"Well, John, what is it?" the master would say.

"Please, sir, I've come to ask what we are to have for dinner," says John.

"O, yes, John, that is a very important question. Let me see—let me see. What did we have yesterday, John?"

To this John would jerk out, "Pea soup, sir."

"Why, yes—of course we did—and it was very good, John; so we will have pea soup again to-day, John."

"Yes, sir," replies the faithful servant, as he backs out of the room and goes off to prepare the monotonous meal.

This daily interview was held with all becoming decorum and gravity between master and servant every day for several months.

Fortunate, indeed, was it for the Indians, and also for the fur-traders and missionaries in those dreary wilds, that the lakes and rivers are so abundantly supplied with fish of various kinds. The white fish is most highly prized, and literally swarms in millions in many of the great lakes. Pike, pickerel, jack, muskallonge, gold-eyes, mullet, enormous and most delicious sturgeon, and many other varieties are caught in great numbers in their season. The finest trout haunts the crystal rivers and forest streams, and

TROUT SPRINGING UP THE RAPIDS

well repaid is the adventurous sportsman who penetrates into these sylvan wilds by the sight of these gamy fish lurking in the dark pools, or with surprising muscular power and skill springing up the falls and rapids of these picturesque, well-stocked rivers. Many of them were until lately unknown, and for years would have so remained if it had not been that the building of the magnificent Canadian Pacific Railway and its many tributaries had brought them within the knowledge and reach of the enthusiastic followers of Izaak Walton.

So dependent were we in our mission homes for our supplies of fish for our daily existence that all the mere pleasurable excitement and sport of fishing soon died away. For many years our principal food was fish. Hardly ever did a day pass without fish being on our table, and often for months together it was the principal and sometimes the only article of food three times a day. And as it was with ourselves so it was frequently with the natives and traders. In our interchange of visits, as we dined with each other, so accustomed were we to this fish diet that the most common form of invitation to dine was to say, "Will you come and eat a white fish with me to-day?"

From many of the officials and employees of the Hudson Bay Company we received help and encouragement in our missionary work. Their posts were ever open to receive us, and much was done to aid us in preaching the Gospel to their servants and the Indians at these different places. But they were extremely sensitive in reference to the fur trade, and were very quick to turn their friendship into open hostility toward any one who in the slightest degree came in collision with what they considered their rights, even long after they had surrendered their charter to the government of the Dominion of Canada.

When we first went to that land where the cold is so great that winter reigns with despotic power from November until May we naturally expected that from our Indian hunters we would secure all the furs we needed for our warmth and comfort. To our surprise and indignation we were told in unmistakable language that if we bought or accepted as a present from an Indian an otter, beaver, mink, marten, or any other fur-skin, the Hudson Bay officials would take it as a personal insult and would do all in their power to oppose and hinder us in our work as missionary and teacher among the people. At first there was a very decided disposition on our part to resent such impertinences and assumptions; but when we seriously considered how much more important were our duties toward the poor Indian than were a few furs for our selfish comfort, my noble wife and I determined to pocket the insult and do nothing that would interfere with our being able to do the greatest amount of good to the souls of the people, both whites and Indians, among whom our lot had been so providentially cast. So what few furs we absolutely needed to help keep us from freezing to death in that cold land, we sent for all the way to Montreal, a distance by the route they had to travel in those days of over three thousand miles, while all around us we saw hundreds of much finer ones caught and sold by our own poor Indians, our own parishioners, for not one tenth the price we had to pay in a distant city.

Some sincere friends have questioned our conduct in thus yielding to the unreasonable demands of this despotic company. But the more we think about it the more thankful are we that we did. It gave us the goodwill of the company, and through having this we had access to hundreds of people whom in all human probability we would never have reached.

We were kindly welcomed at their different forts and trading posts; and great need there was for some of these visits. Couples were married by us who ought to have been married long before, and the Gospel was preached to men who had gone in as servants to the company from Christian lands, but who, for many long years, had not heard a sermon. I well remember at one of the lonely interior posts where, with a couple of Indians with our dog-trains, we had penetrated, after I had preached to the few whites and Indians, who had crowded into the kitchen, an intelligent Scotchman grasped my hand and said, "It is twenty-one years since I heard a sermon. Long years ago," he added, "I used to sit under the ministry of Dr. Chalmers." At another place a hardy Highlander thanked me very cordially for coming to them with the Gospel, saying it was over a dozen years since, amid the hills of old Scotia, he had attended a religious service.

Thus the joy of carrying the Gospel to these neglected white men, as well as to the hundreds of Indians, might have been very much lessened if I had stubbornly stood on my dignity or rights. Paul's testimony was, "To the weak became I as weak, that I might gain the weak: I am made all things to all men, that I might by all means save some." So we had a good precedent, and we were blessed in our own souls personally as well as made a blessing to many others.

SNOWSHED IN THE ROCKY MOUNTAINS ON THE CANADIAN PACIFIC RAILWAY

CHAPTER XX

THE FUR-BEARING ANIMALS OF THE HUDSON BAY TERRITORY

CLEVER FUR-HUNTERS—FOX EASILY SHOT—INDUSTRIOUS BEAVERS—THEIR DAMS—HOUSES BUILT—THE OLD SENTINEL—YOUNG BEAVERS AT WORK ALSO—FUR-HUNTING DANGEROUS WORK—POOR REMUNERATION TO THE INDIAN

MORE than half of the valuable furs of the world are obtained in the wild northern regions of the Dominion of Canada. This fact is worth remembering in view of the wide-spread desire to get as much information as possible of the varied resources of this Canada, which is advancing with such rapid strides to take her place among the great nations of the world.

Far north of the fertile prairies, from which the Indians are gradually retiring before the irresistible march of the white man, there is a vast region of country extending from the Atlantic to the Rocky Mountains, abounding in various kinds of fur-bearing animals. In hunting them the Indian finds congenial employment; and as hunting naturally means isolation, or, at most, living in small companies, there are none of those opportunities for the large tribal gatherings which used to occur among the tribes further south, and which so often resulted in mischievous conspiracies, followed by deeds of blood.

This fur-producing region is a land of broad lakes and rapid rivers, a country so intersected by streams that by making portages occasionally an Indian can go in his light canoe almost anywhere. It is a land of vast forests and immense swamps. In their dark recesses and along the banks of those streams and lakes are to be found a great variety of fur-bearing animals. Among them are the black bears, wolves, wolverines, and six varieties of foxes, namely, the black, silver, cross, red, white, and blue. Here is also the home of the beaver, the most industrious and clever of animals, that builds a house vastly superior to the wigwams of the pagan Indians, and often dams back a stream capable of driving a first-class mill. Of the beaver and his doings we will have more to say further on.

Minks abound in thousands, and the finest of martens, but little inferior to the Russian sables, are also obtained in great numbers. The fisher and lynx, or wild cat, are numerous, and the snow-white ermines yield up their diminutive coats to form some of the robes of royalty, or to decorate those of the judges of some of the highest courts of the land. Numerous otters are often seen swiftly gliding through the water or basking on the shores in the pleasant sunshine, or they may sometimes be seen having rare sport as they climb up the steep clay-bank and then slide down with much apparent delight along the well-worn groove and dive with almost boyish glee into the deep waters below. Many of these animals live on fish, with which those lakes and rivers at times literally swarm. Others of them thrive on rabbits and mice and small birds.

But numerous as these animals are—and of some of them there is no apparent diminution, very much owing to the wisdom of the Indian hunters in leaving some to breed—a great deal of skill and cleverness is required in capturing them. Marvelously endowed with the instincts of self-preservation are most of these animals; and it was always intensely interesting to watch the conflict between man's reason and long experience and the natural gifts of these four-footed creatures which we call instinct— a word which does not begin to cover all their acquirements. Each variety seems to have its own characteristic of cleverness, and along this line it ever seems to work. To overmatch this is the constant study of the Indian hunters, and as a general thing they show themselves apt scholars. Then, like animals of a higher grade, they have their weak points also. To find out these and then triumph over them is also important for those who would capture them. See this as a sample:

"Do you see that red fox there on that shore, missionary?" said one of my Indian canoe-men to me as we were paddling along one lovely summer morning on a beautiful lake in that northern land.

I shaded my eyes, and soon saw the fox several hundreds of yards away. "Yes, I see it," I replied.

"Don't you white folks call the fox very clever?" he asked.

"Yes," I answered; "we have a proverb, 'As cunning as a fox.' We think him very clever or cunning."

With a laugh he answered, "We Indians think the fox is the greatest fool in the woods. Do you see that fox? Well, see now how soon we will have him here in the canoe."

"All right," I said; "go ahead and let me see you catch him."

He instantly sprang up in his canoe and began to sing, while he noisily aided the other Indian and me paddle the canoe

SHOOTING THE FOX

along. As soon as the fox heard the noise, after gazing at us for a minute or two, he trotted up from the shore and disappeared over a bank which rose up from the beach.

"There," I said, "you have lost him."

"O, no; I'll get him soon," said the man, with any amount of assurance.

We had now got within perhaps a hundred yards of the shore when my noisy Indian put down his paddle and, taking up his shot-gun, began making a noise with his mouth or lips exactly like the squeaking of mice. Quietly we two behind paddled nearer and nearer the shore, while the man with the gun kept up his mouse-like squeaking. Soon, to my surprise, I saw the fox coming back over the bank looking for the mice. A report rang out from the gun in the hands of my clever Indian, and the fox, falling dead, was soon transferred to the head of the canoe. All the man vouchsafed to say—and he said it with a quiet smile of triumph—was, "There, missionary, is the red fox which you white men think is so clever."

Another thing which I noticed in the Indians was that while they had pretty good ideas of their own skill and ability as hunters they were also very quick to adopt any thing new that they thought would make them more successful in their work.

The beavers, although not so much in demand as when their fur was required for the manufacture of the famous beaver hats of the past generation, are still much sought after for their really valuable fur. The discovery of the method of making the silk hat has thrown the old high beaver out of the market, and it has also saved this industrious animal from threatened extermination. For years it has been a great pleasure to me to watch and study the habits and characteristics of many animals, and to endeavor to compare the perseverance, intelligence, or industry of one with another, and as the result I have no hesitancy in saying as far as my observations have gone the beaver heads the list. Marvelously clever were some of my dogs, as some of the early articles of this series have shown. And living as I did with dogs that plowed my field, harrowed in my grain, dragged home my wood for mission, church, and schoolhouse, and also were my gallant trains on those long journeys of hundreds of miles, and then often my bed-fellows at night in the wintry camp in the snow, I saw instances of sagacity and intelligence that won my admiration and bound very closely to me my four-footed friends. But in one day's watching of beavers at work, and then in the study and examination of their dams and houses, I have seen that which amazed and astonished me more than the doings of any other of the brute creation. Of course I do not speak of their love or affection. I never tamed one or tried to do so. Others have done so, and say they are affectionate pets. I am writing only of those characteristics that came under my own observation.

I have seen stumps of trees over two feet in diameter that had been cut off by beavers. They can always throw the tree just where they want it to go. When out in the forest with my Indian wood-men chopping down the large trees for our great winter fires, as we had no coal in that land, I have been amused by hearing the men say, as they anxiously watched to see where the trees they had cut would fall, "Beavers are better at this work than we. They know exactly where the tree they have cut will fall. They never even look up as it comes crashing down just where they wanted it to go." I first thought this was some of their nonsense, but I found out after years of inquiry and observation that it was the fact. They are very numerous in the Nelson River country, and there some of their largest houses and dams are to be found.

With the greatest interest I have from a wooded hill-top or bluff watched through a telescope a colony of these clever beavers at work. If the pond was made it was generally quite easy to single out the old watchman who acted as guard for all. His place was frequently on a stump out in the water, which only rose a few inches above it. Apparently he was only lazily sunning himself while all the rest were industriously at work. But to find out his true position all we have to do is to make a slight noise, and instantly his broad tail comes down on the water with a slap so vigorous that it sounds like a pistol-shot. Having sounded his note of danger he quickly dives out of sight into the water, and every one of the colony, no matter how he might have been employed, quickly follows. Where all was activity a few minutes ago now all is apparent solitude. But if our patience will hold out and the wind is blowing from them to us we will soon see them at work again.

As we keep perfectly still, we observe on the quiet glassy water a faint disturbance away off on one side. If our telescope is powerful enough we can see that it is caused by the old sentinel beaver, who is quietly poking up first his nose to smell and then his eyes to see if he can discover what it was that alarmed him. As we are very quiet and completely hid from him he cannot detect us. Still he is very wary, and so he sinks again out of sight and swims to another part of the pond. Here he again comes up very cautiously to the surface and tries to discover any signs of danger.

It is fortunate for us that the wind is blowing from him to us. If it were otherwise he would soon have scented us, and our coming to see them at work would have been in vain. As it is he does not suspect our presence, and as there is much work to be done he soon imagines that his had been a false alarm, and so he quietly swims back to his stump in the middle of the pond. After a cautious survey and intense listening he becomes satisfied that all is right, and then with two sharp, loud slaps on the water with his broad tail he summons the rest to work. Very quickly do they respond.

The quiet waters seem to boil, almost, as twenty or thirty beavers come up to the surface and swim off or walk off to their various duties. Some of them are cutting into logs some large trees that they had recently cut down. Others are rolling or dragging logs into the water, and then floating them down to increase the height and strength of the dam. Others at the dam are moving and packing in stones and gravel and brush and mud at a great rate. See how carefully those two are piling mud on that big fellow's broad tail, and then see how carefully he crawls

to the proper place and there deposits it and slaps it down with his tail, which, having first served as a sled on which to drag it, now serves as a mason's trowel to pack it down. And look at those little beavers. It looks as though in mere sport only they are busy. It may seem but fun to them, but theirs is an important work. You see them running into the dense underbrush and quickly returning with little birch or wallow trees about an inch in diameter and from ten to fifteen feet long. Carefully watch their movements. They come to the edge of the shore, and then, catching the little trees or poles in their mouths, a couple of feet or so from the end, they dive with all the force possible into the water. Down they go, but soon the beavers come up alone. They have succeeded in their work, which was to stick those birches or willows in the mud so that they will remain there. Away they go for more saplings. And very important work this is; for on the bark of those young trees and branches the whole colony will have to depend for their living during the long, cold winter which will soon set in. The older ones will complete the house and pond. The ice will form a thick covering; it may be from four to six feet over the water. Under it in the house and pond the beavers are to live for at least six months. The only door their house, with its two feet of solid walls, has is the one under the water. Hence their only supply of food for that long period is that which the industrious younger ones stuck in mud. When in the spring the ice melts away I have seen as much as would fill several wagons of these sticks floating on the surface, from which the beavers had eaten the bark, which is their principal food.

In all probability but very few ladies as they wrap their warm, luxurious furs around them have any very clear idea of the hardships, as well as the skill, necessary on the part of the Indian hunters as, in the dreary forests, in the bitter cold, day after day and week after week, they pursue their lonely and dangerous vocation.

Very clever and cunning are all of these fur-bearing animals, and so the greatest patience and most thorough knowledge of their various habits are absolutely essential on the part of those Indians who would excel as fur-hunters.

The lives of these Indians are full of hardships and dangers. Into the most remote and desolate places have they to go if they would find the animals for which they seek. Among the many dangers which encompass them, perhaps the greatest is that of starvation. While rich fur-bearing animals may abound, the flesh of most of them is unfit for food. To carry in supplies to regions so remote is an impossibility. The result is that a great deal of the time has to be spent in hunting the deer and other animals whose flesh is good for food. Some years these are not numerous, and then there is want and suffering and even starvation. So at the best these Indian fur-hunters are not to be envied. We have known cases where, when the deer and rabbits failed, the hunters have been reduced to the necessity of scraping the fur and hair off their beaver-skins and then boiling them for food. Some winters they have eaten their dogs, and I have heard of cases where a hunter has been reduced to such extremity that he toasted and then ate his deer-skin moccasins!

In the face of these risks and hardships—and they are not uncommon—it does seem hard that in view of the high prices that people have to pay for their furs so little should go to those who have so often to put their lives in jeopardy and endure such hardships to capture them.

There is an impression abroad that the Indian is a very indolent, lazy, and shiftless creature. Where spoiled by contact with unprincipled whites or where treated only as a "ward of the nation," there is, I am sorry to say, too much truth in the charge. But out in these northern regions there are large numbers of them who in their way are just as industrious and attentive to their daily concerns as are their white brethren anywhere. It was often a great pleasure to be associated with them, and to see the skill and cleverness with which they did their work.

CHAPTER XXI

BLACK BEARS

EASILY TAMED—BEARS FISHING—A TAME BEAR ROCKING
A BABY'S HAMMOCK—AN ADVENTURE WITH ONE—
SHOOTING IT IN THE RIVER—MARVELOUS CLEVERNESS
OF THE INDIANS—DINNER OF BEAR'S RIBS—SUPPER OF
BEAR'S PAWS—CONDEMNED TO DIE—AIDED BY THE BOYS,
CAPTURED A GRIZZLY BEAR—BECAUSE OF HIS BRAVERY
THE SENTENCE OF HIS DEATH WAS REVOKED—LIVED TO
BECOME A CHRISTIAN

THE country between Norway and Nelson River is very wild
and desolate. In its dreary forests many wild animals are found,
and so its hunting-grounds are much prized by the Indians. More
black and silver foxes are here obtained than in any other portion
of the world. Their very beautiful skins are rated, at times, as the
most costly of all furs. Black bears are numerous, and are hunted
by the natives both for their flesh—which they prize as an article
of food—and also for their warm, shaggy skins. Bears' grease was
used by us at the mission as a substitute for lard, and it answered
admirably. The most profitable time to kill bears is in the fall of
the year, just before they den up for the winter. Then their fur is
in prime condition and the oil receptacle around the heart is full
of fat. These bears live on roots, grubs, berries, and small animals.
They are also very expert at catching fish. The only kinds they
succeed in capturing are those that at certain seasons of the year
crowd up the shallow streams or along the marshy shores, such as
the mullet or suckers, jack-fish, pike, and white-fish. They even at
times succeed in capturing the sturgeon, which, in looking for a
spawning-place, has so crowded himself up into the shallows that
his back becomes exposed to the view of watchful bruin.

When in the spring of the year the bear gets hungry for a dinner of fish he looks out for a place where they are swimming up the shallow stream near the shore. Then he sits quietly down on his haunches as near the water as possible. When one comes swimming along near enough to be reached he quickly pushes his hand-like fore-paw under it, and with a sudden jerk throws it over his head on the shore. When fish are numerous, as they are in spawning-time, in those great northern streams and lakes, the bear will sometimes get fifteen or twenty in a short time in this cunning way. Once, when traveling in a birch canoe with a couple of Indians, we disturbed a bear that had adopted the following plan: He had ensconced himself on a flat rock, between which and the shore a rapid little stream, two or three feet wide, was running. As the fish attempted to get up this stream the bear would put one of his paws under it and skillfully toss it from him on the shore. As we were not looking for bear when we turned the sharp corner and came upon him, he, after giving a growl of annoyance at our disappointing him of his supper, sprang from the stone on to the main-land and plunged into the forest ere we were ready to fire. However, he left us fish for supper. These black bears are easily tamed when caught very young.

At Norway House the young clerks in the employ of the Hudson Bay Company had a bear so tame that they frequently harnessed him up to a dog-sled. He seemed to think it great sport to gallop over to the Indian village, two miles away, with two or three persons on the sled.

An Indian family had a tame bear of which they were very fond. They lived in a birch-bark wigwam, and the bear had his share of the little home. He was very gentle, and the children played with him as they would with a large dog.

In these wigwams the baby's principal resting-place is in a little hammock that swings from the tent-poles. One day all the members of this family owning this tame bear were away with the exception of the mother and the baby. The supply of water being exhausted, the mother was obliged to go down to the river, which was not far away, for some. She left her babe in the hammock in the tent and the bear sleeping near it on the ground. When she returned she found the bear sitting up on his hind legs, and, using his fore-paws as hands, was gently rocking the child. The babe was smiling now, but the tears on its cheeks told

A NOVEL NURSE

that it had been crying. This seems to have excited the bear's sympathy, and to have prompted him to endeavor in the usual way to soothe and quiet the little one; and he had succeeded.

Bears are very fond of berries. I have often been amused and interested as, through a good field-glass, I have watched the dexterity with which they would, with their tongue and hand-like paws, gather them in. They are very quick at hearing and full of cunning. These northern black bears, unlike the grizzlies, are very timid, and much prefer to escape into the deep dark forests than to risk an encounter with man. They are very clever in escaping from the hunters. And more than once when, like the Irishman's flea, we thought we had our hands upon him we found he was not there. Still, human skill and the thorough knowledge of their habits have, backed up by good weapons, enabled the Indians to succeed in killing them in large numbers. We killed a bear once in a queer way while on a trip to the encampment of the Nelson River Indians. Two clever natives were my canoe-men. So many and difficult were the portages and other obstructions that we were twelve days in making the journey down. We carried no tent and but little food. But we had a good breech-loading rifle, a couple of shot-guns, and plenty of ammunition. We slept on the smooth granite rocks at night and lived on the game we happened to kill. As in the adventure there was so clearly developed the cleverness of the Indians in reading the bear's intentions and so completely checkmating him, I will try to describe the affair.

We were not far from Split Lake, and were paddling down a large, beautiful river. Our supply of food for dinner was very limited, and so we were delighted to see a large flock of ducks alight down in the reeds on the left side of an island but a short distance ahead of us. We noiselessly paddled our canoe around the head of the island, and keeping close to the shore we cautiously approached them. Just as we were getting within gunshot, and the Indian in the front of the canoe was about to fire, I happened to look up to the bank of the island along which we were now so quietly gliding. Fancy my astonishment at seeing there, within fifteen or twenty yards of us, an enormous black bear. He seemed about as much startled as I was, and from our proximity seemed afraid to run away. So he rose up on his hind legs and began snuffing the air and growling at a great rate. I quietly said to the Indian who was about to fire at the ducks, "Never mind the ducks; take the rifle and shoot the bear." Instead of doing this, or even firing at the ducks, he instantly put down his gun, and, taking up his paddle, he and the other Indian quickly and quietly paddled the canoe backward. Back, back we went, until we were out of sight of ducks and bear, and just opposite the point or end of this long, narrow island. Not until we reached a place where they could see the river on both sides of the island did they stop. Here, resting on their paddles, they began watching and listening.

"Why did you not shoot that bear when I told you to?" I asked of the man in front of me.

"Wait, missionary," he replied. "We will kill that bear."

"I think paddling away from a bear is a queer way to kill him," was my answer.

Good-naturedly he replied, "Wait a little, and you will see how we do it when we get a bear where that one is."

Carefully looking down the two sides of the island and seeing where the river was narrowest, they said, "Do you see that place there?"

"Certainly I do."

"Well," they answered, "in a short time we will shoot the bear in that place."

Having often seen their skill as hunters before, I thought my best plan was to ask no more questions at present, but quietly watch their operations. We had not to wait many minutes in our little craft at the upper end of the island before we heard a great crashing among the underbrush, and then the bear appeared in sight. He came rushing along to the end of the island as near to us as he could get. There he rose up again on his hind legs, and, showing his glittering teeth, began growling fiercely at us. As he was not more than a hundred feet away I wanted to fire at him, but my good fellows said, "Not yet, missionary; we can do better yet with him." So we quietly watched him as he stood there snarling at us. All at once his proud, confident spirit seemed to leave him, and he turned round, and with the actions of a cowardly dog rushed back into the dense woods with which the island was covered.

Now, for the first time, I noticed that my Indians were beginning to get excited. They quickly paddled the canoe around on the right-hand side of the island, so as to have a good view of that narrow channel in the river which they had pointed out to me. It was perhaps half a mile wide. Here we had to wait but a few minutes before we heard a great splash in the water, and then we saw, not many hundred feet from us, the bear swimming as hard as he could. He was making a gallant effort to get from that island to the main-land. As we so quickly paddled toward him he turned back toward the island. Seeing this we retreated, and he turned again for the distant shore. We let him get out a good distance from the island, and, using our paddles, we soon overtook him. My men, conscious of their ability to keep out of his way, paddled up so close alongside of him that they could, and did, frequently tease him with their paddles. The bear resented this, of course, and once when we were very close he made a sudden dash for our canoe. I confess I felt my back hair (I haven't much on the top of my head) suddenly manifesting a desire to get up on the perpendicular just then; for the angry brute succeeded in getting his paws within eighteen inches of the side of our frail birch canoe. But the Indians only laughed out their merry Ho, ho! and skillfully glided away. The bear never tried to follow us any distance. His object was to reach the main-land. Across about three fourths of that river did my Indians tease that bear and play with him as a cat does with a mouse. When nearly across one of the men said, "Missionary, did you ever kill a bear?"

"No," I replied. "I have not been long enough in your country to know much about such game."

"Well, then," they answered, "here is a good chance-to begin; so let us see you shoot this one."

"All right!" I said, and so, taking the rifle, I stood up in the canoe to fire. The river was very rapid and our little boat was tossing on its swift current. As I fired, owing to my excitement and to the fact that I did not allow for the swinging of the canoe, I missed the bear. The bullet just grazed the top of his head and plunged into the river beyond. My Indians laughed, and roguishly looking at each other quietly muttered the word "Monyas" the Cree for greenhorn or "little white man." Another cartridge, however, was soon in, and this time there was no miss. The bullet went crashing through his brain, instantly killing him.*

We dragged him ashore, and the Indians soon skinned him and cut up the best part of his carcass to carry along with us for food. The spare-ribs were cut out and roasted, there and then, at a fire which we kindled on the shore. While picking these bones at our midday meal I asked my Indians to tell me why they adopted the plan they did in killing that bear. They said:

"If we had fired at him when we first saw him we might have only badly wounded him, as it is hard to kill a bear with one shot if you do not hit him in the brain or in the heart. Then, if badly wounded, and he had got away from us, he would have hid in the dense, dark underbrush and trees of that island, and it would have been dangerous work to follow him up without a dog to give us notice when we were close to him."

"Why, then, did you so quickly paddle away from him?" I asked.

"Because," they answered, "a bear is like a cowardly dog. He comes out and growls at you, and if you run from him he thinks you are very much afraid of him, and he will follow you up. So when we first saw that bear he was very much surprised to see us, and before he got afraid we ran away from him. This made him think that he was very brave and we were very much afraid, and

---

*See photo in frontpiece, after title page.

that was why, when we paddled back to the end of the island, he came rushing out to the point and growled so bravely at us."

"Why did you not want me to shoot him then?" I asked.

"For the same reason we did not fire at the first," was the reply. Then they continued: "You saw, when he found we did not run away, but sat there looking at him, he got afraid, and turned round and ran back into the woods. When we saw that he was frightened, as we wanted him to be, we knew that he would soon try to get off from that island, although it is a large one, as bears know they are not safe on such places. Then we know that when bears get frightened on islands they always choose the spot where the river or lake is narrowest, and that is just what this bear did, as we told you."

I listened to their words with about as much pleasure as I had witnessed their clever actions. Some people say that the Indians are inferior in intelligence to the whites. My experience has been that along certain lines they are highly educated, and could easily worst in a great many ways those who so glibly traduce and belittle them.

Soon after dinner we again pushed out our canoe from the shore and resumed our journey. That evening at the campfire, as my Indians were roasting the bear's feet, which are considered a great delicacy, we had from them a variety of stories and adventures. One which they told about an old Indian grandfather, Mis-mis, was so very interesting that I will here record it.

Mis-mis lived in one of the Indian villages much farther west, where the people were still heathens, and consequently very cruel. One of their wicked habits was that just as soon as the men or women grew so old and helpless that they could not snare rabbits or catch fish they were in some quick way put out of existence. The same thing was done to a child who happened to become so injured as likely to be badly crippled or helpless. In their cruel, heartless way the people said they had better kill them at once than have them grow up to be a burden to themselves and their relatives.

Mis-mis, who had been a great hunter and warrior in his

day, had grown old and was no longer able to go on the long hunting excursions and come back loaded with game. While still quite free from sickness, yet, on account of his great age, he was in a measure dependent upon the supplies of food brought in by the younger Indians.

One summer the buffaloes were disappearing very fast, and there was but little food to be obtained. The hunters were sullen and discontented, and one day when starting off on a hunting excursion we overheard them saying that when they came back they would start Mis-mis off on the journey to the happy hunting-grounds. In some way or other Mis-mis got hold of the information that his life was in danger, and it was not very pleasant news. True, in the days when he was a great hunter he had been cruel and heartless, and had been guilty of killing others who were old or helpless, but now, when younger men thought his turn had come, he was quite indignant at it. The more he thought about it the more angry he got. The idea that he, the mighty warrior who had come home with the reeking scalps of his enemies, was now to be strangled like some good-for-nothing old Skwew! Had he not been able to shoot the arrow clear through the body of the buffalo and return to the camp laden down with the choicest meat? Why had he not died in battle long ago, rather than come to this? So, instead of sitting down in sullen indifference and stoically awaiting his fate, he determined that as he was to die he would die in a manner worthy of his record as a brave warrior and a mighty hunter. He resolved that he must die in mortal conflict with some hostile foe or in battle with some savage beast.

While brooding over his resolve the opportunity for carrying it out suddenly presented itself to him one day while the hunters were all away. Back of the village in which he lived in the deep ravines, called "coolies," grew large quantities of sweet berries called by the Indians Sas-ke-too-me-nah-nah Menisuk. These berries grow on bushes, and the bears are exceedingly fond of them.

One day as Mis-mis sat in gloomy thought in his little wigwam a party of boys came rushing in with the news that while they were out in one of the ravines picking berries they saw not very far away a large grizzly bear. Mis-mis sprang up with joy. Here was his opportunity. He would die fighting that great bear. So, clothing, or rather unclothing, himself for the conflict, and sticking as many feathers in his hair as he imagined he had slain enemies in battle, he took his tomahawk and sallied forth for the battle unto death. Of course he expected nothing but death from the monster, as the killing of a full-grown grizzly bear by a great hunter is ever considered equal to the feat of slaying a great warrior of another tribe in a hand-to-hand conflict.

Mis-mis had not far to go before he caught sight of the savage beast, now engaged, however, in the harmless work of picking and eating berries. All bears seem fond of fruit, and with their hand-like paws they can pick them off the bushes very cleverly. Mis-mis resolved to have the thing over as quickly as possible, and so, while loudly singing his death song, he hurried bravely toward him. The grizzly seemed amazed at his audacity, and, enraged at being interrupted in his berry feast —for bears are very quick-tempered—he at once came to meet him. If he had been a black bear in all probability he would have run away, but grizzlies seldom run from any foe. When the bear had come within striking distance Mis-mis, who had resolved to sell his life as dearly as possible, raised his glittering tomahawk and struck as savagely as he could at the bear, which had quickly risen up on his haunches before him. Bears are skillful boxers. They can parry the blows aimed at them like trained pugilists, and this enormous old fellow was no exception. So when Mis-mis struck at him he struck out with one of his paws so cleverly that he knocked the sharp tomahawk out of the hand of the old Indian with such force that it went flying through the air and landed in the grass yards away. It looked hopeless for poor old Mis-mis now. There he stood, disarmed before the angry, savage bear. But he had come out to die, and while sorry that he had not been able to have at least wounded the bear that was to kill him he resolved to stand his ground bravely and receive the terrible stroke of the paw that would about tear him to pieces. Black bears in close conflict try to hug their victims to death, but grizzlies strike out with their fore-paws as they rise up on their hind legs. In this way they can with their terrible paws, armed with claws larger than the fingers of a man's hand, strike down a horse or a buffalo.

Great was Mis-mis's astonishment to find that, when he received the blow of the bear that he thought was to tear him in pieces, while the weight of it fairly staggered him it did not even scratch him. The reason was the claws were all gone, and so the bear's paw was only like a great ball of fur. Quickly recovering himself, the old warrior, with his blood getting up, clinched his fist and hit the bear, and got another blow in return. Thus it went on, fists against an old bear's paws robbed of the claws. Then a thought came into the head of the old man, and it was this: "I will capture this old bear, and thus show the hunters that I am worth something yet." So he jumped back and ran away as fast as he could. The old bear did not chase him very far, and soon returned to his berries.

When Mis-mis reached the camp he told the boys about this old bear that had lost all his claws, and how it was possible for them to capture him. Under his guidance they entered eagerly into the attack, for were they not the sons of hunters and warriors longing for the time and opportunities when they could emulate the deeds of the bravest of their tribe? So, leaving behind them their bows and arrows, they took only their lassos, which are made of strong green hide and fixed with a running noose or slip-knot at one end. The other end is tied to the belt of the person using it. The boys as well as the men become very skillful in throwing these lassos. Accompanied by about a dozen of these boys, armed only with their lassos, Mis-mis returned to the scene of his conflict, and after a little search they observed the bear a short distance away, again eating berries. As quietly as possible they crawled through the grass and surrounded him. Then at a given signal each boy sprang up, and almost before the bear realized that he was attacked the lassos began whizzing through

Mɪs-Mɪs AND OLD GRIZZLY

the air and falling over his head and tightening on his neck. He plunged this way and that way, but all in vain. The sturdy boys held bravely on, and each struggle only more securely tightened the slip-knots on his neck. When he found he could not shake the things off he put up one of his paws, and, pulling some of the lassos in his mouth, tried to bite them off. But as he had lost most of his teeth, as well as his claws, he could not succeed in cutting any of them off, as they are made of very tough leather, and the boys kept jerking them out of his mouth. Vainly did the old grizzly struggle and roar. Mis-mis and the boys had him securely enough, and after a good deal of excitement and struggling they got him into the village, to the consternation of the women and girls. They drove down some strong stakes on different sides of him and tied him down so securely that he could not get away. When the hunters returned great was their excitement at this capture. Here was a feat never equaled in the history of the tribe—a live grizzly captured and tethered with lassos in the midst of their village.

A great council was called. Mis-mis was voted to be a brave man still. Mis-mis was not to die; the threat to kill him was revoked, and it was decided that as long as there was food in the camp old Mis-mis was to have his share. Then the grizzly was killed, and there was a great feast.

Soon after the missionaries arrived at this village and preached the Gospel of peace and good-will. The people became Christians, and now, as every-where when the Gospel of the Son of God is accepted, the old and feeble and crippled are kindly cared for, and there will never be a return to those old cruel, sinful times when it was considered a crime worthy of death to grow old.

CHAPTER XXII

THE MOOSE-DEER

VALUABLE TO THE INDIANS—METHODS OF CAPTURE—
BIG TOM'S CAMP-FIRE STORY—HIS METHOD OF HUNTING
THEM—THE REINDEER—MIGRATORY HABITS—POND
OF SWIMMING—EASILY KILLED IN THE LAKES—WOMEN
HUNTERS—A TRAGIC STORY—THREE LIVES LOST BY THE
REINDEER SMASHING THE CANOE—WANTED, A CHRISTIAN
WIFE—SUCCESSFUL IN THE UNDERTAKING—A SHORT
COURTSHIP WITH VERY HAPPY RESULTS

OF the several varieties of deer which abound in the northern part of the Dominion of Canada the moose is the largest and the one most highly prized both by Indian and white hunters. He is also found in the State of Maine and in the Province of New Brunswick. Moose have been found standing over seventeen hands high, and, when in good condition, have yielded about as much meat as a large, fat ox. Their enormous horns are very broad and heavy, yet when they are alarmed and wish to retreat in silence, which is not always the case, they can effect their purpose with marvelous cleverness, no matter how dense may be the forest through which they glide. Throwing back his head so that his antlers seem to rest on his neck, the moose can flit away among the trees without breaking a twig or branch.

The hide, which is much thicker than ordinary buckskin, when well tanned, makes the best of moccasins and the warmest of leather suits. The preparation of the moose-skin, which is generally the work of the Indian women, ere it is considered fit for use, is a work of great labor and patience, and requires a good deal of time and skill. First, the coarse, thick hair, which is very brittle and inelastic, is carefully scraped off by a chisel-like instrument made out of the shinbone of a reindeer. Then the skin is again stretched in a large frame and scraped and rubbed until every particle of flesh or foreign substance is removed from it. Then, to aid in the tanning, the brains of the deer are carefully rubbed in, after which the skin is subjected to an amount of rubbing, pulling, and scraping that would wear out the patience of any white tanner. However, the result is a skin so tough and enduring that nothing can tear it.

To make it so that it will always remain soft and pliant and acquire the valuable property of being uninjured by the sun's rays or the drenching rains, another operation has to be performed upon it as well as upon all kinds of deer-skins. This is called smoking the skins, and is done in various ways, according to the facilities of the operators. Mary, the old Indian woman nurse, who made all our moccasins, used a large kettle, in which she placed pieces of a peculiar kind of rotten wood, which, when ignited, made a most pungent smoke but no flame. Over this she would fasten the mouth of the skin, which she had sewed up into the form of a sack. The dense smoke poured into this bag-like affair, and, not being able to get out, soon permeated the whole concern, and the skin was tanned. When a number were to be prepared in this way a hole would be dug in the ground and filled with burning pieces of this rotten wood. Over this smoking mass the skins were carefully placed, and then the whole was covered over by a tent, which was made so tight that none of the smoke could escape. For a day or two the skins were left in this way, and then were generally considered to be in prime condition for various purposes. For nine years I wore a coat made out of moose-skin tanned in this way. It was then still considered to be good enough in which to appear before enthusiastic crowds at Ocean Grove and elsewhere in America, and also on the platform at some of the great May meetings in Exeter Hall, London, and in many other places in England. It is good for at least nine years of hard service yet, and nothing would give its owner greater joy than to have the pleasure of again fastening it around him with an Indian sash, and once more for years go back to that same arduous but delightful work among these poor but grateful Indians.

The moose, although so large and powerful, is one of the most cautious and timid of animals. Any unusual sound, such as the cough of the hunter or the snapping of a stick under his feet, even when the high winds may be bringing down the dry branches, will alarm him. Hence the greatest possible caution has to be observed by those approaching him if they would get within range. If once alarmed and started the moose generally goes many miles ere he stops. He has not the graceful movements of some others of the deer tribe. His gait seems to be an awkward, swinging trot, but, uncouth as he looks, no Indian hunter, be he ever so fleet of foot, thinks of trying to overtake him.

The moose, when captured young, can be easily tamed. He can also be trained to trot in a sulky or cart, and there holds

A FLEET TROTTER

his own with some of the fleetest trotters in the world. An acquaintance of the writer in Trenton, Canada, had one in his possession for years. He was very gentle, thoroughly broken in, and was a great pet among the hostlers and drivers.

Successful hunters of the moose are very rare. Many Indians who are able to shoot the reindeer and other animals often fail most signally in their efforts to get within range and bring down, by what is known in hunting parlance as honest stalking, this most wary animal.

Of course, many of them are easily killed in winter, when the deep snow makes it possible for the active hunter, on his snow-shoes, to run them down. Others are killed by the use of a fire-light in the head of a canoe or skiff. The Indians say that the moose, generally so clever, becomes fascinated by a brilliant light, and often allows a cautious hunter to float down very near to him, if he keeps very still and the wind is in such a quarter that it does not carry the scent of the hunter to the deer.

In the fall of the year, when the males are roaming about, many of them are killed by the clever hunter who is able to imitate the call of the female moose. Some Indians can do this with the unaided voice, so great are their powers of imitation, but the majority generally provide themselves with a horn or trumpet of birch-bark, with which they can the more thoroughly deceive these naturally suspicious animals.

None of these methods of hunting the moose are considered as tests of skill by the regular hunters, although they are often adopted for the purpose of capturing the valuable animal. What is considered an achievement of which to be proud is for an Indian or white man to go out with his gun and return laden with moose-meat, which he has obtained by the fair, sportsman-like way of getting on the animal's track and then following it up until he was clever enough to get within range and there shoot him.

Ma-ma-nowatum, or "Big Tom," as we generally called him, was one of our best moose-hunters at Norway House. When he returned from some of his successful hunts it used to be a pleasure to hear him and others talk of their successes. Big Tom was the steersman who let me fall over his head once in Lake Winnipeg, after offering to carry me ashore on his back. Coming in one day from a successful hunt, he gave us, at his camp-fire, in his slow, measured style, his experience in killing one of these wary old moose. He told us that he had been out traveling two days before he struck the traces of the animal. He found where the moose had been browsing the tops of the young birch and willows. "For, you know, or ought to know," he added, "that the moose does not eat hay or grass, but lives on the twigs, branches, sprouts, and leaves of the trees. He can easily bite through branches an inch thick, and then, without any trouble, can crush the pieces up in his mouth ere he swallows them. He is also fond of some kinds of ferns, and considers the shoots and roots of the water-lilies very great delicacies, for which he will dive like an otter, big and awkward as he looks." Said Tom:

"It was quite early in the forenoon when I found out where the young twigs and branches had been bitten off, and, as the ends were dry—that is, there was none of the saliva upon them—I knew the moose was not very close at hand. So I followed on, keeping as low down as I could, so as not to be easily seen if he were near."

As he found the track went this way and that way, he said he did not need to be so very, very careful as he had to be soon after. Toward noon he found saliva on the ends of the willow and birch branches left, and then he knew the trying time had come. So he added:

"I took off my moccasins and most of my clothes, so as to get more easily through the bushes and be less liable to make any noise. Soon I found where he had stopped eating and had begun to look for a good place where he could have his noonday sleep. For," said Tom, with a merry twinkle in his eye, "these moose, like some people, love to have a big sleep after a good dinner. But he knows that he has enemies who would like to catch him napping, and so he makes his plans that he may escape, if possible. This is the way he goes to work: When he is eating he keeps moving about from side to side, wherever he sees the best food, but always on the watch for enemies. Now he stops and looks around, and finding out which way the wind is, he generally goes in as straight a line as possible, for perhaps a mile or so, in the most open part of the forest, and then, on a little hill or rising ground, with some dense trees or underbrush behind him, he turns his face toward the line of straight trail he has made, and there he lies down, with his big ears fixed to catch any sound from the rear, while his eyes and wonderful nose guard the path he has just made. He does not depend so much upon his eyes as upon his nose to tell him of any taint that may come in the air while he sleeps.

"Now," said Tom, "if a greenhorn should be out hunting a moose, and got on his track when the moose was eating, he would, perhaps, follow all night, and do well as long as the trail went zigzag; but it would never do, when the track began to go straight, to get on it and begin to follow it up. That would be just the thing for which the deer had prepared himself, and no hunter could get him, for the moose would detect him and be off long before the man could get within range.

"No, no!" said Tom, as he laughed. "Lots of hunters, good moose-hunters, get this far, and then they fail, and so have to come home, their belts drawn tight, and no moosemeat."

"Well, go on, Ma-ma-nowatum, and tell us what you did."

After he had pulled a few vigorous puffs through his big pipe he proceeded:

"As soon as I saw that the twigs and branches were not bitten off I knew that the moose had gone away to have his noon sleep, and that perhaps even now he was looking toward me, although too far away to see me yet. So I dropped flat on the ground, very quiet, and thought what to do. I was glad the wind had nearly gone down. I studied the way of the land, and then I crawled back, where I could get behind a big tree, and there I thought some more. Then from behind that tree I looked away along the track, and far off I saw a little hill, perhaps half a mile away, with some dense bushes. I said to myself, 'Mr. Moose is sleeping there, and there I must try and kill him.' But of course I was not sure, and so, after fixing my gun all right, I began crawling on, keeping some distance from the track the deer had made, but sometimes coming back to see if it was still straight and how long since he had gone over it. Of course, I had to keep very flat on the ground, and only came to the path where there was a hollow or some bushes to hide me from being seen.

"Five or six times I went away and then came back to the path; each time I was perhaps three or four hundred feet nearer to the moose. Then I made up my mind that I was so near him I must not come to the track again. So I moved away to one side again, and looking carefully through the branches I could see the hill very plainly, and I made up my mind that he was near that spot, although I could not see him. Now I had my hardest work. I knew I must move very quietly, for if I even broke a little twig with one of my feet, or hit my gun against a tree, even when hundreds of yards away, the moose would hear it and be off.

"Very carefully then I made a big circuit, so as to come in right behind where I thought the moose was lying. Sure enough, when I got round where the track ought to have been, if it had gone on straight from where I had followed it so long, there was no track there. Then I knew I was ahead of the moose. But the question was, 'How far am I from him?' Of course I did not know, but I still thought I would find him where I said. So I took off some more of my clothes and crawled on like a snake until I got in the rear of those bushes which I had seen when at the other end of the track. Here I waited and listened, but I neither heard nor saw any thing of the moose. As I felt I had gone far enough I very carefully examined my flint-lock gun, and then slowly got upon my feet. Certain that my deer was close at hand, I sharply snapped off a dry stick by stepping on it. Instantly, as I had expected, there sprang up the big moose, not fifty yards from me. He quickly turned sideways toward me to see what the danger was. I instantly fired and killed him on the spot, and felt very glad to have my two days' hunt end so well."

We who had listened to Big Tom's story congratulated him on his cleverness and rejoiced with him at his success, for he is one of the best and bravest of men, as well as one of the kindest.

Compared with some of the more graceful species of the deer family the reindeer appears ungainly and thick-set. Yet he is quick and fleet in his movements, and when in his prime carries gracefully a magnificent pair of antlers. Although not as large as the moose, yet many of them are very fine-looking animals and are much prized by the Indians, who, however, do not train them to draw their sleighs as do the Laplanders, but hunt them solely for their flesh and skins.

During the greater part of the year they live principally in what are known in the far North as the "Barren Lands." These inhospitable regions, although destitute of nearly every species of vegetable life, yet abound in different kinds of lichen or Iceland moss, which is the food most prized by these wandering bands of reindeer, or caribou. These deer differ from many other species in that they are essentially migratory animals. Some years they will collect in great herds and wander hundreds of miles from their ordinary feeding-grounds. The colder the winter the further south they come. Although not as fond of water as the moose, yet when on their migrations they do not hesitate to cross large rivers and deep bays. Impelled onward by some unknown impulse, they will even pass through settlements and crowd up so close to human habitations that for the time being they seem to have almost lost their fear of man. One winter, so close did immense herds pass by one of the largest Hudson Bay Company's posts, that many were shot by the officials and employees from the doors and windows of the different buildings. During the cold winter months many of the herds of these valuable animals wandered into the regions hunted over by my Cree Indians. Hundreds of them were killed, and the venison thus obtained was an agreeable addition to the "bill of fare" of

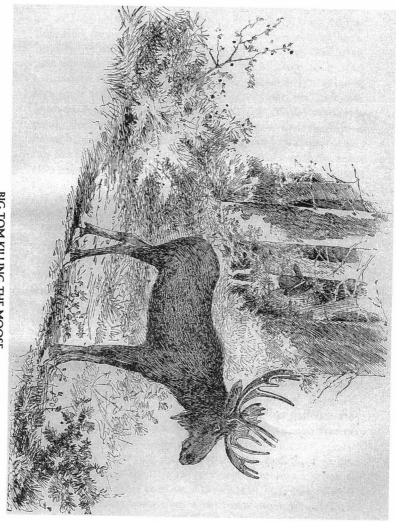

BIG TOM KILLING THE MOOSE

a people whose principal article of food was fish.

When a hunter gets on the track of a herd of them he will sometimes follow them up for days without firing a shot, even if he is frequently in range of some of the finest of them. His object in reserving his fire is to wait until he can shoot the leader of the herd. If he succeeds in this the whole band is thrown into disorder, and becomes so bewildered that they seem to lose their senses and run this way and that way in the greatest confusion. The hunter, meanwhile, avails himself of this mad panic and keeps loading and firing his gun as rapidly as possible. Soon, however, a great big-antlered deer seems to appoint himself as leader, and, rushing off with a snort, is quickly followed by all that is left of the herd, while the clever hunter, as the reward of his patience and shrewdness, is perhaps the fortunate owner of enough venison to keep him and his family for months.

The reindeer are very much pestered by a kind of gadfly, which not only causes them very much annoyance but so punctures their skins that often they are of but little value to the Indians or any body else. I have seen them, when tanned by the Indian Skwews, so full of holes that they looked more like the bottom of a colander than any thing else. Often there was not enough good leather in one skin out of which to make a pair of moccasins. On account of the persecutions which they suffer from these flies the deer are frequently observed swimming in the lakes or rivers. Many of them are killed while thus in the water by watchful Indians. In killing them when in the water the hunters very seldom use their guns, but gliding up swiftly near them in their fleet canoes they strike them on their heads with their axes or spear them with their long, sharp hunting knives which they have lashed to poles. By killing them in this noiseless way they do not frighten away others that may be feeding near the shore. Even the women will sometimes in the absence of the men glide out noiselessly where they see the deer swimming, and successfully attack them and drag their bodies in triumph at the stern of their light crafts to the shore, where their wigwams are

WOMEN SPEARING REINDEER IN THE WATER

pitched. But there are times when they are not so successful, as the following tragic story will explain.

I was interrupted one day while sitting in my study by the quiet entrance of a stalwart Indian whom I had not seen for a year. I had met him the previous summer in his own wigwam on the banks of a beautiful lake a couple of hundred miles north. After a few words of kindly greeting I asked about his family, when, to my surprise, he exclaimed, almost passionately, "Missionary, my heart is sad, and I have come to ask you to get me a wife from one of the Christian families of your village."

Somewhat annoyed, I said: "Do you not know that I do not believe in a man having two wives at the same time? When I visited your wigwam and had religious services among your people last summer I thought you had a very good wife and a pretty babe, and that you were very fond of them."

"Yes," he said, passionately; "all true, missionary!" and then his spirit broke, and he wailed out, "Non pimatissit!" which means, "Not among the living."

This is the pagan Cree Indian way of referring to the death of friends. Having none of the consolation which Christianity gives in reference to death, the very word itself is to them one of such terror that they seldom utter it. When obliged to speak of those that are gone they use the Cree phrase non pimatissit not among the living. Shocked at this sad news, and pitying the poor fellow, we made him sit down with us to tea, and then after a while we got him to tell us his sad story. He said:

"Missionary, a short time after you left us I started from the place where you had met our people on the Burntwood River to go far away to my own hunting-grounds to catch beaver. I pitched my wigwam on the bank of a fine large lake in which there were plenty of fish, and there I left my wife and babe and my wife's mother. They had every thing they needed to make them comfortable. There were fish in the lake and rabbits in the woods. With plenty of food in the wigwam I left them light of heart, for I was glad to see them so well. The last thing I saw of them was the baby laughing in the hammock and my wife sitting beside him and busy making the new white fish net for the fall fishing. I went up the lake for some miles until I reached a large stream that flowed down into the lake. As I had seen before this time plenty of signs of beaver up this creek I went up it a few miles and there set my traps. I hunted around for a few days and did very well. Then I packed up my furs and beavermeat, and started on my trip home. My load, which I carried on my back, supported by the carrying-strap from my forehead, was heavy, but my heart was light, for I had been successful as a hunter, and then I was also on my way to see my wife and baby boy. I hurried along on the side of the stream until it entered into the lake, and then I turned to walk along the shore. I had not gone very far before I was surprised to find lying in the water at the edge of the lake the body of a large dead reindeer. I examined him to see if he had been shot, but instead of any bullet marks I found that he had been badly cut about his head with an ax. As he was not fit for food I left him there for the wild beasts to eat and hurried on toward my wigwam. I had not gone very far before I found on the shore one of my canoes badly broken. This very much surprised me, and so I hurried on faster than before, for my heart began to feel strange and heavy; and there was reason for it, missionary, for I had not gone on much farther before I found at the shore in the water the bodies of my wife, babe, and wife's mother. They were cold and dead, although there were no wounds on their bodies. They had been drowned all drowned."

The poor fellow had been able to control himself fairly well up to this point while in his simple yet eloquent manner he had told his pathetic story. But here even the Indian's stoical nature was overcome, and his heart was stirred to its depths by the memory of his great loss. So for a time in a hushed silence my sympathetic wife and I sat with him until he had mastered his emotions and could proceed with his narrative. He said:

"I carried the bodies home to my empty wigwam, and as they lay there so still I could but think of how different when

I left them a few days before. I hurried away to the wigwams of some of my people miles away, and they came to see me in my sorrow and helped me to bury my dead."

In answer to our questions as to his impressions or ideas as to the manner in which his loved ones had met their death he said nobody had seen how it happened, as all the people were in other places, hunting or fishing, but he and his relatives had talked it over, and they had all come to one mind about it. And this was how they thought it happened: The women in the tent must have seen that large reindeer swimming in the lake, and, being anxious to kill him, they had launched the canoe to go after him. As there were sometimes gray wolves or other wild animals prowling about they were afraid to leave the baby behind, and so they took him with them in the canoe. They only took with them their paddles and a couple of axes.

The reindeer has good lungs, and so he can swim high in the water, and sometimes he will make a desperate fight, even in the water, for his life. So it seemed in this case that, while the

THE BROKEN CANOE

women succeeded in so striking him in the head with their axes as to mortally wound him, he succeeded in breaking the canoe, perhaps with his hind feet, for they are able to kick very savagely, even when swimming. The result was, the boat sank, and the women becoming entangled with their clothing, and perhaps trying to save the baby, all were drowned together.

We listened to the recital of this sad story, and would not have been human if we had not been moved by it and also by the simple, pathetic way in which he tried to tell us how he felt when he reached his wigwam and found the fire out, the hammock empty, and the wooden needle still dangling in the last mesh of the net which his wife had been weaving ere she had doubtless hurried out to try and show how bravely she and her mother could kill the deer. We kept the poor fellow all night, and in the morning were better prepared to sympathize with him in his desire to obtain a wife than when he had in such a strange way referred to the matter the previous evening at the beginning of our interview.

"Why," I said to him, "have you come hundreds of miles for a wife? Why did you not go to Nelson River, or to some other place nearer to your home?"

His prompt answer was: "Because I want a Christian wife. I am convinced that what you told me is true. I am trying to believe in your religion, and know more about the true God and his Son, and as you can only come once or twice a year to teach us and preach to us I thought a good Christian wife might help me along in the good Christian way."

Still anxious to draw him out, for I saw that I had here a man of more than usual character and thoughtfulness, I said: "But I cannot forget that although I manage to get down once or twice a year by canoe or dog-train to visit your people, and they have always received me kindly and listened very attentively to what I say, yet it is only a very short time since they began to hear about the true way, and many of them are still pagans; so you see there might be a good deal of fear that if a Christian young woman went to live there they would persuade her to return to the old Indian way."

"No, no!" he said very earnestly. "We have all lost faith in the old way, and she would be able to help us to be good Christians all the sooner."

So, after my good, judicious wife and I had listened to the story and talked the matter over, we thought of a family where there were several marriageable daughters dependent on a sickly father, one of whom we thought would make this fine-looking fellow a good wife and help him to be a Christian. Soon after, I escorted the suitor over and introduced him to the family, and had him tell his story and plead his loneliness and make his promise of how good and true he would be. As it did not take Rebekah long to make up her mind, in the ancient primitive times, to consent to be the wife of Isaac, and to start off on a long journey, so it was here. A few days after there was quiet marriage in our little church and a happy wedding-feast. Then the bride and the bridegroom embarked in their birch canoe for their far-distant home. With machine-like precision their paddles rose and fell together as they rapidly propelled their beautiful craft along. We could not help but breathe the prayer that their lives might move along in equal unison. If so, they were assured of many days of sunshine.

I visited them years after. They are consistent Christians, as well as the majority of the Indians in that section of that vast country.

CHAPTER XXIII

THE MODEL MISSIONARY SUPERINTENDENT, THE REV. GEORGE YOUNG, D.D.

BEGINNING THE WORK IN MANITOBA UNDER HARDSHIPS AND DIFFICULTIES—HIS GENUINE SYMPATHY WITH THE ISOLATED MISSIONARIES—HIS TWELVE-HUNDRED MILE TRIP BY DOG-TRAIN—NARROW ESCAPE FROM A CRACK IN THE ICE—VARIED TRAVELING EXPERIENCES—THE CAMP IN THE SNOW—THE MISSIONS VISITED—NORWAY HOUSE—OXFORD HOUSE—MISSIONARY DISCOMFORTS—NELSON RIVER MISSION—REV. J. SEMMENS—BEREN'S RIVER MISSION—DIFFICULTIES THAT HAVE TO BE OVERCOME IN CHRISTIANIZING THE INDIANS—DR. YOUNG'S RETURN HOME—LONG SICKNESS AS THE RESULT OF THE HARDSHIPS OF THE JOURNEY—CLOSING WORDS QUOTATION FROM THE REV. DR. PUNSHON

IN December of one of our coldest winters I went in to the Red River Settlement with my dog-trains to bring out our beloved chairman, the Rev. George Young, D.D., who had long promised, much to our delight, to pay us a visit in our lonely northern mission field. Dr. Young was the first Methodist missionary appointed to the *white work* in the Northwest. When he and his family reached the Red River Settlement there was not a single Methodist in the country to bid him welcome. No comfortable parsonage awaited him. Chilling and discouraging indeed was the outlook. But Dr. Young was just the man for the place. As soon as possible he secured a little log-cabin house of only one room, and in it he and his household lived for months. A good lot of land for a church was obtained, and amid many discouragements Dr. Young began to gather materials for the first Methodist sanctuary. A great deal of the work in the build-

REV. GEORGE YOUNG, D.D

ing he did with his own hands. Once, as I came in on business from my northern mission, in response to my inquiry as to Dr. Young's whereabouts, I was told that he was somewhere gathering materials for the new church. After quite a search I found him with a yoke of oxen attached to a stone-boat hauling stones for the foundation of the new church. As I looked at him, sunburnt and bronzed, but happy in this work, and remembered how I had seen him but lately as the honored pastor of one of the largest congregations in Toronto, I rejoiced that we had such men, and saw that success was already assured. Such men succeed.

The church was soon erected, and for such a new country it was one of rare beauty. Its windows of the finest stained glass were the gifts of different Sunday-schools in Canada. So charmed in after years were some Indians whom I had brought in from Nelson River to meet Dr. Punshon and the missionary secretaries, who had come to that land to meet the missionaries, that, as these children of the forest stood gazing at the gorgeous colors as the western sun so grandly illumined them, they turned to me and cried out, "O, missionary, is the heaven you have described to us as beautiful as this?"

Great and marvelous have been Dr. Young's successes. A conference of over a hundred ministers, with a membership of many thousands, now flourishes where amid many difficulties and discouragements he began the seed-sowing. From the beginning of his labors in that new country he took the greatest interest and showed the most tangible sympathy in the Indian missions and for the missionaries on their lonely, remote fields of toil. My long journeys by canoe in summer and dog-trains in winter were always of great interest to him, and the promise was given that as soon as help reached him, and he could safely leave his work among the whites, he would come out and gladden the hearts of the toilers on the field and personally inspect the work. Years passed before this could be carried out. The Riel rebellion occurred, and during those dark days which tried men's souls Dr. Young had much to endure. His only son for a time was a

IN MY TRUSTY SUIT OF MOOSE-SKIN

prisoner in Fort Garry, and his wife suffered intensely from the bitter cold, as she was obliged in the depths of a severe winter to return to Toronto, crossing the storm-swept trail through Dakota and Minnesota, ere she reached the most northern railroad station.

Dr. Young, although at times his life was in jeopardy, bravely remained at his post and at much personal risk did all he could to alleviate the sufferings of the loyal Canadians who were imprisoned in Fort Garry by the rebel half-breeds. And when Scott, for the sole crime of being loyal to his flag and country, was condemned to be shot by these miscreants Dr. Young demanded from them the right to visit and pray with him in the cold bastion in which he was confined; and when the unfortunate man was taken out and shot he bravely stood by him with words of cheer until the foul murder took place. Sir Garnet Wolseley's march into the country with his British troops and Canadian volunteers quickly ended this stupid rebellion amid the rejoicings of every loyal heart. Dr. Young was publicly thanked in different ways for the brave, patriotic stand he had taken and maintained.

Peace and prosperity having returned to the country, and Dr. Young having secured the services of an earnest missionary as his colleague, he was now able to carry out his promise of years before, to visit us in our northern wilds. It was a perilous journey, as the official letter written to the missionary secretaries which we include in this chapter will show. Dr. Young was a brave traveler and stood the journey well. My trusty Indians aided me in doing all we could to mitigate the hardships and privations of the trip. We made a cariole out of a dog-sled by putting parchment sides, made out of deerskins upon it, and adding a stiff back. In this long, narrow vehicle we packed our honored visitor, well wrapped up in blankets and fur robes. We carried with us an abundant supply of the fattest of food suitable for such a cold journey. Our dogs were in splendid condition and well trained for the work. We tried to arrange our hours of travel so as to reach the best camping-places, but in spite of all we could do the trip was a severe one and beset with many dangers and much suffering. Here is an account of one little adventure which will give a faint idea of some of the perils of traveling during the night vigils with dog-trains in this northern land. One night Sowanas, the Indian runner, complained of a swelling in one of his knees which made it impossible for him to keep running ahead of the trains at the rapid rate we wished to travel. This was a serious matter, but it could not be helped. So I arranged him a place where he could ride on my dogsled, and I took his place at the head as runner. We left our wintry camp very early, as I was anxious to make at least twenty-five miles before sunrise. Our course was due north up Lake Winnipeg. The stars shone out with wondrous brilliancy, and the fitful auroras flashed and scintillated in the heavens. As we knew the ice was from three to six feet thick we hurried along without any fear. So vigorous was the exercise in keeping ahead of my spirited dogs that I had thrown off my overcoat, and in my trusty suit of mooseskin found that it taxed my energies to the utmost to fill the place of an Indian runner. While rushing along I was startled at the strange phenomenon of the stars being, as I thought, very vividly reflected from the transparent ice just before me; but, providentially, I was enabled to suddenly observe that what I had thought was transparent ice was open water of unknown depths, into which we had come within a foot or two of falling. Suddenly checking myself, I turned and threw myself on the leader dog, which was close to my feet, and shouted "Stop!" to both men and dogs, who were close at hand, and who, like myself, were in imminent danger of plunging into the open lake never to be seen again. With grateful hearts we offered up in quiet tones our sincere thanksgiving to God for the wonderful deliverance from plunging into this open crack in the ice.

So bitterly cold is it at times that the ice, although several feet thick, suddenly cracks by the terrible frost. The seam or opening is often many miles long and from six to twenty feet wide. The water suddenly rushes up to the surface, and, until frozen over, which soon occurs, is a dangerous trap for the unwary. Fortunately our good chairman, well wrapped up in the robes of his cariole, was sound asleep and knew nothing of the narrow escape of the whole party. Years after, when he and I were at a great missionary meeting in the Metropolitan Church, Toronto, in my address I described the perils we had been in, and then for the first time he heard of our narrow escape. Great indeed was his astonishment at the recital.

The following is his letter, written after his return to his work in Winnipeg, prefaced by the editorial remarks of the late venerable Dr. Wood, the senior missionary secretary:

"The chairman's narrative of his journey to Beren's River, Rossville, and Oxford House, depicting, as it does in detail, the state of our missions in that sterile country, is full of interest. Can any benevolence be more pure than that which has prompted the establishment and maintenance of Christian ordinances among a people so placed by divine Providence, far away from, the advantages and pleasures of civilized life? Whatever may be thought of Brother George Young's prudence in undertaking such a journey at that season of the year, all must admire his courage and self-denial and rejoice in his safe return to his family and charge in Winnipeg."

"On the 7th of December last it was my privilege to assist in the opening services of a new church on the High Bluff Mission, about forty-eight miles west of Winnipeg. On my return home, Monday evening, I found the Rev. E. R. Young waiting, with Indians, dogs, and sleds, to take me to Beren's River, on my long trip to visit the Indian missions of the North. I was led to decide on making this trip by a conviction, long felt, that I could not discharge aright my duties either to the missionary committee or the missionaries without such a knowledge of the field and the work as can be secured only by actual observation. My purpose had been to make the journey during the summer, but I chose the winter instead from a wish to get in my report before next Conference, because of a saving of time in making the trip, larger numbers of Indians to be met at certain points, and greater press of duties in Manitoba in the summer; besides which I desired, as a means to an end, a just appreciation of the toils, privations, exposures, and expenses inseparably connected with the long winter trips in this 'wild north land,' which are being made by my brethren in the prosecution of the great work of evangelization.

"The journey extended to a distance of well-nigh one thousand two hundred miles, occupied twenty-eight traveling days, and was performed by some walking and a good deal of riding in dog-sleds. The sixteen dogs, four sleds, four Indians, and two missionaries made up such a procession, as we left in the early morning of December 9, as would have brought to the front a crowd of spectators had it appeared on King Street, Toronto, instead of the Red River of the North. Let me describe: Foremost of all was the runner, Jake Sowanas, or South-wind, a fat young Indian, a good runner, a still better feeder. Then came the Rev. E. R. Young, with his valuable train of dogs and a sled heavily laden with supplies needed at home. Next in order my cariole, with its one hundred and eighty pounds, more or less, of humanity, and how much of bedding, clothing, pemmican, etc., I know not; and then two other trains, loaded with flour, pork, and fish, either for use on the trip or to meet the wants of the people at Beren's River.

"Two of the four teams of dogs and sleds were required for my use; the other two were independent, though 'attached,' for reasons sufficiently apparent. The dog-sled, used as a cariole, is made of thin oak about an inch thick, fourteen or eighteen inches wide, and about ten or twelve feet long, with the front end turned up like a skate, while the sides and back are made of parchment drawn tightly around a frame-work and so hinged to the bottom of the sled as to yield a little when it runs against blocks of ice or trees and thereby escape being wrecked, even though the passenger experiences an unpleasant squeeze from the collision. The whole thing is very light, and runs easily and rides smoothly on smooth ice or a well-beaten road; otherwise, not. My experience in dog-sledding was of the following order: First period, quite amusing; the thinness of the oak-bottom and the pliability of the sides render it a springy sort of thing; and as it runs over an uneven surface, the bottom changing quickly from the straight to the convex and then to the concave and back to the straight again—the sides, meanwhile, working like the leather sides of a bellows—it seems most like a thing of life, and might easily suggest to a half-awaked passenger the idea of being a sort of second Jonah who by some hook or crook had got inside some monster who, though on the ice, was making desperate strides toward an opening through which to plunge with his victim into his native element—the 'vasty deep.' Two months before this, to a day, I was enjoying a ride on one of the beautiful and comfortable Pullman cars between Chicago and St. Paul. Between that ride and this there was but little semblance save that in each one is conscious of being strangely jerked, feet foremost, toward some place, he scarcely knows where. The second period, barely enjoyable, with interruptions; sitting for hours, not as in a chair, but after the fashion of a jack-knife, half open, with an occasional let-down when the sled drops from a cake of ice or log while the dogs are at a trot, and to be capsized and find one's self as an Indian babe in a 'moss-bag,' to say nothing of the cool attentions of Jack Frost when thermometers indicate forty and fifty degrees below zero. These things act as interruptions, the barely enjoyable, in a dog sledder's experience. The third period is one of desire to have done with dog sledding forever. This I reached while yet far away from the home-side end of my journey. The dog-train is managed by a driver running behind without any reins, but with many words, of which 'yee,' 'chaugh,' and 'marche' are among the most important and in some instances the least objectionable. To these words are added certain *persuasive measures* in which a whip, often loaded with shot, is brought into painful requisition. Unlike the horse or ox, the dog speaks out his feelings in relation to these passing matters. By 'running,' in this connection, I do not mean that either Indians or dogs literally run, nor do they walk much; both take a kind of shack, a kind of nondescript gait, which they can do very well, even to the extent of sixty or seventy miles per day *on a pinch*. In that case they set off from camp at two or three in the morning, and deducting simply brief rests, during which two meals are taken by the men, they continue running until sunsetting, or even late in the evening when the end of the journey is to be reached. These long-day journeys can only be made with good dogs and smooth roads. To those who have not witnessed it, the statement that these men can travel so far in a day seems incredible; but so much for *use*. The Indians are not alone in being able to do it. I saw the Rev. E. R. Young, after suffering all night from toothache, and being engaged from 11 P. M. to 2 A. M. in keeping up our camp-fire to keep us from freezing to death, lead off with his dogs across a bay twenty-five miles, making that distance in running before the sun rose. When the other trains came up, three-quarters of an hour later, he had our breakfast nearly ready, and then before sunset he traveled about thirty miles more; nor was this, by any means, equal to what he has done. There are but few Indians who can out-travel him; and but few of his brethren and the patrons of this great Missionary Society know or can appreciate the full amount of toil, privation, and exposure which have been involved in his missionary life in the North. And let no one imagine that all this is done quite *easily*; not so these achievements and results of straining, fatiguing, and *wearing* efforts, which in many cases are followed by an early break-down.

"The camp for the night is quickly made by all hands setting to work; some scraping back snow, some cutting spruce boughs and carpeting the place, building up a back wall with them about three feet high, and others getting fuel for the fire. Thawing fish for the dogs, getting supper, getting frost and ice from clothes, preparing flat cakes, and cooking pork for the next day constituted the work of the evening around the camp-fire.

Then after our evening hymn and prayer the weary ones retired for rest in the open wild, sometimes with snow falling thickly and wind blowing sharply, with 'spruce feathers' under them and a blanket or two over them to sleep comfortably *sometimes*. I found that as long as I could avoid turning in bed I could keep warm; but to turn or to strike a match to see my watch—for I kept time for the men—was to give the cold an entrance, and then to sleep or to shiver became the question. Among the last things to be done before sleep and the first on waking, by most of the men, was to drink strong tea and smoke tobacco, large quantities of which have to be supplied them. Nor can such exertions be sustained and such intense cold endured without frequent replenishings with nourishing food. Four meals a day are requisite; a strong cup of tea, with some pemmican or pork or venison or fish, with flat-cakes, often baked in fat, are necessary. In these almost arctic regions such a head of steam as is requisite can be kept up only by a heavy supply of fuel. This will account for the fact that the supplies for one of these trips, in the land of 'magnificent distances' and high prices, run up to an amount that cannot but astonish the uninitiated. The different stages in my journey were from Winnipeg to Beren's River, about five days; thence to Norway House, four days; thence to Oxford House, five days; the return trip occupying about the same time. During these twenty-eight days I encamped out some twenty-three or twenty-four nights, some of which were colder than any I had ever before experienced. My aim was to walk about five or six miles a day; but in crossing a long, rough portage I made one day about fifteen miles, and suffered for it, too.

"The missions I visited belong to the Methodist Church; no other denomination has ever occupied this ground.

"The Rossville Mission is very pleasantly situated on the shore of a beautiful little lake, within two miles of Norway House Post, and is the oldest and by far the strongest of our Indian missions in the Northwest. It was established in 1840 by the Rev. Mr. Rundle, Wesleyan missionary from London. In looking over the register of baptisms and marriages, which has been carefully kept from the first, I found the first baptism recorded on the 28th day of May, 1840, by Mr. Rundle, and the last on the 3rd of January, 1875, by myself. Between these dates one thousand five hundred and sixty baptisms were registered. Mr. Rundle was succeeded by the late Rev. James Evans, who, in labors and travels and successes, was 'more abundant,' and whose name is ever mentioned by these Christian Indians with profoundest respect and gratitude. Probably one thousand Indians or more consider this place, and neighborhoods adjacent, their home. The mission itself embraces a large number of families who live in very comfortable and clean-looking little houses, not far from the church and school and mission house. The church, which has been enlarged once, was built by Mr. Evans, and is at present about sixty feet by forty feet, and, as it is closely seated, I suppose contains occasionally some four hundred, little and big, of a congregation.*

"Since the Rev. Mr. Evans the mission has been occupied by Messrs. Thomas Hurlburt, Brooking, George McDougall, String-fellow, E. R. Young, and their present pastor, Mr. Ruttan, all of whom have been made great blessings to this once benighted people. At present there is a membership of three hundred and eighty-one, of whom forty-seven are on trial, making a net increase this year of sixty-four. There are eighteen classes with leaders and assistant leaders, one day school and one Sunday-school at Rossville, and one day-school and a Sabbath-school at Crooked Turn, about eight miles away; in these schools there are about one hundred and fifty scholars. At the love-feast there were present about three hundred people, while nearly two hundred came to the Lord's table, among whom one was over one hundred years of age, and one came one hundred miles to attend the services. New Year's day was 'a high day' with the Indians at

---

*This church has, since this was written, been replaced by a much better structure.

Rossville, over five hundred of whom feasted on 'fat things,' all of which were 'gratis' to the feasters. From morn till evening the eating went briskly on amid indications of good appetites and great enjoyment and but little weariness. I reached the mission on my return trip from Oxford about 10 A. M., just in time for the feast. In the evening they had a public meeting, with 'Big Tom' as chairman, who, by the way, is a good man and true, but, O so slow in getting up to speak, and in speaking exceedingly slow. Just imagine a great, tall man getting up an inch at a time, and waiting between the inches. But he got all the way up at last and spoke, I presume, very sensibly, which is more than many a white man does who gets up with less hesitancy. A number of speeches were made, and a very enjoyable meeting indeed terminated in good time. I visited both schools, and was much pleased with the appearance of the children.

"The mission at Jackson's Bay, near Oxford House, and about two hundred miles north-east from Norway House, was established at a more recent period, and has been occupied by Rev. Messrs. Steinhaur, Brooking, Stringfellow, Sinclair, and the present missionary, Mr. German. It has been a great blessing to hundreds of Indians. We reached the mission on the evening of Christmas day after a very fatiguing day's run from early dawn till long after dark. On Sunday I preached and gave communion, and then we crossed over to the fort, fourteen miles, and held service there. The night was the coldest I ever experienced, and when we set out the next morning before sunrise to cross the lake, a distance of about forty miles, it is said, with wind sharp ahead, neither present experience nor future prospects for that day were very pleasing. The Indians with me froze cheeks and ears in a general way, but said very little about it, while I felt the cold very much with all my mummy-like wrappings, till finally I had to get out and run to keep my feet from freezing. The thermometer at the fort was useless in such intense cold. I have no doubt it should have gone down to fifty or sixty degrees below zero. I mention this to show under what circumstances of discomfort and peril our devoted missionaries are often placed. Dr. Taylor, one of the missionary secretaries, once in his life endured the most purgatorial sufferings occasioned by the swarms of mosquitoes which gave him such a warm reception in this same region, and gloriously did he depict his sufferings; once in my life, for a little while, I have felt the discomfort and faced the peril and endured the toil of a trip through there in midwinter; but what is all this in either case to what our dear brethren stationed out here have to meet with every summer and every winter? And are they not equally susceptible to suffering as either of us? Let our good brethren in the more comfortable home-work bear them up in their prayers and use all allowable means to secure to them the most liberal appropriations. These are the toilers who earn and really need the highest salaries going. High prices prevail, hungry Indians clamor, and perquisites and presents are unknown. These are noteworthy facts.

"The Nelson River mission is situated about three hundred miles north from Norway House, and is the most northerly point of our mission-field. The work of instructing these poor pagans was commenced by Rev. E. R. Young during his occupancy of Rossville, and by him a large number were converted and baptized. Through his representations and influence mainly the authorities of the Church were led to open a mission there and to appoint the Rev. J. Semmens as their first missionary. Upon him rests the heavy responsibility of making this mission a success, and his will be the honor in that case from the Church of the future. As I understood that the Indians were generally away in their hunting-grounds I decided not to extend my long and tedious and costly trip to that point, but during my visit to Oxford House the missionary, the Rev. John Semmens, with his splendid train of five dogs, arrived at Norway House, so that on my return I met him there and received from him a full statement of the work done and of his plans for the future. During the last few months he has baptized fifty-five persons and conducted services regularly on Sunday, with congregations not very large but attentive, some of whom have become communicants. According to returns made to the Hudson Bay Company there are over five hundred Indians to whom our missionary there can preach the blessed Gospel.

"The new mission at Beren's River is situated on the shore of a pleasant little bay which puts in from Lake Winnipeg, on the east side of the lake, and about midway from the mouth of Red River and Norway House. The mission was opened by Rev. E. R. Young in 1873. When the statement of Rev. John Ryerson, as published in his book of travels through this land in 1854, is remembered, that this point ought to be made a mission, that the Indians and the company's officials desired it, and that missionaries in passing had promised they should have a missionary, and then the fact noted that despite the importunity and recommendation of promise no missionary was sent until 1873, the old adage, 'Large bodies move slowly,' will be apt to occur to the mind. On Sunday, December 13, I reached this pleasantly situated mission in time to enjoy a service in the 'tabernacle,' as they call it, erected a few months ago. Our arrival was followed by no small stir among the natives, who, upon the call of the beautiful bell given by James Ferrier, Esq., of Montreal, assembled and gave earnest attention to my message from 'Behold, I bring you glad tidings,' etc. A number of buildings—a mission-house (a very good one), school-house, place of worship, kitchen, wood-house, fishhouse, cow-stable, house for interpreter and bell-tower, etc.— have been erected during the last summer, and a large quantity of building material for a church, when required, collected, all of which, as well may be supposed, has not been done without a heavy outlay. But in this case the 'end justifies the means.' The missionary has secured a grant of three or four hundred acres of land, about one hundred of which he reports pretty good, ten of which are partially cleared and one under cultivation. Sunday services are conducted in the tabernacle—at 11 A. M. an Indian service for the natives, and at 7 P. M., at the fort, in English. Class and prayer meeting and Bible-class are conducted in the afternoon or during the week. At the three services I attended the congregations were very encouraging; about twenty received communion and three were baptized. As a center the mission is of great importance. Large bands of Indians yet unchristianized can be easily reached, as at Poplar River, Jack's Head, Sandy Bar, Pigeon River, and Grand Rapids, many of whom will settle near the mission erelong. The fisheries and hunting-grounds are the best, I suppose, on the lake, being about midway between Norway House and the Red River. They will afford our missionaries, as they pass to and fro, a much-needed and quiet resting-place, securing to the mission a visit and to the weary travelers a home and a Sabbath's rest. To my mind a field here is attractive and the prospects of a mission are cheering.

"Mr. and Mrs. E. R. Young are toiling hard, and even with weeping, to scatter 'precious seed.' May they soon realize and 'come again with rejoicing, bringing their sheaves with them!' During my journey I had several conversations with uninstructed pagans, all of whom professed to feel dissatisfied with their position, and to desire more light and to be anxious for instruction in doctrines of Christianity. From several I got a promise that they would pray to the great and good Spirit to lead them into the true light. Polygamy, a superstitious dread of their medicine-men and conjurers, wandering habits, and an idea that he who would *teach* them ought to *feed* them to a considerable extent—*these* are obstacles in the way of their Christianization, but they are surmountable and have been surmounted in thousands of instances. The difficulty of mastering their language so as to preach in it, or of getting the truth properly before them through an interpreter, is felt by all our missionaries. From them we need now fear neither violence nor opposition. The term 'savages,' if by any applied to Indians of this country, whether Christian or pagan, is a misnomer in these latter days. Openings for schools and missionaries abound, 'the fields are white unto the harvest,' the laborers are comparatively few, and the funds are not as plentiful as they should be in the treasury of a Church bought with the Redeemer's blood.

REV. JOHN SEMMENS AND HIS SPLENDID DOG-TRAIN

"After parting with the kind people at Beren's River on January 11, I reached home on Friday, the 16th, weary and sore indeed, better, as I suppose, in health; and yet after the Sunday services the reaction came, and for several days it seemed uncertain whether an attack of fever or inflammatory rheumatism awaited me. However, deliverance came, and, as has been usual with me, through the infinite mercy and goodness of God. I am thankful that I have been enabled to make the trip in the winter, but this one, with its fatigue and exposure, must suffice for me. "Were I possessed of the vigor and activity and endurance and *lightness* which were mine thirty years ago, I might decide otherwise. It affords me great pleasure to state that my brethren are not only in health, but, as I believe, energetically, faithfully, and successfully prosecuting their great work. Our district meeting is appointed to be held in Grace Church, Winnipeg, on the 9th and 10th of March, when we hope to make our full returns for Conference, and trust that they may prove in every way satisfactory."

To attend this district meeting some of the missionaries from the remote Indian missions had to travel over a thousand miles with their dog-trains ere they reached their homes again. So deep was the snow that most of that distance was walked on snow-shoes, and over twenty nights did these missionaries have to sleep in the wintry camps in the forest, which they made each night when the day's toilsome trip was ended. But bravely and uncomplainingly did they accomplish the journey, and, with hearts cheered and refreshed by fellowship with their brethren, with renewed zeal they again grappled with the work and the difficulties inseparably connected with it.

Some of these brethren with whom I have had the joy of being associated in the blessed work are still on those northern fields. Others have in the mutation of years, or from broken health, been assigned to other places, and some have finished their course and have entered into rest. And so, in closing, to whom can we more appropriately apply Dr. Punshon's eloquent words than to these our Indian missionaries who, in regions so lonely, work so arduous, sufferings so terrible, and yet with triumphs so signal, have gone up from the battle-field to the rich reward? "Bravely they bore the banners while they lived, but the nerveless hand relaxed its hold and they have passed them on to others. We, too, must pass them on. We received unfinished labors from our fathers and transmit them to our children. Watchers in the night, it may not be given to us to tarry until the morning. We can but wave the battle-flag gallantly for a while, but our hands will stiffen and our comrades will bury us before the fight is done. O, to be kept faithful unto death! From their elevation in heaven they seem to whisper us, 'Be ye followers of us as we have been followers of Christ.'"

How beautiful upon the mountains are the feet of him that bringeth good tidings, that publisheth peace; that bringeth good tidings of good, that publisheth salvation; that saith unto Zion, Thy God reigneth! (Isaiah 52:7)

Also by Lighthouse Trails Publishing

BOOKS

Another Jesus (2nd ed.)
by Roger Oakland, $12.95

A Time of Departing, 2nd ed.
by Ray Yungen, $12.95

Castles in the Sand–A Novel
by Carolyn A. Greene, $12.95

Faith Undone
by Roger Oakland, $12.95

For Many Shall Come in My Name
(2nd ed.) by Ray Yungen, $12.95

Foxe's Book of Martyrs
Lighthouse Trails Edition
$14.95, illustrated

Laughter Calls Me
by Catherine Brown
$10.95, Illustrated, photos

Let There Be Light
by Roger Oakland
$13.95, photos

Muddy Waters
by Nanci Des Gerlaise
Released in 2012

Stolen from My Arms
by Katherine Sapienza
photos

Strength for Tough Times
by Maria Kneas, $7.95

The Color of Pain
by Gregory Reid, $10.95

Things We Couldn't Say
1st Lighthouse Trails Edition
by Diet Eman, $14.95, photos

The Other Side of the River
by Kevin Reeves, $12.95

Trapped in Hitler's Hell
by Anita Dittman with
Jan Markell
$12.95, illustrated, photos

DVDs
The Story of Anita Dittman
with Anita Dittman
$15.95, 60 minutes

The New Face of Mystical Spirituality
with Ray Yungen
3-DVDs, $39.95 or $14.95 ea.

For a complete listing of all our
books and DVDs, go to
www.lighthousetrails.com,
or request a copy of our catalog.

To order additional copies of:
*Stories from Indian Wigwams
and Northern Campfires*
Send $15.95 per book plus shipping
($3.95 for 1 book, $5.25 for 2-5 books) to:

Lighthouse Trails Publishing
P.O. Box 908
Eureka, Montana 59917

For bulk rates of 10 or more copies, contact Lighthouse Trails Publishing, either by phone, online, e-mail, or fax. You may order online at www.lighthousetrails.com or for US & Canada orders, call our toll-free number: 866/876-3910.

For international and all other calls: 406/889-3610
Fax: 406/889-3633

Stories from Indian Wigwams and Northern Campfires, as well as other books by Lighthouse Trails Publishing, can be ordered through all major outlet stores, bookstores, online bookstores, and Christian bookstores. Bookstores may order through: Ingram, SpringArbor or directly through Lighthouse Trails.

Libraries may order through Baker & Taylor.
Quantity discounts available for most of our books.

For other resources, visit our website at:
www.lighthousetrails.com

Also check out our new product line:
Shepherd's Organic Bible Verse Tea
"A Bible verse with every tea bag"
www.theshepherdsgarden.com

Made in the USA
Charleston, SC
28 April 2012